Hiking

Lassen Volcanic National Park

Tracy Salcedo-Chourré

FALCON®

A FALCON GUIDE®

Falcon® Publishing is continually expanding its list of recreation guidebooks. All books include detailed descriptions, accurate maps, and all the information necessary for enjoyable trips. You can order extra copies of this book and get information and prices for other Falcon® books by writing Falcon, P.O. Box 1718, Helena, MT 59624, or calling toll free 1-800-582-2665. Also, please ask for a free copy of our current catalog. Visit our website at www.Falcon.com or contact us by e-mail at falcon@falcon.com.

1 2 3 4 5 6 7 8 9 10 MG 05 04 03 02 01

All photos by author unless otherwise noted.
Cover photo by Laurence Parent.
Project Editors: Jay Nichols and Glenn Law
Production Editor: Heidi Gutesha
Copyeditor: Virginia Hoffman
Page Compositor: Darlene Jatkowski
Maps by Trapper Badovinac.
Book design by Falcon Publishing, Inc.

Cataloging-in-Publication data is on record at the Library of Congress.

CAUTION

Outdoor recreational activities are by their very nature potentially hazardous. All participants in such activities must assume the responsibility for their own actions and safety. The information contained in this guidebook cannot replace sound judgment and good decision-making skills, which help reduce risk exposure, nor does the scope of this book allow for disclosure of all the potential hazards and risks involved in such activities.

Learn as much as possible about the outdoor recreational activities in which you participate, prepare for the unexpected, and be cautious. The reward will be a safer and more enjoyable experience.

♻ Text pages printed on recycled paper.

Contents

Dedication

For Martin

Acknowledgments

This guidebook would not have been possible without the help of a number of people. Central to the process were Steve Zachary, Education Specialist for Lassen Volcanic National Park, and Anne Dobson, Business Manager for the Lassen Loomis Museum Association, both of whom reviewed the manuscript for me. Thanks are also due Ned Farnkopf and his family, for letting us use their cabin as base camp. Finally, the key to my ability to complete this project was the enthusiastic participation of my husband, Martin, and my sons, Jesse, Cruz, and Penn, who have enjoyed hiking in Lassen Volcanic National Park as I have. I could not have done it without them.

Overview Map

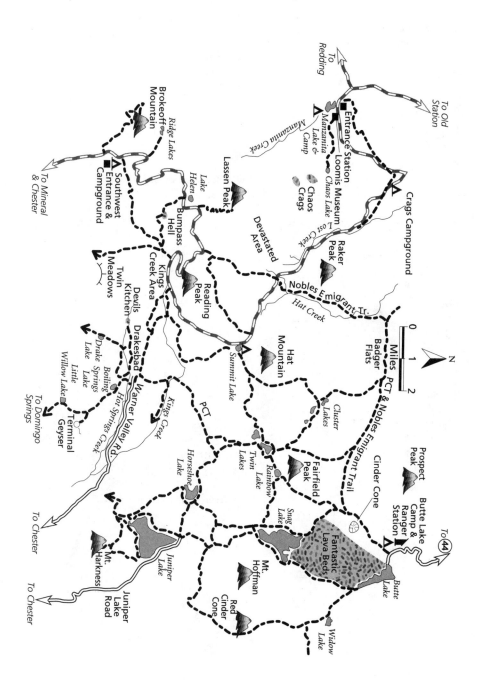

Legend

State or Other Principal Road	(00) (000)	Peak	9,782 ft.
Forest Road	4165	Pass/Saddle	) (
Paved Road		Elevation	9,782 ft. X
Gravel Road		Overlook/Point of Interest	◨
Trailhead	○	National Forest/Park Boundary	
Parking Area	Ⓟ		
Main Trail(s)/Route(s)		Picnic Area	🛆
Alternate/Secondary Trail(s)/Route(s)		Ranger Station	
River/Creek		Snowfield	
Lake		Lava Beds	
Falls	//	Hydrothermal Area	
Spring			
Marsh		Crater	
Meadow		Cliffs	
Boardwalk			
Campground	⛺	Direction of travel	
Cabins/Buildings	▪	Map Orientation	N
Gate			
Bridge		Scale	0 0.5 1 Miles

viii

Introduction

I've never known a wild place as completely as I've come to know Lassen Volcanic National Park. They say familiarity breeds contempt, but in this case, the opposite is true. In the course of compiling this guidebook, I have walked nearly every inch of every trail within the park, and I have come to love it dearly. I can't wait to go back.

My hope for those who use this guidebook is that hiking on these trails will inspire the same kind of passion. It could be a mixed blessing, because more love means more people, which means more impacts, and the potential for more noise, more litter, too many hikers on the trails. Indeed, one of the things I found most wonderful—if sometimes enervating—about hiking in the park was that, even in the height of the summer season, I could find myself absolutely alone in the wilderness. In this time of overcrowded wildernesses and packed national parks, it was a rare and savory treat.

I also pray that, as more people recognize the value of places like Lassen Volcanic National Park, they will fight to preserve and protect other wilderness sanctuaries. Big, beautiful parks and monuments inspire and nurture all of us, and, as the pace of life continues to quicken, provide a much-needed retreat for world-weary souls. Lassen Volcanic National Park is just such a retreat. Explore and rejoice.

—Tracy Salcedo-Chourré

GEOLOGY

Standing on Lassen Peak, you know the world is living. Its surface is quiet, but the mountain boils deep within, revealing its energy in the fumeroles, mud pots, and cauldrons that simmer in hydrothermal areas on its flanks.

Lassen, generally believed to be the world's largest plug dome volcano, last erupted nearly 90 years ago. For three years, from 1914 to 1917, it threw clouds of steam and ash thousands of feet into the air, spewed poisonous gasses, ejected hot rocks, and belched other volcanic detritus, startling and thrilling both those who lived in its shadow and those who read about it in newspapers.

Its most notorious eruptions came in 1915. On the night of May 19, a massive mudflow coursed down the northeast face of the mountain, roaring down the Hat Creek and Lost Creek drainages and causing homesteaders in these valleys to flee for their lives. On May 22, a second eruption, this one a pyroclastic flow of sizzling steam and ash, poured down the same slope, leaving in its wake the Devastated Area, a swath of denuded earth upon which the forest is only now beginning to regenerate.

Lassen is one of the famed Cascade volcanoes, which includes mountains that thrust up more than 14,000 feet, including Mount Shasta and Mount Rainier. The Cascades are part of "The Ring of Fire," a girdle of volcanoes and seismic activity encircling the Pacific Ocean. From Malaysia to Alaska to the Andes, tectonic plates, pieces of the fractured shell of the planet, bump and

A snow plant fades in the forest below Prospect Peak.

slide and surrender to one another in wrenching cataclysms. Every feature within the park—even the gentlest, like Prospect Peak—was born of the movements of these plates. Look around you: Every single peak you see is a volcano—cinder cones, shield volcanoes, plug domes, even the remains of Mount Tehama, a composite volcano that has long since collapsed.

These days, Lassen slumbers. This deep sleep, whether permanent or temporary, offers the hiker a wonderful opportunity to explore the mysteries and wonders of the volcanism that has shaped northern California and the rest of Cascadia.

NATURAL HISTORY

In addition to its fascinating geology, Lassen Volcanic National Park is unique because plant and animal communities common to several different regions—the Cascades, the Great Basin, and the Sierra Nevada—reach a confluence within the area.

As you climb through the park, you pass through four natural communities. In the park's lower reaches, the mixed conifer (yellow pine) forest predominates. Jeffrey pines, ponderosa pines, sugar pines, incense cedars, and white firs take root at elevations below 6,500 feet. A wide variety of understory plants, including an abundance of wildflowers and low-growing shrubs, thrives in this forest, which also supports a number of animal and bird species, including black bears and songbirds.

Between 6,500 and 8,000 feet, the upper montane forest, or red fir forest, takes over. Little grows below the canopies of these dense red fir forests, but in open areas, domain of the western white pine, you find a colorful undergrowth of wildflowers and manzanita, an evergreen shrub featuring bright green leaves and red, smooth bark. The lodgepole pine finds purchase on thinner soils in this zone. Though this forest supports less diversity, you still encounter most of the fauna found in the mixed conifer forest, with the addition of elusive creatures like the pine marten and the red fox.

Higher still, between 8,000 and 10,000 feet, the subalpine complex thrives. At this altitude, whitebark pine and mountain hemlock dominate a forest that is often stunted by heavy loads of snow—sometimes flattened into knee-high krummholz. A greater variety of wildflowers takes hold here, including vibrant Indian paintbrush, pink and white heathers, and purple penstemons. This is the territory also of the yellow-bellied marmot and the chirpy pika.

Finally, in the park's highest reaches (generally above 9,000 feet and above treeline), you find the alpine natural community. It's basically a desert, with water often staying frozen except for a brief summer season, when low-growing wildflowers like pink pussy paws thrust their blooms toward the sunshine. The pika and several rodents, as well as some hardy birds and insects, also visit the high ground.

HISTORY

As with all early habitation of North America, placing an exact date on the arrival of human beings in Lassen country is next to impossible. Several

Native American tribes, however, were present in the area when the first Europeans came on the scene. Two of those tribes, the Yana and the Yahi, were obliterated by disease and conflict with the white settlers. The story of the Yahi Indian Ishi, who emerged from the woods south of Lassen early in the twentieth century and spent his final years helping anthropologists from the University of California document his culture, is told with grace and care in the book *Ishi in Two Worlds,* by Theodora Kroeber. The other two tribes from the area, the Maidu and the Atsugewi, were nearly decimated by disease and warfare, but there were survivors, some of whom still live in the region.

Settlement by nonnatives in Lassen country has been relatively sparse when compared to the rest of California, but has still produced its share of characters. Chief among those is the namesake of both park and peak, Peter Lassen. A blacksmith from Denmark, Lassen immigrated to America in 1829, then continued his migration west, finally acquiring a large Mexican land grant in the upper Sacramento Valley. Hoping to establish a town called Benton City on his land, he recruited emigrants from the east, leading them back to his rancho via a circuitous route. The Lassen Trail turned out to be of dubious quality—yes, the emigrants got where they wanted to go, but they were so hammered by hunger and exhaustion that the trail blazer earned himself not fame, but infamy.

Another emigrant trail, established by William H. Nobles, saw considerably more success. Used by thousands of travelers in the 1850s and 1860s, present-day park visitors can hike on the sections of this route that are preserved within the national park.

The spectacular country around Lassen Peak was the focus of preservation efforts for at least ten years before it became a national park. There was some commercial development in the region—in addition to logging operations, resorts were operated at Drakesbad in the Warner Valley and at Juniper Lake, and the Supan family had some success mining in the area of Sulphur Works—but most of the landscape remained in a wild state. As part of ongoing efforts to preserve the unique natural features of the area, both Lassen Peak and the Cinder Cone were designated national monuments in 1907.

But Lassen Peak might never have become the centerpiece of a national park if it hadn't blown its top. Congressman John Raker, who vacationed in Drakesbad with his family, had first petitioned Congress to set aside the area as a national park in 1912, and other movers and shakers, including newspaperman Michael Dittmar and businessman Arthur Conard, were also pressing for preservation when the eruptions began. During its active phase, between 1914 and 1917, Lassen Peak drew a number of intrepid scientists and thrill seekers to its summit, which only bolstered the case presented by the politicians and boosters. One of its greatest champions, Benjamin F. Loomis, a local resident and photographer, climbed to the 10,457-foot summit of the peak on several occasions, and snapped a number of pictures of the mountain. It was partly because of Loomis's startling and spectacular pictures of a 1914 eruption that Lassen and its environs were preserved as a national park in 1916.

How to Use This Guide

HOW THE INFORMATION WAS GATHERED

The research for this book was done in the summers of 1998 and 1999. I hiked almost every trail within the park, save a section of the Nobles Emigrant Trail, which my husband covered while I nursed blisters. The only trails that haven't been described are a couple of little-used routes that lead out of the park.

MILEAGES

The mileages of hikes were difficult to discern exactly. Distances listed on trail signs didn't necessarily mesh with maps, or with one another, for that matter. I relied mostly on the park's trail signs, but in some cases the mileages listed in the book will vary from distances listed on signs and/or maps based on my on-the-ground observations, and for consistency's sake. These variations are very slight and shouldn't affect a hiker's ability to gauge the difficulty or duration of a given hike.

DIFFICULTY RATINGS

The hikes are rated easy, moderate, or strenuous. In assigning a label, I took into account elevation gains and losses, hiking surfaces, and distances. Generally speaking, easy hikes are short and relatively flat. Moderate hikes involve greater distances and (perhaps) greater elevation changes. Strenuous hikes include the ascents of mountains, and long-distance loops or shuttles.

Keep in mind that every trail is only as difficult as you make it. If you keep a pace within your level of fitness, drink plenty of water, and stoke up on good, high-energy foods, you can make any trail easy.

ROUTE FINDING

Trails within Lassen Volcanic National Park are very well marked and nicely maintained. But, as you will see on maps of the area—those in this guide, as well as USGS and other maps of the park—the trails don't have names or numbers, and they seldom lead to a single destination. On some maps in this guide, I have labeled trails for clarity's sake, but keep in mind that these are not official trail names.

Instead, Lassen's trail system is a web of interlocking routes. I have broken these routes down into logical, easy-to-follow day hikes and short backpacking trips, both loops and out-and-back affairs. But you will no doubt find, as I did, that there are myriads of combinations that can be traveled. This guide covers just about every trail, but not every combination. If you've the inclination, pick up a good park map and compass, and explore.

MAPS

There are a number of good maps covering the park. The USGS topographic maps that pertain to each route are listed in hike descriptions, as are two excellent composite maps of the park, one by Earthwalk Press and one by Wilderness Press. The Lassen Volcanic National Park map, which is also listed in hike descriptions, is very general, serving mostly as a useful tool for locating trailheads, but can serve as a trail map in a pinch. The Lassen National Forest map also shows some of the park's trails, as well as access roads to trailheads that are off the beaten track, but it has no topographic detail and is not the best map source for these hikes.

These maps and several others are available at all sales outlets within the park, or can be ordered through the Lassen Loomis Museum Association; (530) 595-3399.

ELEVATION PROFILES

I have created elevation profiles for each of the hikes, using USGS topographic maps as my source. These graphs illustrate the general ups and downs of the hike, but do not show every nuance, and elevations in some cases have been rounded to the nearest 10 feet. Loop trails are graphed in their entirety; out-and-back trails are graphed to the stated destination, but not back.

Backcountry Safety and Hazards

MAKE IT A SAFE TRIP

The Boy Scouts of America have been guided for decades by what is perhaps the single best piece of safety advice—Be prepared! For starters, this means carrying survival and first-aid materials, proper clothing, a compass, and topographic map—and knowing how to use them.

Perhaps the second-best piece of safety advice is to tell somebody where you're going and when you plan to return. Pilots must file flight plans before every trip, and anybody venturing into a blank spot on the map should do the same. File your "flight plan" with a friend or relative before taking off.

Along with filing your flight plan and being prepared with proper equipment, consider physical conditioning. Being fit not only makes wilderness travel more fun, it makes it safer.

Here are a few more tips:

- Check the weather forecast. Be careful not to get caught at high altitude in a bad storm or along a stream in a flash flood. Watch cloud formations closely so you don't get stranded on a ridgeline during a lightning storm. Avoid traveling during prolonged periods of cold weather.

- Avoid traveling alone in the wilderness and keep your party together.

- Don't exhaust yourself or other members of your party by traveling too far or too fast. Let the slowest person set the pace.

- Study basic survival and first aid before leaving home.

- Before you leave for the trailhead, find out as much as you can about the route, especially the potential hazards.

- Don't wait until you're confused to look at your maps. Follow them as you go along, so you have a continual fix on your location.

- If you get lost, don't panic. Sit down and relax for a few minutes while you carefully check your topo map and take a compass reading. Confidently plan your next move. It's often smart to retrace your steps until you find familiar ground, even if you think it might lengthen your trip. Lots of people get temporarily lost in the wilderness and survive—usually by calmly and rationally dealing with the situation.

- Stay clear of all wild animals.

- Take a first-aid kit that includes, at a minimum, a sewing needle, snakebite kit, aspirin or over-the-counter pain reliever, antibacterial ointment, antiseptic swabs, butterfly bandages, adhesive tape, adhesive strips, two triangular bandages, two inflatable splints, moleskin or Second Skin for blisters, 3-inch gauze, CPR shield, rubber gloves, and lightweight first-aid instructions.

- Take a survival kit that includes, at a minimum, a compass, whistle, matches in a waterproof container, cigarette lighter, candle, signal mirror, flashlight, fire starter, aluminum foil, water purification tablets, space blanket, and flare.

Lastly, don't forget that knowledge is the best defense against unexpected hazards. Read up on the latest in wilderness safety information in Falcon's *Wild Country Companion*.

BE BEAR AWARE

The first step of any hike in bear country is an attitude adjustment. Being prepared for bears doesn't only mean having the right equipment, it also means having the right information. Black bears do not, as a rule, attack humans, but they may pose a danger if you handle your food improperly. At the very least, letting a bear get human food is like contributing—directly— to the eventual destruction of that bear. Think of proper bear etiquette as protecting the bears as much as yourself.

CAMPING IN BEAR COUNTRY

Staying overnight in bear country is not dangerous, but the presence of food, cooking utensils, and garbage adds risk to your trip. Plus, bears are usually most active at night. A few basic practices will greatly minimize the chance of encounter.

To be as safe as possible, store everything that has any food smell. Ziplocked bags are perfect for reducing food smell and keeping food from spilling on your pack, clothing, or other gear. Store food in airtight, sturdy, waterproof bags to prevent food odors from circulating throughout the forest. You can purchase dry bags at most outdoor specialty stores, but you can get by with a trash compactor bag. Don't use regular garbage bags as they can break too easily.

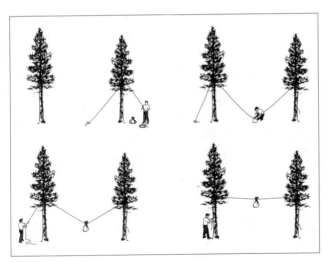

Hanging food and garbage between two trees.

8

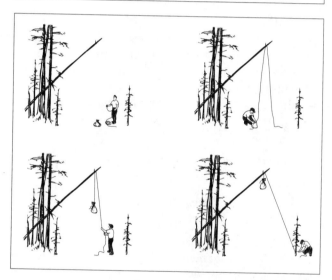

Hanging food and garbage over a tree branch.

Hanging food and garbage over a leaning tree.

If you have spilled something on your clothes, change into different clothes for sleeping and treat the clothes with food smells as you would food and garbage. If you take them into the tent, you aren't separating your sleeping area from food smells. Try to keep food odors off your pack, but if you fail, put the food bag inside and hang the pack outside. Campers should use the bear-proof lockers provided at campgrounds and never bring food into their tents. If no lockers are available, hang your food-smelling items in a tree (see diagrams).

Be sure to finalize your food storage plans before it gets dark. It's not only difficult to store food after darkness falls, but it's easier to overlook some juicy morsel on the ground.

See the diagrams for different ways to hang a bear bag. If you have two bags to hang, divide your food into two equal sacks. Use a stone to toss the end of a piece of nylon cord (parachute cord is fine; under most circumstances there is no need for the heavier stuff) over a limb at least twenty feet high and well out from the trunk, then tie half your food to the end. Pull the food up to the limb, then tie your remaining food sack onto the cord as high as you can reach. Stuff the excess cord into the food sack, then use a stick to push the second sack several feet higher than your head. The first sack will act as a counterweight and descend a few feet, but it should remain at least as high as the second sack. In the morning, use a stick to pull down one of the sacks.

Don't get paranoid about the types of food you bring—all food has some smell. By consciously reducing the number of dishes and the amount of packaging, and consuming everything on your plate (pack out all food scraps), as well as by paying careful attention to storage, you will not only make your backpacking culinary experience more enjoyable and hassle-free for yourself, but also more bear proof.

Read *Bear Aware* by Bill Schneider for complete information on camping in bear country.

BE MOUNTAIN LION ALERT

Though many people consider themselves lucky to see a mountain lion in the wild, the big cats—nature's perfect predator—are potentially dangerous. Attacks on humans are extremely rare, but it's wise to educate yourself before heading into mountain lion habitat.

To stay as safe as possible when hiking in mountain lion country, follow this advice:

1. Travel with a friend or in a group, and stay together.

2. Don't let small children wander away by themselves.

3. Don't let pets run unleashed.

4. Avoid hiking at dawn and dusk—the times mountain lions are most active.

5. Know how to behave if you encounter a mountain lion.

In the vast majority of mountain lion encounters, these animals exhibit avoidance, indifference, or curiosity that never results in human injury. But it is natural to be alarmed if you have an encounter of any kind. Try to keep your cool and consider the following:

Recognize threatening mountain lion behavior. A few cues may help you gauge the risk of attack. If a mountain lion is more than 50 yards away, and it directs its attention to you, it may be only curious. This situation represents only a slight risk to adults but a more serious risk to unaccompanied children. At this point, you should move away, while keeping the animal in your peripheral vision. Also, look for rocks, sticks, or something to use as a weapon, just in case.

If a mountain lion is crouched and staring at you less than 50 yards away, it may be assessing the chances of a successful attack. If this behavior continues, the risk of attack may be high.

Do not approach a mountain lion. Give the animal the opportunity to move on. Slowly back away, but maintain eye contact if close. Mountain lions are not known to attack humans to defend young or a kill, but they have been reported to "charge" in rare instances and may want to stay in the area. It's best to choose another route or time to hike through the area.

Do not run from a mountain lion. Running may stimulate a predatory response.

Make noise. If you encounter a mountain lion, be vocal and talk or yell loudly and regularly. Try not to panic. Shout to make others in the area aware of the situation.

Maintain eye contact. Eye contact presents a challenge to the mountain lion, showing you are aware of its presence. Eye contact also helps you know where it is. However, if the behavior of the mountain lion is not threatening (if it is, for example, grooming or periodically looking away), maintain visual contact through your peripheral vision and move away.

Appear larger than you are. Raise your arms above your head and make steady waving motions. Raise your jacket or another object above your head. Do not bend over, as this will make you appear smaller and more "prey-like."

If you are with small children, pick them up. Bring children close to you, maintain eye contact with the mountain lion, and pull the children up without bending over. If you are with other children or adults, band together.

Defend yourself and others. If attacked, fight back. Try to remain standing. Do not feign death. Pick up a branch or rock; pull out a knife, pepper spray, or other deterrent device. Individuals have fended off mountain lions with rocks, tree limbs, and even cameras. Keep in mind this is a last ditch effort. Defending pets is not recommended.

Respect any warning signs posted by agencies.

Teach others in your group how to behave in case of a mountain lion encounter.

Report encounters. Record your location and the details of any encounter and notify the nearest landowner or land-managing agency. The land management agency (federal, state, or county) may want to visit the site and, if appropriate, post education/warning signs. Fish and wildlife agencies should also be notified because they record and track such encounters.

If physical injury occurs, it is important to leave the area and not disturb the site of attack. Mountain lions that have attacked people must be killed, and an undisturbed site is critical for effectively locating the dangerous mountain lion.

See Falcon Publishing's *Mountain Lion Alert* for more details and tips for safe outdoor recreation in mountain lion country.

WEATHER

Depending on the severity of the winter, Lassen Peak can remain draped in snow into August. Hiking trails melt off more slowly as the altitude increases;

thus, trails on the mountain's lower slopes are accessible earlier than those reached from the park road near Lake Helen.

Weather during the hiking season, from late May to October, is generally good, with sunny skies and moderate temperatures predominating. The mountains are occasionally beset by thunderstorms, which may include hail and lightning. At higher altitudes, you may encounter wind and dropping temperatures, so be sure to pack layers of additional clothing.

Lightning: You might never know what hit you

Mountains are prone to sudden thunderstorms. If you get caught in a lightning storm, take special precautions.

- Lightning can travel ahead of a storm, so take cover before the storm hits.

- Don't try to make it back to your vehicle. It isn't worth the risk. Instead, seek shelter even if it's only a short way back to the trailhead. Lightning storms usually don't last long, and from a safe vantage point, you might enjoy the sights and sounds.

- Be especially careful not to get caught on a mountaintop or exposed ridge; under large, solitary trees; in the open; or near standing water.

- Seek shelter in a low-lying area, ideally in a stand of small, uniformly sized trees.

- Avoid anything that attracts lightning, like metal tent poles, graphite fishing rods, or pack frames.

- Crouch with both feet firmly on the ground.

- If you have a pack (without a metal frame) or a sleeping pad with you, put your feet on it for extra insulation against shock.

- Don't walk or huddle together. Instead, stay 50 feet apart, so if somebody gets hit by lightning, others in your party can give first aid.

- If you are in a tent, stay in your sleeping bag with your feet on your sleeping pad.

Hypothermia: The silent killer

Be aware of hypothermia—a condition in which the body's internal temperature drops below normal. It can lead to mental and physical collapse and death.

Hypothermia is caused by exposure to cold and is aggravated by wetness, wind, and exhaustion. The moment you begin to lose heat faster than your body produces it, you're suffering from exposure. Your body starts involuntary exercise, such as shivering, to stay warm and makes involuntary adjustments to preserve normal temperature in vital organs, restricting bloodflow in the extremities. Both responses drain your energy reserves. The only way to stop the drain is to reduce the degree of exposure.

With full-blown hypothermia, as energy reserves are exhausted, cold blood reaches the brain, depriving you of good judgment and reasoning power. You won't be aware that this is happening. You lose control of your hands. Your internal temperature slides downward. Without treatment, this slide leads to stupor, collapse, and death.

Logs offer an alternative to wading Kings Creek.

To defend against hypothermia, stay dry. When clothes get wet, they lose about 90 percent of their insulating value. Wool loses relatively less heat; cotton, down, and some synthetics lose more. Choose rain clothes that cover the head, neck, body, and legs and provide good protection against wind-driven rain. Most hypothermia cases develop in air temperatures between 30 and 50 degrees, but hypothermia can develop in warmer temperatures.

If your party is exposed to wind, cold, and wet, watch yourself and others for uncontrollable fits of shivering; vague, slow, slurred speech; memory lapses; incoherence; immobile, fumbling hands; frequent stumbling or a lurching gait; drowsiness; apparent exhaustion; and inability to get up after a rest. When a member of your party has hypothermia, he may deny any problem. Believe the symptoms, not the victim. Even mild symptoms demand the following treatment:

- Get the victim out of the wind and rain.

- Strip off all wet clothes.

- If the victim is only mildly impaired, give her warm drinks. Then get the victim into warm clothes and a warm sleeping bag. Place well-wrapped water bottles filled with heated water close to the victim.

- If the victim is badly impaired, attempt to keep him awake. Put the victim in a sleeping bag with another person—both naked. If you have a double bag, put two warm people in with the victim.

HYDROTHERMAL AREAS

Some of these trails lead to hydrothermal areas, where fumeroles (steam vents), hot springs, and mud pots exist. The park has posted warning signs about these potential hazards. Please heed these warnings, remaining on established trails, to avoid serious injury.

General Park Information

Lassen Volcanic National Park is a fee area. Entrance permits may be purchased at either the Manzanita Lake or Southwest Entrance Stations. When these stations are not manned, or at self-registration areas at the other three park entrances, Butte Lake, Juniper Lake, and Drakesbad, follow posted directions to self-register. All permits must be clearly visible in the front windshields of vehicles.

More than 79,000 of Lassen Volcanic National Park's 100,000 acres are designated wilderness. Please respect this designation by not invading it with mechanized vehicles of any sort.

CONTACTS

For general park information, contact:

Lassen Volcanic National Park
P.O. Box 100
Mineral, CA 96063
(530) 595-4444

In case of emergency, call 911.

You can reach the **Loomis Ranger Station** at (530) 595-4444 ext. 5187.

The **Southwest Information Station,** located adjacent to the Lassen Chalet, can be reached at (530) 595-3308 during the summer months only. You can obtain publications, wilderness permits, and horse permits here.

The **Loomis Museum,** which also serves as the park's visitor center, is at Manzanita Lake. It is open daily from 9 A.M. to 5 P.M. from mid-June to late September, and on weekends beginning with the Memorial Day weekend. Call (530) 595-4444 ext. 5180. The museum/visitor center offers exhibits, orientation films, publications, wilderness permits, and horse permits.

The **Lassen Loomis Museum Association** is a nonprofit educational organization that assists the National Park Service in promoting Lassen Volcanic National Park and educating its visitors. The organization publishes a variety of educational materials, which can be obtained at the Loomis Museum, the Lassen Chalet, the Manzanita Lake camper store, and other outlets, as well as through the association itself. For mail order purchases or to become a member, write to P.O. Box 220, Mineral, CA 96063; (530) 595-3399, or e-mail llmassoc@aol.com. Appendix C includes a listing of some of the titles offered by the association.

The **Lassen Park Foundation,** a private, nonprofit organization, provides funding for projects within the park and the surrounding national forest. For more information or to make a donation, write to P.O. Box 3155, Chico, CA 95927-3155, or call (530) 898-9309.

Lassen Volcanic National Park is surrounded by the Lassen National Forest, and is bordered on the east by the Caribou Wilderness. The USDA Forest Service administers both the forest and the wilderness. The nearest forest service offices are:

Hat Creek Ranger District
P.O. Box 220
Fall River Mills, CA 96028
(530) 336-5521

Almanor Ranger District
P.O. Box 767
Chester, CA 96020
(530) 258-2141

ROADS

Roadways within the park generally open once winter snows have melted. Call the park at (530) 595-4444 for road information.

The Lassen Park Road (California 89) is the main route through the park, offering access to the hiking trails and campgrounds in the park's western section. It is generally clear of snow and open by mid-June and closes by late October. During the winter, the road is plowed to the Lassen Chalet on the southwest side and to the Loomis Ranger House on the north side. Call the main park number for up-to-the-minute road conditions.

The Butte Lake Road, a good gravel road that leads 7 miles from California 44 to the Butte Lake Campground, is usually open by mid-May and closes in November.

The Juniper Lake Road (Plumas County 318) is paved for its first 5.5 miles, then becomes gravel. It is not suitable for trailers. It is usually open by mid-June and closes in late October.

The Warner Valley/Drakesbad Road (Plumas County 312) is generally open between late May and November. It is paved for the first 14 miles, then is gravel for 3 miles. It is not suitable for trailers.

CAMPING

Campgrounds within the park generally open as the winter snows melt off. Manzanita Lake is usually the first to open, and Summit Lake the last. Check with park officials about whether a specific campground is open by calling (530) 595-4444.

The following regulations apply to all campsites:

- Sites are available on a first come, first served basis. Camping in all campgrounds is limited to 14 days per year, except for Summit Lake, where overnight stays are limited to 7 per year.

- Campfires are permitted in formal fire rings only, and the use of chainsaws to collect firewood is prohibited.

- Two vehicles are permitted per campsite, and must park on the designated parking pad.

- Six adults (10 people total with children) are allowed per site. Quiet hours are from 10 P.M. to 6 A.M.

- There are seven formal campgrounds in the park. Specific information about each follows:

Manzanita Lake: There are 179 sites available, at $14 per night. Facilities include fire rings, flush toilets, showers, tables, bear-proof cabinets for food storage, piped water, and garbage collection. Additional attractions include non-motorized boating, fishing, and swimming. Some sites accommodate trailers up to 35 feet in length; the trailer dumping fee is $5. Other amenities include a camper store, laundry facilities, pay telephones, and ranger-led programs at the amphitheater. The Loomis Museum/visitor center is also in the area.

Crags: There are 45 sites available, at $8 per night. Facilities include fire rings, vault toilets, tables, bear-proof cabinets for food storage, piped water, and garbage collection. Trailers up to 35 feet in length can be accommodated.

Summit Lake: There are two campgrounds at Summit Lake, with a total of 94 sites. Fees are $14 per night in the north campground, $12 per night in the south. Facilities include fire rings, vault and flush toilets, tables, bear-proof cabinets for food storage, piped water, and garbage collection. Additional attractions include swimming, non-motorized boating, a ranger station, and ranger-led programs.

Southwest: There are 21 sites available, at $12 per night. Facilities include fire rings, flush toilets, tables, bear-proof cabinets for food storage, piped water, and garbage collection. The Lassen Chalet, with restaurant and concession services, is open during the summer. Trailers may use the chalet parking lot for self-contained camping for $8 per night, and should register at the campground.

Butte Lake: There are 45 to 101 sites available, at $10 per night. Facilities include fire rings, vault toilets, tables, bear-proof cabinets for food storage, and garbage collection. Water is slated to be available for the 2001 or 2002 summer season. Other attractions include swimming and non-motorized boating. There is a ranger station.

Juniper Lake: There are 18 sites available, at $12 per night. Facilities include fire rings, vault toilets, tables, bear-proof cabinets for food storage, and garbage collection. Other attractions include swimming and non-motorized boating. Trailers are not recommended.

Warner Valley: There are 18 sites available, at $10 per night. Facilities include fire rings, vault toilets, tables, bear-proof cabinets for food storage, piped water, and garbage collection. Other attractions include stream fishing. Trailers are not recommended. There is a ranger station at Warner Valley.

MISCELLANEOUS REGULATIONS

• Bicycles are permitted on park roads and in campgrounds, but are prohibited on trails. Skating, skateboarding, and in-line skating are prohibited.

• Pets are not permitted on trails, in the backcountry, or in any body of water within the park. If they are kept on leash, pets are allowed in campgrounds and picnic areas, on established roadways and in other developed areas. Clean up after your pet, and take responsibility for its behavior.

• Fishing is permitted in most lakes and streams within the park, with the exception of Emerald Lake, Manzanita Creek, and the portion of Manzanita Lake within 150 feet of the inlet. Catch-and-release fishing only is permitted on Manzanita Lake; artificial lures and single, barbless hooks may be used.

• Horses are allowed in the park by permit only. No overnight camping is allowed in the backcountry. Permits may be obtained through the park offices. Corrals are available by reservation at Summit and Juniper Lakes.

Backcountry Permits and Regulations

Backcountry permits are required for overnight camping in Lassen's backcountry. There is no self-registration. You may obtain a permit by mail in advance by calling the park at (530) 595-4444. Allow at least two weeks for the permit to be processed and sent out.

Permits may also be obtained in person from the Loomis Museum at Manzanita Lake, park headquarters in Mineral, the Southwest Information Station at the Lassen Chalet, and the entrance stations at Manzanita Lake and the Southwest Entrance. You can also obtain a backcountry permit through the USDA Forest Service at its offices in Old Station and Almanor. Call (530) 595-4444 for more information.

Other important regulations:

- A maximum of 10 people is allowed per permit, though up to 20 people may hike in a group.
- Camping is limited to 14 days per year.
- Fires are prohibited. Use a portable camp stove for cooking.
- Hang food and garbage out of reach of animals (see Be Bear Aware section).
- Purify water from lakes and streams before drinking by boiling, filtering, or chemically treating it.
- Do not wash clothing or utensils, or use any cleansing agents, in lakes or streams.
- Camp at least 300 feet from other backcountry groups.
- Do not camp in meadows or on fragile vegetation.
- Camp at least 100 feet from the lakes, springs, and streams.
- Camp at least one mile from campgrounds, park roads, and other developed areas.
- Some areas, like Echo Lake, are closed to backcountry camping. Check with a park ranger about these areas.

Zero Impact

Nowadays most wilderness users want to walk softly, but some aren't aware that they have poor manners. Often their actions are dictated by the outdated habits of a past generation of campers who cut green boughs for evening shelters, built campfires with fire rings, and dug trenches around tents. In the 1950s, these practices may have been acceptable. But they leave long-lasting scars, and today such behavior is absolutely unacceptable.

Because wild places are becoming rare and the number of users is mushrooming, a new code of ethics must be employed by the unending waves of people seeking a perfect backcountry experience. Today, we all must leave no clues of our passage. Enjoy the wild, but leave no trace of your visit.

THREE FALCON PRINCIPLES OF ZERO IMPACT
- Leave with everything you brought in.
- Leave no sign of your visit.
- Leave the landscape as you found it.

Most of us know better than to litter—in or out of the backcountry. Be sure you leave nothing, regardless of how small it is, along the trail or at your campsite. This means you should pack out everything, including orange peels, flip tops, cigarette butts, and gum wrappers. Also, pick up any trash that others leave behind.

Follow the main trail. Avoid cutting switchbacks and walking on vegetation beside the trail. Don't pick up "souvenirs," such as rocks, antlers, or wildflowers. The next person wants to see them too, and collecting such souvenirs violates many regulations.

Avoid making loud noises on the trail (unless you are in bear country) or in camp. Be courteous—remember, sound travels easily in the backcountry, especially across water.

Carry a lightweight trowel to bury human waste 6–8 inches deep and at least 200 feet from any water source. Pack out used toilet paper.

Go without a campfire if you can't find an established fire pit. Carry a stove for cooking and a flashlight, candle lantern, or headlamp for light. For emergencies, learn how to build a no-trace fire.

Camp in obviously used sites when they are available. Otherwise, camp and cook on durable surfaces such as bedrock, sand, gravel bars, or bare ground.

Details on these guidelines and recommendations of Zero Impact principles for specific outdoor activities can be found in the FalconGuide *Leave No Trace.* Visit your local bookstore, or call Falcon Publishing at (800) 582-2665 for a copy.

Leave no trace—and put your ear to the ground and listen carefully. Thousands of people coming behind you are thanking you for your courtesy and good sense.

Lassen Volcanic National Park Trail Finder

	EASY	MODERATE	STRENUOUS
Lovely Lakes	11 Cold Boiling Lake 30 Reflection Lake 33 Manzanita Lake 36 Bathtub Lake 53 Boiling Springs Lake	4 Ridge Lakes 8 Terrace and Shadow Lakes 12 Crumbaugh Lake 14 Sifford Lake 20 Echo Lake 21 Upper and Lower Twin Lakes 23 Big and Little Bear Lakes 32 Chaos Lake 43 Juniper Lake 44 Crystal Lake	9 Cliff Lake 22 Rainbow Lake 24 Cluster Lakes 37 Widow Lake 40 Butte and Snag Lakes 46 Jakey Lake 48 Indian Lake 51 Drake Lake
Wonderful Waterfalls		2 Mill Creek Falls 16 Kings Creek Falls	
Get an Education	29 Devastated Area Interpretive Trail 31 Lily Pond Nature Trail	6 Bumpass Hell Nature Trail	
Go Climb a Volcano		38 Prospect Peak 39 Cinder Cone 42 Mount Harkness	1 Brokeoff Mountain 7 Lassen Peak
Boiling Pools, Mud Pots, and the Smell of Sulphur	5 Sulphur Works	6 Bumpass Hell Nature Trail 53 Boiling Springs Lake 54 Terminal Geyser	52 Devils Kitchen
Bring the Kids	5 Sulphur Works 29 Devastated Area Interpretive Trail 31 Lily Pond Nature Trail 36 Bathtub Lake 50 Dream Lake	11 Cold Boiling Lake 44 Crystal Lake	6 Bumpass Hell Nature Trail 39 Cinder Cone

	EASY	MODERATE	STRENUOUS
Spend the Night in the Backcountry	21 Upper and Lower Twin Lakes 46 Jakey Lake	24 Cluster Lakes Loop 40 Butte and Snag Lakes Loop 41 Rainbow and Snag Lakes Loop 58 Nobles Emigrant Trail—Eastern Section	57 Pacific Crest Trail

Author Picks

Best Meadow	26 Paradise Meadow
Best Lakes	41 Rainbow and Snag Lakes Loop
Best Little Volcano	39 Cinder Cone
Best Big Volcano	1 Brokeoff Mountain
Best Famous Volcano	7 Lassen Peak
Best Waterfall	15 Kings Creek Falls
Best Hydrothermal Area	52 Devils Kitchen
Best Zen Hike	58 Nobles Emigrant Trail—Eastern Section

Southwest Entrance

Lassen Volcanic National Park is a kaleidoscope of wilderness. It is volcanic and glacial, barren and densely forested, marshy and sandy, peaceful and frightening. What you see in any part of the park is dependent on the force that has most shaped that area, and that force varies from place to place.

In the southwest corner of the park, the dominant dimension is prehistoric. Mount Tehama, a long-defunct composite volcano in the tradition of Mount Shasta, is the foundation upon which the panoramas throughout this portion of the park are built. The volcano, which topped out at more than 11,000 feet, formed between 600,000 and 400,000 years ago, and was gradually whittled away by an earth mover as powerful as volcanism—water, in the form of glaciers and creeks.

Today, the remnant of Mount Tehama displays its legacy in the ragged peaks sprawling south and west in a half-moon: Brokeoff Mountain, Mount Diller, Pilot Pinnacle, and Mount Conard. It hisses from the fumeroles at the Sulphur Works, and its minerals stain the bed of Sulphur Creek. Its presence is felt on each of the hikes described in this chapter, from the craggy summit of Brokeoff Mountain to the interpretive signs along the boardwalks at the Sulphur Works, which describe the volcano's rise and fall.

The Southwest Entrance to the park is located off California Highway 36, which runs between Red Bluff to the west and Chester to the east, and passes through Mineral, where the park's headquarters are located. To reach the entrance, turn north off CA 36 onto CA 89, the Lassen Park Road, which leads 5 miles to the entrance station.

Amenities near the Southwest Entrance include the Southwest Walk-in Campground, where you will find 21 walk-in campsites with fire rings, water sources, and restrooms. The fee is $12 per night. The café and gift shop in the Lassen Chalet is open for business from the end of May through the end of October.

1 Brokeoff Mountain

Highlights: From the summit of Brokeoff Mountain, views stretch in every direction: north to Lassen Peak, east and south to the foothills of the Sierra Nevada and Lake Almanor, and west across the upper Sacramento Valley.

Type of hike: Day hike; out-and-back.

Total distance: 7 miles.

Difficulty: Strenuous.

Best months: Late June–late September.

Maps: USGS Lassen Peak quad; Lassen Volcanic National Park maps by the National Park Service, Earthwalk Press, and Wilderness Press; USDAFS Lassen National Forest map.

Special considerations: You gain a lot of altitude on this hike, reaching a summit of 9,235 feet. Watch for symptoms of altitude sickness, including fatigue, headache, and nausea. Descend immediately should any of these symptoms materialize. The summit, and parts of the approaches, also features some thrilling exposure, so watch your step.

Parking and facilities: There is a parking area at the trailhead, but no other facilities. You can find restrooms and other amenities, including a café, 0.5 mile farther north on the Lassen Park Road (California Highway 89) at the Southwest Walk-in Campground and at the Lassen Chalet.

Finding the trailhead: The trailhead is located 0.5 mile south of the Southwest Entrance Station and Southwest Walk-in Campground, and 5 miles north of the intersection of CA 89 and CA 36 east of Mineral.

Key points:

0.0 Brokeoff Mountain Trailhead.

1.5 Pass Forest Lake.

2.5 Traverse the rocky upper face of the mountain.

3.5 Arrive on the summit.

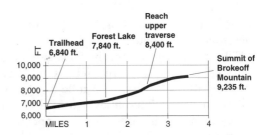

The hike: No doubt some will find this blasphemous, but Brokeoff Mountain is arguably the best mountain climb in Lassen Volcanic National Park. Yes, Lassen Peak is higher, and yes, the summit of Lassen Peak is wonderfully dramatic, with its staggering views and evocative crater. But Brokeoff Mountain features sublime hiking through varied terrain, a thrillingly exposed traverse along its summit ridge, and views of Lassen Peak that are unparalleled. Plus, even in the height of summer, when the trail up Lassen is a human highway, you may find yourself

Brokeoff Mountain

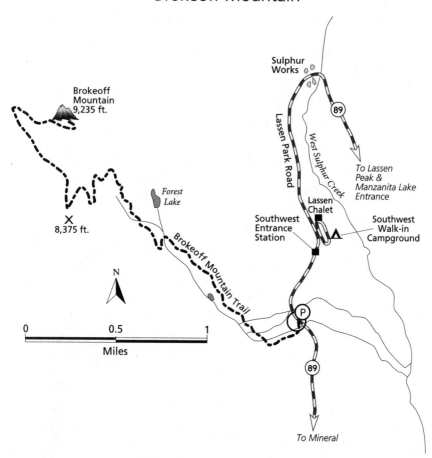

alone on the summit of Brokeoff Mountain. Just you, and the wind, and the views, and the wonder.

The trail departs from the west side of California Highway 89 opposite the trailhead parking area. The climb begins immediately, but mellows briefly within the first 0.25 mile as you cross several small streams that fall from Forest Lake above to Mill Creek in the valley below. As you ascend, you catch glimpses of the spectacular summits in this portion of the park: Lassen Peak, Mount Diller, Pilot Pinnacle, and, of course, your ultimate destination.

The trail passes through alternating evergreen groves and small meadows as it climbs alongside the Forest Lake outlet stream. The thick red fir forests provide welcomed shade for hard-working hikers, and the meadows are alluring, thick with wildflowers, and buzzing with insects. The trail steepens as it climbs over a bench and into a shallow basin. A small pond lies to the left (west) of the trail; beyond, the trail crosses to the west side of the stream over two small log footbridges.

The path traverses above the meadow-lined stream, then arcs to the south, and switches back as it climbs onto a sunny knoll at 1.5 miles. Forest Lake is tucked in the trees to the right (northeast) of the knoll, almost the same deep green as the forest that embraces it. A brief cross-country trek along the lake's outlet stream will lead directly to its shores.

Above the lake, the terrain changes. There is still a stream running near the trail—for a little while, at least—but the trees become sparser, and fade from red fir to whitebark pine as you ascend into a dry, open basin. The barren, east-facing slope of Brokeoff Mountain serves as the headwall of the basin. The trail crosses from the south to the north side, skirts the north wall, then crosses back to the south, and climbs switchbacks out of the basin onto the wooded southern shoulder of the mountain.

From this high point, you can look back and marvel at how far you've already come. The trail bends west through a shimmering bowl of silver-leaf lupine; from here, you can see how far you've got to go. Above the bowl, swing through a talus field and onto an exposed ridge, where winter weather has bent and gnarled the few trees that cling to the rocky soil.

The narrowing ridge leads to a traverse of the rocky, south-facing slope of the mountain at 2.5 miles. The incline is relatively gentle, but given the altitude and the distance already traveled, it is less than easy. The trees get thinner and thinner, and the views more and more impressive as you ascend westward, then round a switchback and climb toward the east. A few hardy trees and wildflowers find purchase here, while the crickets abound in late summer, scattering from footfall into the crevices in the talus.

The trail passes between a silvering stump and a patch of living krummholz as it attains the summit ridge. The talus slope sweeps steeply away to

Lassen Peak as seen from near Brokeoff Mountain's summit.

the south, but the mountain drops precipitously to the north. It is an odd feeling to know you are on solid ground on the south side of the summit ridge, but 100 yards up and over, you would drop into the void.

That void is glimpsed at a break in the ridge. You can look down through Brokeoff's broken rock into Brokeoff Meadows; the distant lake more than a thousand feet below looks like a small sapphire. Lassen Peak, rising to the north, is framed perfectly in this rugged window.

The trail continues along the south face of the summit ridge to the flat top of the mountain at 3.5 miles, where, on a clear day, the vistas are unbeatable, reaching to the snowy summit of Mount Shasta to the northwest, and southwest across the low, forested summits into the upper Sacramento Valley. Back to the east, you can look down into the maw of ancient Mount Tehama, then up and away into the Sierra Nevada.

A cluster of rocks on the west side of the summit "plateau" holds the register, along with a U.S. Geological Survey earthquake marker. When you are ready, you can return the way you came.

2   Mill Creek Falls

Highlights:	A shaded overlook offers great views of the sharp spill of Mill Creek Falls.
Type of hike:	Day hike; out-and-back.
Total distance:	3 miles.
Difficulty:	Moderate.
Best months:	Late May–October.
Maps:	USGS Lassen Peak; Lassen Volcanic National Park maps by the National Park Service, Earthwalk Press, and Wilderness Press; USDAFS Lassen National Forest map.
Special considerations:	Walk with care around the cascade's overlooks, as a misstep could lead to a nasty fall.
Parking and facilities:	There is plenty of parking, as well as restrooms and a water source, at the Southwest Walk-in Campground. Food and other amenities are located in the nearby Lassen Chalet.

Finding the trailhead: From the Southwest Entrance, follow the Lassen Park Road (California Highway 89) north for 0.1 mile to the Southwest Walk-in Campground entrance. The trailhead is on the east side of the parking lot, about 50 yards north of the restrooms.

Key points:

0.0   Mill Creek Falls Trailhead.
0.2   Cross West Sulphur Creek.
0.5   Enter the East Sulphur Creek drainage.
1.5   Arrive at the Mill Creek Falls overlook.

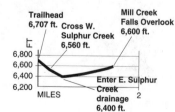

Mill Creek Falls • Conard Meadows and Crumbaugh Lake

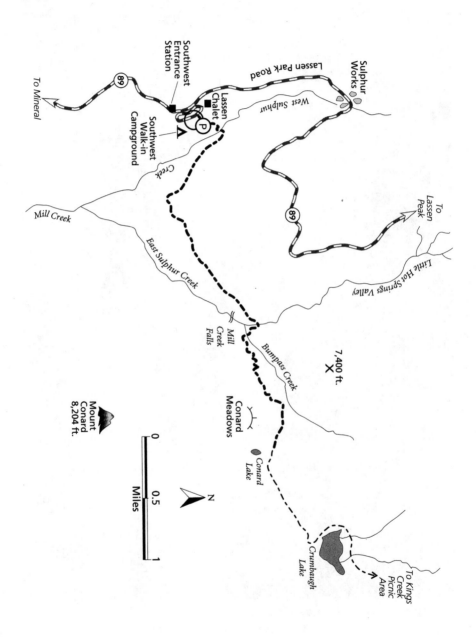

Mill Creek Falls as seen from the trailside overlook.

The hike: Mill Creek Falls is a vigorous whitewater spill of nearly 100 feet. The spray from the falls darkens the cream- and gold-colored rock of the cliff over which it cascades, and the narrow gorge of East Sulphur Creek resonates with its splendid roar. The falls can be enjoyed from a shady overlook along the Mill Creek Falls Trail, or from a thrilling perch at the very brink of the falls, where the creek gathers itself into a frothy fury before taking the plunge.

The trail begins in the picnic area of the Southwest Walk-in Campground, and winds down through big pines and firs to West Sulphur Creek, which meets with East Sulphur Creek downstream to form Mill Creek. At 0.2 mile, a bridge allows an easy crossing of the creek. Climb up onto the hillside on the north side of the creek, and traverse southward through the knee-high mule ear that flourishes on the sunny slope.

The trail dips into a dense fir forest as it bends east, then northeast into the East Sulphur Creek drainage at 0.5 mile. Like a ride on a roller coaster, the route bucks in and out of gullies as it follows the contours of the creek's ravine, but the trend is generally upward. A gentle roar accompanies you up the canyon, but it can be hard to discern whether what you hear is the falls, or the creek below, or the wind in the trees. Regardless, it's a sweet, wild sound.

The trail emerges from the forest briefly to overlook the canyon, then begins a steep descent to the overlook of Mill Creek Falls, which is at 1.5 miles. This is as good a place as any to stop and enjoy the sight of the falls as it tumbles down terraces into a milky green pool, with the rock on either side of the cascade streaked orange with mineral deposits and green with moss. If you choose, you can hike left (north) on the trail to the bank of East Sulphur Creek above the falls, where a spur trail splits off to the right (south) and downstream to a rocky perch right above the top of the falls.

Return as you came, or, if you are in the mood for a climb, continue to Conard Meadows (Hike 3).

3 Conard Meadows and Crumbaugh Lake

See Map on Page 27

Highlights:	Quiet, colorful Conard Meadows is a restful destination between raucous Mill Creek Falls and peaceful Crumbaugh Lake.
Type of hike:	Day hike; out-and-back or shuttle.
Total distance:	5.6 miles.
Difficulty:	Strenuous.
Best months:	June–October.
Maps:	USGS Lassen Peak and Reading Peak; Lassen Volcanic National Park maps by the National Park Service, Earthwalk Press, and Wilderness Press; USDAFS Lassen National Forest map.
Special considerations:	Take care around Mill Creek Falls, as a misstep could result in a nasty fall.
Parking and facilities:	There is plenty of parking, as well as restrooms and a water source, at the Southwest Walk-in Campground. Food and other amenities are located in nearby Lassen Chalet. There are also restrooms and picnic facilities at the Kings Creek Picnic Area trailhead at the northern terminus of the trail.

Finding the trailhead: To reach the Mill Creek Falls Trailhead from the Southwest Entrance, follow the Lassen Park Road (California Highway 89) north for 0.1 mile to the Southwest Walk-in Campground entrance. The trailhead is on the east side of the parking lot, about 50 yards north of the restrooms. To reach the Kings Creek Picnic Area trailhead from the Southwest Entrance, follow the park road for 11.2 miles, turn right (south) onto the paved picnic area access road, and follow this to the trailhead.

Key points:

0.0	Mill Creek Falls Trailhead.
0.2	Cross West Sulphur Creek.
1.5	Arrive at the Mill Creek Falls overlook.
1.7	Cross East Sulphur Creek and begin to climb.
2.3	Reach Conard Meadows.
2.8	Arrive on the southwest shore of Crumbaugh Lake.
4.0	Reach the Kings Creek Picnic Area.

The hike: When bathed in sharp sunlight, the lush grass of Conard Meadows glows like an incandescent bulb through a green glass shade. It shines in direct contrast to the darker green of the surrounding forest, and complements

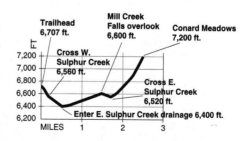

30

Conard Meadows spreads toward Mount Conard.

perfectly the deep blue of the alpine sky. The meadows' overseer, 8,204-foot Mount Conard, guards the southeastern borders of the meadows. Both meadows and mountain are named for Arthur Conard, a resident of Red Bluff who was instrumental in the movement that led to the preservation of Lassen country as a national park.

The meadows can be reached from either the Mill Creek Falls trailhead or the Kings Creek Picnic Area. It is described here from the Mill Creek side; you climb steeply to reach the meadow, but the descent is swift, and the terrain is pleasantly wild. See the description of the hike to Crumbaugh Lake (Hike 11) in the Kings Creek Picnic Area chapter for a detailed route description from this trailhead.

The trail begins at the Southwest Walk-in Campground, plunging down through the fir forest to cross the bridge over West Sulphur Creek at 0.2 mile. The footpath leads onto the hillside on the north side of the creek, traverses this briefly to the south, then bends northeast into the East Sulphur Creek drainage. Follow the trail up the drainage to the Mill Creek Falls overlook at 1.5 miles (see Mill Creek Falls, Hike 2, for more details).

From the overlook, the trail climbs left (north) to the bank of East Sulphur Creek. Stay left (north) at the trail intersection, and head upstream to where two narrow footbridges allow safe crossing of the creek at the mouth of the Little Hot Springs Valley. Switchbacks lead up and southeast away from East Sulphur Creek. A yellow dot on a tree marks the route; the trail drops to cross Bumpass Creek.

More yellow trail markers keep you on the right path as you climb switchbacks out of the Bumpass Creek drainage and into the woods on the south side of the stream. It's a steep ascent, tracing the edge of the deep defile carved by Bumpass Creek, but the pitch lessens once you reach a meadowy area that spills down the slope on the right (southeast) side of the trail.

Finally, at 2.3 miles, the trail emerges from the trees at verdant Conard Meadows. The path drops across a streamlet that flows out of the northwest corner of the meadow, then leads to the north side, where views across the open expanse are best. A rustic sign noting the meadows' altitude, 7,200 feet, confirms your location. Conard Lake lies hidden in the grasses at the head of the meadow, but is out of sight from the trail.

If this is the end of the line for you, return as you came. To continue to Crumbaugh Lake, the trail traces the northern border of the meadow, wedged between the lodgepole pine woodland and the grasses, before immersing itself completely in the forest. You are still climbing, but the pitch is so much less than that ascended earlier that it feels absolutely flat. Occasional clearings allow patches of meadow or clusters of silverleaf lupine to take hold.

At 2.8 miles, you emerge from the woods on the southwest shore of Crumbaugh Lake. Enjoy the peaceful shores before returning as you came. If you have arranged for a shuttle to pick you up at the Kings Creek Picnic Area trailhead, follow the trail around Crumbaugh Lake's north shore, then climb past Cold Boiling Lake to this trailhead at 4 miles (see Hike 11 for more details).

4 Ridge Lakes

Highlights:	These small alpine tarns are cupped in a basin below Brokeoff Mountain and Mount Diller.
Type of hike:	Day hike; out-and-back.
Total distance:	2 miles.
Difficulty:	Strenuous.
Best months:	June–October.
Maps:	USGS Lassen Peak quad; Lassen Volcanic National Park maps by the National Park Service, Earthwalk Press, and Wilderness Press; USDAFS Lassen National Forest map.
Parking and facilities:	There is abundant parking at the trailhead. Restrooms, water, and food are available at the Southwest Campground and Lassen Chalet, located 1 mile south on the Lassen Park Road (California Highway 89).

Finding the trailhead: From the Southwest Entrance, head north on CA 89 for 1 mile to the well-marked trailhead parking area, which is on the left (west) side of the road. From the Manzanita Lake Entrance Station, you'll have to drive nearly the entire length of the park road—28 miles—to the parking lot and trailhead.

Ridge Lakes • Sulphur Works

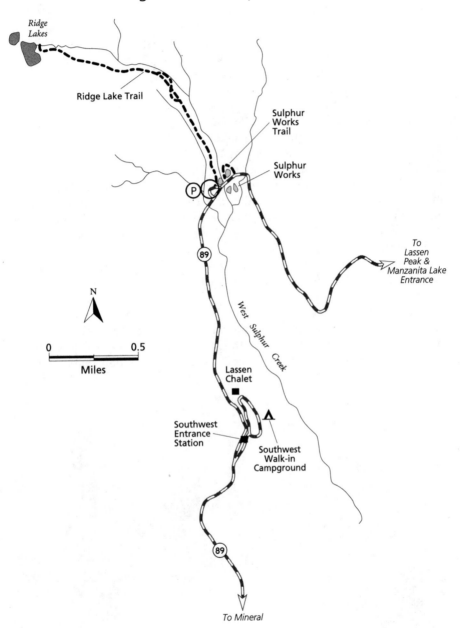

Key points:

0.0	Ridge Lakes Trailhead.
0.5	The trail splits.
1.0	Reach the first Ridge Lake.

The hike: Want that alpine high with a minimum of effort? Hiking to Ridge Lakes might be right up your alley. But don't misunderstand: A minimum of effort doesn't mean you won't have to work to reach these airy heights. While this route hardly compares to an ascent of any of the surrounding mountains, including Lassen Peak, you will have to climb nearly 1,000 feet in 1 mile to reach the lakes.

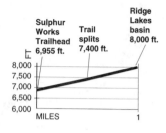

The trail is clean and easy to follow, traveling up a steep wooded ridge to a ravine, then up the ravine to the lake basin. Once there, you can rest on the first lake's rocky shores, enjoying the steep, rosy slopes that spill down from Brokeoff Mountain to the south and Mount Diller to the north.

The Ridge Lakes Trail begins on the north side of the Sulphur Works parking area, and is marked with a trail sign. Head up through the fragrant ferns and grasses onto a narrow ridge that overlooks the Sulphur Works to the northeast. Here, a different fragrance—that of rotten eggs—permeates the air.

After about 0.2 mile, leave the Sulphur Creek drainage behind. The trail curves to the west, following another drainage. Arc back northeast toward Sulphur Creek and continue upward, occasionally catching glimpses of Mount Diller through the trees.

The trail swings back and forth on the ridge between the creek drainages two more times as it continues upward, before finally settling into the northernmost drainage. The footpath splits at about 0.5 mile. Choose either path; they rejoin shortly. Another split lies ahead, in a meadow that in summer

Looking west through the sparse basin holding Ridge Lakes.

is thick with lupine, clover, aster, and skunk cabbage. Again, pick either path as they merge again after a short distance.

Two switchbacks break up the climb at about the 0.7-mile mark. These are followed by an upward traverse through more little meadows, with shade provided by small stands of evergreens. The trail grows rockier as it ascends. A steep pitch leads over a bench into a meadow thick with lupine, then a final pitch takes you into the Ridge Lakes basin at 1.0 mile.

Both lakes are cupped in a stark high-country bowl. The bigger lake lies at trail's end; you'll have to hike cross-country over the rocky terrain to the west to reach the second, smaller lake. A smattering of mountain hemlocks crowns the steep slopes guarding the southern shore of the bigger lake. To the north, Mount Diller stretches along a bony ridge toward the Pilot Pinnacle; to the south, a rounded, rocky slope leads up toward Brokeoff Mountain. If the weather is warm enough, and you are brave enough, you may choose to swim in the lake, or you may decide that simply resting on its shores, enjoying the beauty of the high ground, is reward enough. When you are ready, return to the trailhead on the same route.

5 Sulphur Works

See Map on Page 33

Highlights: This interpretive trail illustrates the evolution and demise of a volcano, with an intense sulphurous smell adding to the ambiance.

Type of hike: Day hike; out-and-back.

Total distance: 0.5 mile.

Difficulty: Easy.

Best months: The Sulphur Works can be visited year-round, though the boardwalks may be icy or completely buried under snow in the height of winter.

Maps: USGS Lassen Peak quad; Lassen Volcanic National Park maps by the National Park Service, Earthwalk Press, and Wilderness Press; USDAFS Lassen National Forest map.

Special considerations: This path wanders through a dangerous hydrothermal area. For your safety, stay on the boardwalks.

Parking and facilities: There is abundant parking at the trailhead. Restrooms, water, and food are available at the Southwest Walk-in Campground and Lassen Chalet, located 1 mile south on the Lassen Park Road (California Highway 89).

Finding the trailhead: From the Southwest Entrance, head north on CA 89 for 1 mile to the well-marked trailhead parking area, which is on the left (west) side of the road. From the Manzanita Lake Entrance Station, you have to drive nearly the entire length of the park road—28 miles—to the parking lot and trailhead.

Key points:
- 0.0   Sulphur Works Trailhead.
- 0.2   Reach the end of the boardwalk.

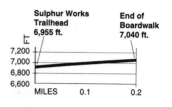

The hike: This remarkable little hike follows boardwalks around the steaming remains of Mount Tehama, a composite volcano whose remnants define the skyline of the southern reaches of Lassen Volcanic National Park. Because it is short, flat, and offers intimate encounters with the geothermal lifeblood of Lassen, this hike is immensely popular, suitable for hikers of all abilities, and often crowded. Interpretive signs describe the sites.

From the parking area, follow the sidewalk adjacent to the park road up and left (northwest) to where the boardwalk begins. Go left (west) at the red warning sign, and climb on the wooden walkway through the sulphurous steam that envelops the trail. The first sign, adjacent to aptly named Sulphur Creek, describes how water and acid are tearing down what remains of Mount Tehama, exposing crystals of sulphur and opal.

Pass another interpretive sign and the boardwalk splits; take the branch to the left (west), which leads to an overview of a bubbling mudpot. Return to the fork, climb the stairs past the stinking fumeroles, traverse along the orange hillside, then cross a bridge over a streamlet tinged an improbable shade of green. The overlook just beyond, at 0.2 mile, features signs describing Tehama's demise at the hands, if you will, of other volcanoes and hungry glaciers, and its spectacular legacy.

Return as you came. When you reach the roadway, carefully cross to the boardwalk on the opposite side, where you can view the beefy steam vent and other fumeroles that erupt from the side of the steep ravine, spilling boiling water into Sulphur Creek. The parking lot, which was never out of sight, is about 100 yards to the southwest.

Looking down on the Sulphur Works.

Lake Helen

This is it, the epitome of Lassen Volcanic National Park's high country. The landscape is stark, shaped by snow that never completely melts, draped with trees hunched over against the extremes. There are four colors here: white (snow), green (trees), blue (sky), and pink (rock). The colors fade into different shades, but always stand in contrast to one another, as though each is outlined in black.

Lake Helen, a small alpine tarn wedged between the Lassen Park Road and the south-facing slope of Lassen Peak, brims with icy meltwater, a patch of turquoise cradled in the mountain's rosy arms. Named for Helen Brodt, historically the first woman to summit the peak, the lake gathers visitors to its shores like a lovely lady attracts suitors—by the droves. Its equally charming sister, Emerald Lake, lies less than 0.5 mile to the west.

While only two formal hikes depart from near Lake Helen, their importance warrants special consideration. The first is the hike up Lassen Peak itself, the ultimate hike within the park. The second leads to Bumpass Hell, a pocket of hydrothermal activity that, given its location in the shadow of the volcano, is a perfect showcase for the forces that have shaped the terrain.

I've included a couple of other hikes in this chapter that, while not immediately adjacent to Lake Helen, are reached from a trailhead high enough on the mountain to impart an alpine feel. Terrace and Shadow Lakes lie just below Lassen Peak's east face, and Cliff Lake lies in a rocky basin beneath the north face of Reading Peak, just off the trail that leads down to Summit Lake.

There are picnic facilities at both Emerald Lake and Lake Helen, and restrooms at the Bumpass Hell Trailhead and the Lassen Peak Trailhead. Both trailheads have large parking areas, but these fill quickly on weekends during the summer. If full, you can park in safe locations along the Lassen Park Road (California Highway 89). A much smaller parking area is available at the Terrace Lake Trailhead, and there are no restrooms at this locale.

To reach the Lake Helen area from the Southwest Entrance, follow the Lassen Park Road (CA 89) north and west for about 6 miles. The lake is on the left (north) side of the road. Bumpass Hell's parking lot is on the right (south) at 5.8 miles, and the Lassen Peak Trailhead is about 1 mile farther north on the park road, on the left (north) side. Terrace Lake is beyond the road's apex, about 9 miles from the Southwest Entrance.

From the Manzanita Lake Entrance Station, follow the Lassen Park Road (CA 89) for about 22 miles to the Lake Helen area. The Terrace Lake Trailhead is at about the 19-mile mark, the Lassen Peak Trail at about 21 miles, and Bumpass Hell at about 22 miles.

6 Bumpass Hell

Highlights:	This trail leads to a large, colorful hydrothermal area that is arguably the most spectacular in the park.
Type of hike:	Day hike; out-and-back.
Total distance:	3 miles.
Difficulty:	Easy.
Best months:	June–October.
Maps:	USGS Lassen Peak and Reading Peak quads; Lassen Volcanic National Park maps by the National Park Service, Earthwalk Press, and Wilderness Press; USDAFS Lassen National Forest map. An interpretive leaflet is available at the trailhead for a fee.
Special considerations:	Bumpass Hell is an active hydrothermal area. Heed signs advising that you stay on the boardwalks for your safety.
Parking and facilities:	There is a large parking lot at the trailhead, but this can be full on busy summer days. If no parking is available, choose a safe spot along the Lassen Park Road (California Highway 89). There are restrooms and picnic sites at the trailhead.

Finding the trailhead: From the park's Southwest Entrance, travel up the Lassen Park Road (CA 89), north and east for about 5.8 miles to the large, paved parking area on the right (south) side of the road. From the Manzanita Lake Entrance Station, follow the Lassen Park Road for about 22 miles to the parking area.

Bumpass Hell as seen from the trail above.

Bumpass Hell

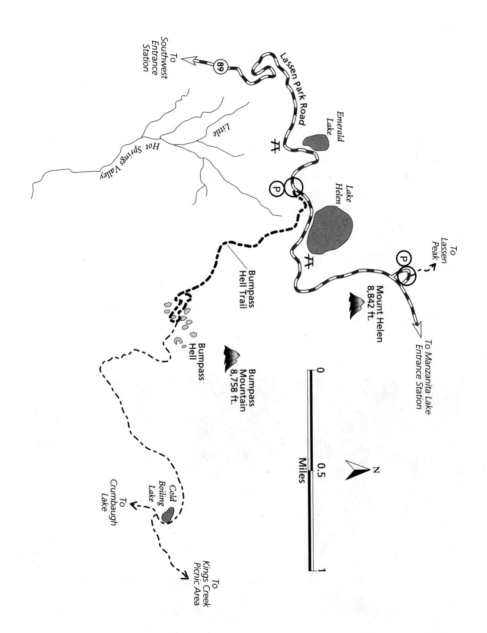

Key points:

- 0.0   Bumpass Hell Trailhead.
- 1.2   The traverse ends and the descent into "hell" begins.
- 1.5   Reach the boardwalks.

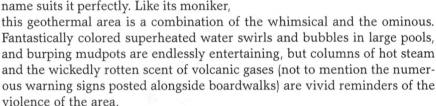

The hike: Bumpass Hell's evocative name suits it perfectly. Like its moniker, this geothermal area is a combination of the whimsical and the ominous. Fantastically colored superheated water swirls and bubbles in large pools, and burping mudpots are endlessly entertaining, but columns of hot steam and the wickedly rotten scent of volcanic gases (not to mention the numerous warning signs posted alongside boardwalks) are vivid reminders of the violence of the area.

Heed the warning signs well, or you may suffer the fate of the area's namesake, Kendall Vanhook Bumpass. He learned about the dangers of hydrothermal areas the hard way, losing a leg after stepping in one of the pools. Be careful, and closely supervise your children.

This trail is very popular, and can be crowded on summer weekends. Finding a spot in the trailhead parking area may require patience or prove impossible; if no parking is available, park along the highway, safely out of the traffic lanes.

The trail begins in the northeast corner of the parking area. Drop gently past a trail sign and pick up a pamphlet that is keyed to the numbered markers that you'll find along the route.

The trail is flat as it meanders by posts 1 through 4, traversing above East Sulphur Creek to the southwest and below Lassen Peak, which rises to the

Bumpass Hell is scenic and educational.

north. Looking southwest across the Little Hot Springs Valley, you'll enjoy great views of the remnants of Mount Tehama, including Brokeoff Mountain, Mount Diller, and Pilot Pinnacle.

A gentle upward traverse leads through a talus field to a trail fork at a saddle shaded by mountain hemlocks. Take the right (west) trail 50 yards to the overlook and an interpretive sign that describes the rise and fall of the Tehama volcano. Return to the main trail and turn right (southeast) to continue.

The brief, gentle climb ends in a colonnade of evergreen trees at 1.2 miles. Wind around a switchback to the first warning sign, and your first glimpse of the milky turquoise pools of Bumpass Hell below. A second overlook, with a bench, lies about midway between the start of the descent and the hot springs; a sign here describes the mishap that befell Kendall Bumpass upon discovery of this "hell." The route descends fairly quickly from the overlook, passing marker 16 as it drops.

Cross the bridge at the base of the descent at 1.5 miles, and you will have arrived. Boardwalks lead to the major features of the hydrothermal area, and eventually circle to the trail that leads back to the parking area. A sign at this point shows you the loops that you can take along the boardwalks, which lead to milky East Pyrite Pool, the steaming Big Boiler, peridot-green West Pyrite Pool, and the thumping mudpots area.

Option: The trail to Cold Boiling Lake, 1.9 miles to the east, begins across the bridge that spans the slate-colored creek that drains the area. This is a nice shuttle hike: Follow the trail to the lake and then up to the Kings Creek Picnic Area. From here, you can either meet a ride, or hike back the way you came to the Bumpass Hell parking area. The round-trip distance is about 6.8 miles.

7 Lassen Peak

Highlights: This is the quintessential hike in the park, leading to the summit of Lassen Peak. On a clear day, you can see the summit of Mount Shasta to the northwest.

Type of hike: Day hike; out-and-back.

Total distance: 4.4 miles.

Difficulty: Strenuous.

Best months: Late July–late September.

Maps: USGS Lassen Peak and Reading Peak quads; Lassen Volcanic National Park maps by the National Park Service, Earthwalk Press, and Wilderness Press; USDAFS Lassen National Forest map.

Special considerations: The summit of Lassen Peak is at 10,457 feet. Symptoms of altitude sickness may develop as you climb, including headache, nausea, and fatigue. If such symptoms arise, retreat immediately to a lower elevation. Carry layers of clothing to protect yourself from wind and changing weather conditions on the summit. Bring plenty of water, as none is available along the trail.

Parking and facilities: There is a large parking lot at the trailhead, but this can be full on busy summer weekends. If this is the case, park in safe areas alongside the Lassen Park Road. Portable restrooms are available in the parking area.

Finding the trailhead: From the Southwest Entrance, follow the Lassen Park Road (California Highway 89) north and east for about 7 miles to the large parking lot, which is on the left (north) side of the road. The parking area is about 21 miles from the Manzanita Lake Entrance Station.

Key points:

0.0 Lassen Peak Trailhead.

1.2 Pass above treeline to the first interpretive sign.

2.2 Reach the summit.

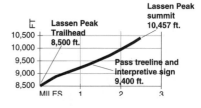

The hike: This is why you came to Lassen Volcanic National Park. You wanted to climb the mountain that gave the park its name. You wanted to enjoy the views from the park's highest point. You wanted to stand near the gaping maw of a volcano. This trail will lead you there.

If you pick your summit day carefully, with a forecast of clear skies, and start early, you can be virtually guaranteed a sublime experience, with unsullied views in all directions. From a vantage point on the rim of Lassen's crater, you can see west across the Sacramento River Valley to the blonde Yolla Bolly range; to the northwest, the snowy cone of Mount Shasta dominates the vista. The northern reaches of the rugged Sierra Nevada lie to the

Lassen Peak

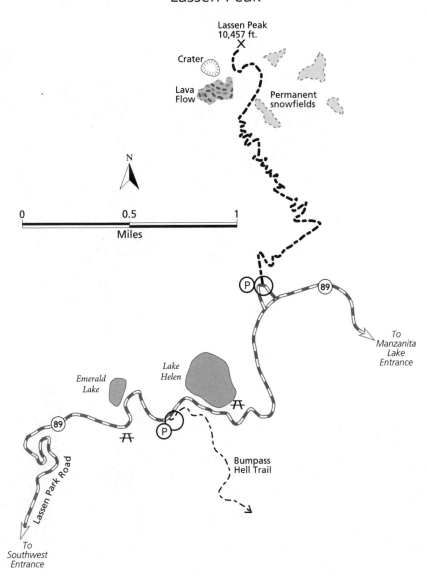

southwest, across the shimmering surface of Lake Almanor. And under your feet is the volcano itself, its crater appearing innocuous, sloping gently into the depression on the west side of the summit, with nary a rumbling to breach the sound of the whistling wind.

The trail itself is very straightforward, well maintained, and popular. It follows sharp switchbacks up the steep, south-facing ridge of the mountain. Handling the altitude is the major challenge, though if it's early in the season, or if it has been a heavy snow year, patches of ice and snow may increase the level of difficulty. Beating the effects of altitude requires plenty

The beginning and end of the Lassen Peak climb.

Looking across the saddle to the summit of Lassen Peak.

of water and time, and pausing on the trail to catch your breath will make it all the easier to enjoy the lovely vistas.

From the trailhead, the broad sandy path begins by reaching up and north. At the first switchback, witness the scar left by the boots of thoughtless hikers who decided to blaze their own trail up the mountain. Remain on the trail, and leave no trace of your passage along the route.

A clump of hardy mountain hemlocks guards the next switchback. Enjoy a fleeting flat section of trail, pausing at the 2-mile marker to enjoy views southwest of Lake Almanor and the Sierra foothills. At the next switchback, a jagged dacite rampart obscures the views northward and a snowfield spills from the summit ridge. As the trail switchbacks upward, the trees become more stooped and gnarled, and then bow to the wind and snow as low-lying krummholz.

At about 1.2 miles, reach the first interpretive sign, about the birth of Lassen Peak, then continue upward. A series of tight switchbacks winds up through the talus—make it easy on both yourself and the mountain by staying on the trail. Pass the 1-mile marker and two more interpretive signs as you continue the climb.

The trail switches back before a melon-colored wall of serrated dacite; just above these crags, you'll pass the 0.5-mile marker. Climb along the summit ridge until you reach the false summit, where chains keep you from harming the fragile plants that find purchase on the heights, and an interpretive sign describes Lassen's most recent eruptions.

To reach the actual summit, climb down into the saddle, cross the snowfield, and ascend the talus on the northern rim of the crater. The views of

Mount Shasta to the northwest, and the Devastated Area on the northwest-facing slopes of Lassen, are best from here. The white cone of the radio tower is the single sign of human influence on the summit; the lookout pictured on the interpretive sign is long gone. It's you, the wind, and the views, and it is wonderful.

Return to the trailhead via the same route; you'll find it easier to respond to the parade of hellos from fellow hikers on the descent.

8 Terrace and Shadow Lakes

Highlights:	Each of these two lovely lakes offers great views of Lassen Peak, as well as opportunities for wading and, for the hardy, swimming.
Type of hike:	Day hike; out-and-back.
Total distance:	1.6 miles.
Difficulty:	Easy.
Best months:	July–October.
Maps:	USGS Reading Peak quad; Lassen Volcanic National Park maps by the National Park Service, Earthwalk Press, and Wilderness Press; USDAFS Lassen National Forest map.
Parking and facilities:	There is a small parking area at the trailhead, but no restroom or picnic facilities.

Finding the trailhead: From the Southwest Entrance, follow the Lassen Park Road (California Highway 89) north and east for about 9 miles, over the summit pass, to the Terrace Lake Trailhead, which is on the left (north) side of the road. From the Manzanita Lake Entrance Station, follow the Lassen Park Road for 19 miles to the Terrace Lake Trailhead.

Key points:

- 0.0 Terrace Lake Trailhead.
- 0.4 Pass the trail that leads north to Paradise Meadow.
- 0.5 Reach Terrace Lake.
- 0.8 Drop over the shelf to Shadow Lake.

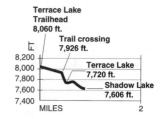

The hike: Cupped at the northern edge of a narrow basin, with nothing but the sky and the forested summits of faraway peaks visible over the basin's lip, Terrace Lake appears to sit on the edge of the earth. This is far from the truth, but the lake's location is high and airy, a perch like that of a raptor on a cliff. The lawn-like meadow that rims the lake's south shore invites hikers to rest for a spell, and perhaps even take a dip in the clear, shallow waters.

Shadow Lake, by comparison, earns its extraordinariness from its views rather than its setting. Reached by diving over the rim of the Terrace Lake

Terrace and Shadow Lakes • Cliff Lake

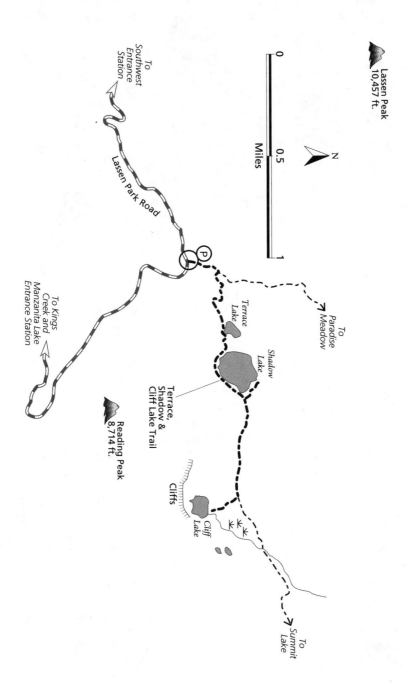

A young hiker skips stones on Terrace Lake.

basin, a seat alongside Shadow Lake's east shore offers unsurpassed views of Lassen Peak's steep, east-facing slopes. This lake, its surface an icy, reflective turquoise, extends an invitation to swim to only those with the thickest skins. Take a deep breath. . . .

From the trailhead, the footpath descends quickly through the open forest, which is laid with park-like precision on the sun-bleached, rolling terrain. This landscape is typical of the park's highest country, where broad, rocky swales are draped with lacy sheets of silverleaf lupine and separated by narrow strips of whitebark pine and mountain hemlock.

At 0.4 mile, reach the intersection with the trail that leads left (north), down to Paradise Meadow and the Hat Creek Trailhead (see Hike 27 in the Emigrant Pass and Hat Creek chapter for a detailed description). Turn right (east) to continue to Terrace Lake.

The trail dives into a rocky ravine, then drops into a meadow that is wedged between the lakeshore to the northeast and the foot of a steep talus field to the southwest. The trail leads north through the meadow to the lakeshore.

To reach Shadow Lake, follow the footpath through the talus that litters the east shore of Terrace Lake, then climb up and over the rim of the lake's basin. The descent to Shadow Lake is quick and decisive, traversing down a steep north-facing slope to the shoreline. A brief swatch of grassy beach on the southeastern side of the lake is perfect for contemplation of Lassen Peak, which looms above, or for napping, if you are so inclined.

Return as you came, or see Hike 9 for a description of the trail's continuation to Cliff Lake.

9 Cliff Lake

See Map on Page 47

Highlights: Separated from the more easily reached Terrace and Shadow Lakes by a length of little-used trail, Cliff Lake offers blissful solitude and lovely panoramic views of the north face of Reading Peak.

Type of hike: Day hike; out-and-back.

Total distance: 3.4 miles.

Difficulty: Moderate.

Best months: July–October.

Maps: USGS Reading Peak quad; Lassen Volcanic National Park maps by the National Park Service, Earthwalk Press, and Wilderness Press; USDAFS Lassen National Forest map.

Parking and facilities: There is a small parking area at the Terrace Lake trailhead, but no restroom or picnic facilities.

Finding the trailhead: From the Southwest Entrance, follow the Lassen Park Road (California Highway 89) north and east for about 9 miles, over the summit pass, to the Terrace Lake Trailhead, which is on the left (north) side of the road. From the Manzanita Lake Entrance Station, follow the Lassen Park Road for 19 miles to the Terrace Lake Trailhead.

Key points:

0.0   Terrace Lake Trailhead.

0.4   Pass the trail that leads north to Paradise Meadow.

0.5   Reach Terrace Lake.

0.8   Pass Shadow Lake.

1.4   Reach the trail that leads to Cliff Lake.

1.7   Arrive at Cliff Lake.

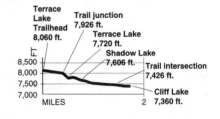

The hike: This sweet little lake is made all the more tempting because it lies off the beaten path. Even on the busiest summer weekends, this secluded tarn sees little traffic, as hikers often skip past it as they hike between Summit Lake and Terrace Lake.

Even if such a traverse is your goal, make time to check out Cliff Lake. The shallow, gray-green pool rests in a depression at the base of the west-facing cliffs of Reading Peak, from whence (obviously) comes the name. The cliffs present two faces: they are crumpled into spills of talus on the southeast shore of the lake, and rear in great, black-streaked domes on its southwest shore. Below all this, the lake is clear, sandy, and inviting.

Cliff Lake can be reached from the trailheads at Terrace Lake, Summit Lake, and the Hat Lake/Emigrant Pass area. The trail described here is from Terrace Lake, which may not be the easiest route but is arguably the most scenic. For details on how to reach Cliff Lake from Summit Lake, see the trail description for Hike 10.

The steep slopes encircling the basin give Cliff Lake its name.

From the trailhead, drop through the rolling, sparsely forested terrain below Lassen Peak's east face to the intersection with the trail that leads to Paradise Meadow at 0.4 mile. Head right (east), and descend into the basin that holds Terrace Lake at 0.5 mile. Circle the east side of Terrace Lake, climb over the basin's lip, and hike down to Shadow Lake at 0.8 mile. This is a very scenic stretch of trail; see the description in Hike 8 for the details.

Circle the east shore of Shadow Lake to continue. The trail, wedged between the turquoise water and the talus slope that spills from the western reaches of Reading Peak, leads to the northeast corner of the lake. At this point, it breaks away from the lakeshore; an informal path continues around the lake.

Drop into the open woodland to the right (east). Yellow dots on the trees mark the way. Reading Peak dominates the southeast horizon as you make a quick and easy descent to a narrow swath of meadow and a creek crossing. Small ponds dot the terrace upon which the meadow lies; beyond the ponds, the trail rolls down through a mixed evergreen forest to the intersection with the trail to Cliff Lake, at 1.4 miles.

Turn right (south) on the trail to Cliff Lake, which continues to descend through the tangle of trees. The lake is well-screened by the forest until you approach its shoreline, where the trees part to reveal a colorful strip of wildflowers watered by the outlet stream.

Walk another 100 yards, and at 1.7 miles you stand on the lake's grassy shore. Pick a spot on a sun-warmed rock or fallen snag, and rest a spell before either returning as you came, or continuing down and northeast to Summit Lake (see Hike 10).

10 Terrace Lake to Summit Lake

Highlights:	Enjoy great views of the northern reaches of Lassen Volcanic National Park as you descend from one spectacular lake to another.
Type of hike:	Day hike; shuttle.
Total distance:	3.7 miles.
Difficulty:	Moderate.
Best months:	July–October.
Maps:	USGS Reading Peak quad; Lassen Volcanic National Park maps by the National Park Service, Earthwalk Press, and Wilderness Press; USDAFS Lassen National Forest map.
Parking and facilities:	There is a small parking area at the Terrace Lake trailhead, but no restroom or picnic facilities. At the Summit Lake Trailhead, you will find parking, restrooms, and water sources, as well as a staffed ranger station.

Terrace Lake to Summit Lake

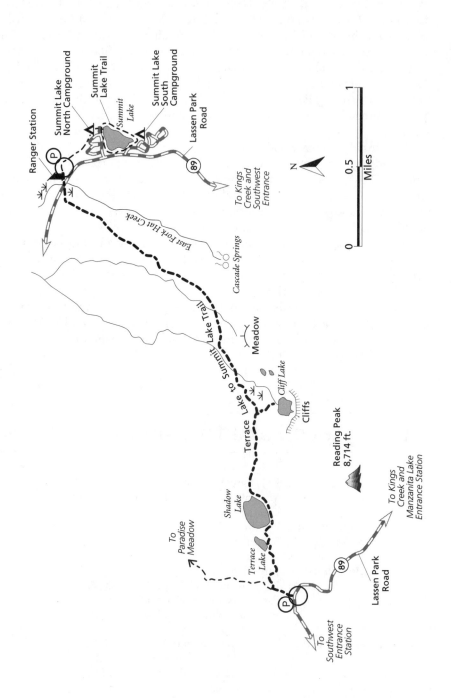

Ranger Station

Summit Lake North Campground

Summit Lake Trail

Summit Lake

Summit Lake South Campground

Lassen Park Road

89

To Kings Creek and Southwest Entrance

East Fork Hat Creek

Cascade Springs

Meadow

Cliff Lake

Cliffs

Reading Peak 8,714 ft.

Terrace Lake to Summit Lake Trail

Shadow Lake

To Paradise Meadow

Terrace Lake

To Kings Creek and Manzanita Lake Entrance Station

89

Lassen Park Road

To Southwest Entrance Station

N

Miles

0   0.5   1

Finding the trailhead: From the Southwest Entrance, follow the Lassen Park Road (California Highway 89) north and east for about 9 miles, over the summit pass, to the Terrace Lake Trailhead, which is on the left (north) side of the road. From the Manzanita Lake Entrance Station, follow the Lassen Park Road for 19.5 miles to the Terrace Lake Trailhead. The Summit Lake end of the trail is at the Summit Lake Ranger Station, which is 16 miles north and east of the Southwest Entrance, and 12 miles south and east of the Manzanita Lake Entrance Station.

Key points:

0.0 Terrace Lake Trailhead.
0.5 Reach Terrace Lake.
0.8 Pass Shadow Lake.
1.7 Arrive at Cliff Lake.
2.0 Return to the trail intersection.
4.0 Arrive at the Summit Lake Ranger Station.

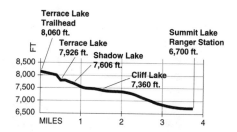

The hike: The trail between Terrace Lake and Summit Lake is a wonderful and easy trek through some of the most accessible "off the beaten path" terrain in the park. The route takes you past Terrace and Shadow Lakes, with their marvelous views of Lassen Peak, down to secluded Cliff Lake, then on a rolling descent to the welcoming shores of Summit Lake. This route is most often done with a shuttle. If you want to make this a round-trip journey, start at Summit Lake so you walk downhill on the return.

The trail begins at the Terrace Lake Trailhead on the eastern flank of Lassen Peak, and drops swiftly to an intersection with the trail that leads north to Paradise Meadow at 0.4 mile. Turn right (northeast), and continue down to Terrace Lake at 0.5 mile. Enjoy the views at Terrace Lake, then forge ahead to Shadow Lake by skirting Terrace Lake's east shore and climbing up and over the lip at its northern edge. Shadow Lake is at 0.8 mile. See Hike 8 for more details.

The trail continues around the east shore of Shadow Lake, departing from the lake's north shore to head northeast toward Cliff Lake. Descend over rolling terrain, crossing a meadow-covered terrace dotted with ponds, to the intersection with the trail that leads to Cliff Lake at 1.4 miles. Turn right (south), and go 0.3 mile to visit this lovely tarn (see Hike 9 for details). Backtrack to the trail intersection at the 2-mile mark, and turn right (northeast) to continue the descent to Summit Lake.

From the Cliff Lake trail intersection, the route heads downhill through mixed fir forest, then bursts free of the trees into a large meadow. Cross a section of the meadow, then skirt its northwest edge. If you walk with care, you can observe wildlife browsing in the meadow—perhaps a shy deer, almost assuredly songbirds and butterflies.

Cross the clear stream that waters the meadow, then follow the creek northeast as it quickens, until the trail breaks away to the right (east). Re-enter the woodland, and continue downhill on a gradual descent that seems almost flat. The eastern shoulder of Reading Peak slopes down and parallel to the trail on the right (southeast).

As the mountain fades from view, you will pass another small meadow, and when you are clear of Reading Peak's shadow, views open to the wooded old volcanoes of Lassen's northern backcountry. Hat Mountain, an aptly named cinder cone, lies directly ahead.

The descent becomes a bit more aggressive as you continue, and sounds of the park road occasionally waft upward. The open canopy allows manzanita to flourish on the forest floor. A steep switchback marks the boundary between the open woodland and a denser forest of lodgepole pines. The trail weaves through the pines to its inauspicious end along the side of CA 89 at about the 4-mile mark.

To reach the Summit Lake Ranger Station, you can follow the park road right (east) for 0.1 to the ranger station access road, which is on the left (north) side of the park road. Or, you can cross the road directly from the trailhead, and pick your way eastward through the roadside meadow, crossing the narrow stream, to the ranger station parking area.

Kings Creek

Several creeks originate on Lassen Peak, fed by snowmelt and springs, filling ponds and lakes, and watering sprawling meadows and strips of riparian habitat. Kings Creek, which drains the southeast slopes of the mountain, is one of the more substantial of these streams. Over the centuries, it has helped to sculpt dramatic scenery along its course, making it a great destination for those seeking visual fireworks without the fire.

As you head downstream on trails that loop through the vicinity of Kings Creek, you can watch the creek evolve from gurgling streamlet to substantial waterway. Near its headwaters in the park's upper reaches, it is a shallow winding ribbon that can be stepped over easily. Lower down, the creek is funneled between rock walls into an exhilarating cataract, then tumbles over a 70-foot precipice. Below the falls, Kings Creek widens and deepens as tributaries, including Summit Creek and the nameless stream that spills out of the Grassy Swale, feed it. By the time it reaches Corral Meadow, it presents a sizable obstacle to the hiker who wants to cross.

From the meadow, the creek rushes southeast out of the park, eventually spilling into the Feather River and Lake Almanor. A little-used path, which is not described in this guide, follows its course to where it flows over the park's boundary at Kelly Camp.

At the end of this chapter, I've described a couple of loop hikes, as well as a shuttle hike, that offer wonderful, longer trekking opportunities in this area of the park. These can be expanded or modified into even longer loops and shuttle trips; consult a good park map or the USGS Reading Peak map to plan more extensive or varied excursions.

There are two trailheads in the Kings Creek area. The Kings Creek Picnic Area features plenty of parking, restrooms, and picnic facilities, and serves as the trailhead for short hikes to Cold Boiling Lake and Crumbaugh Lake, and longer hikes to Twin Meadows, Conard Meadows, and Bumpass Hell. It is located about 16.5 miles south and east of the Manzanita Lake Entrance Station on the Lassen Park Road (California Highway 89), and 11.5 miles north and east of the Southwest Entrance Station. The Kings Creek Trailhead, with parking alongside the Lassen Park Road, has no amenities, but the trails that depart from here lead to a number of lovely spots, including Kings Creek Falls, Sifford Lake, Bench Lake, and Corral Meadow. This trailhead is located about 15.5 miles south and east of the Manzanita Lake Entrance Station along CA 89, and 12.5 miles north and east of the Southwest Entrance Station.

11 Cold Boiling Lake

Highlights:	This easy trek leads to an odd, but lovely, bubbling lake.
Type of hike:	Day hike; out-and-back.
Total distance:	1.4 miles.
Difficulty:	Easy.
Best months:	July–September.
Maps:	USGS Reading Peak quad; Lassen Volcanic National Park maps by the National Park Service, Earthwalk Press, and Wilderness Press; USDAFS Lassen National Forest map.
Parking and facilities:	There are restrooms and picnic facilities at the trailhead.

Finding the trailhead: To reach the Kings Creek Picnic Area Trailhead, take the Lassen Park Road (California Highway 89) north and east from the Southwest Entrance Station for 11.5 miles to the Kings Creek Picnic Area signs. Turn right (south) onto the access road, and drive 0.1 mile to the parking area. From the Manzanita Lake Entrance Station, drive 16.5 miles south and east on the park road; the Kings Creek Picnic Area access road is on your left (south).

Key points:

0.0   Kings Creek Picnic Area Trailhead.
0.5   Pass the trail to Twin Meadows.
0.7   Arrive on the shores of Cold Boiling Lake.

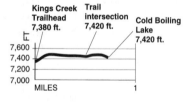

The hike: Cold Boiling Lake is unique in this volcanic park for its subtlety. It lies quietly in its alpine basin, surrounded by a still forest and black-streaked dacite cliffs. Its shores are placid and its waters inviting—you may wonder, as I did, how this seemingly normal tarn could be in any way volcanic. Then, you see them: tiny bubbles gurgling relentlessly among the grasses in the lake before bursting noiselessly on the surface. Caused by the gases escaping Lassen's turbulent innards, the bubbles are a relatively benign reminder that indeed, you are standing on the slopes of a volcano.

The hike begins in the Kings Creek Picnic Area, heading up and southeast past the informational billboard into an open woodland of mountain hemlock. Climb over the rise, then drop gently through a forest of snow-twisted and stunted trees. Beyond, the route skirts the edge of a meadow thick with silverleaf lupine, a low-growing plant with purple flowers and velvety leaves that thrives in the harsh volcanic soils of the park's high country. Yellow dots on the trees mark the route, which rolls over a brief, forested hummock into another clearing.

A trail intersection lies at the border of this open area. Stay right (straight/southwest) to Cold Boiling Lake, which lies 0.2 mile ahead. This distance is

Cold Boiling Lake • Crumbaugh Lake

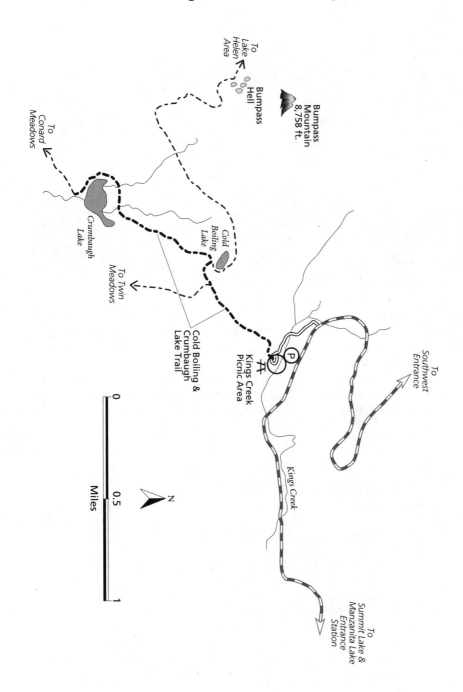

The scene from the southwest shore of Crumbaugh Lake.

swiftly covered; an easy descent leads to the meadow-lined rim of the lake. A couple of brief interpretive signs describe the volcanic workings of the lake; you can get good views of the boiling waters by circling counterclockwise along the shore.

From Cold Boiling Lake, you can continue for 1.9 miles to Bumpass Hell, or descend to Crumbaugh Lake and beyond. If you choose not to continue to another destination, retrace your route to the trailhead.

12 Crumbaugh Lake

See Map on Page 57

Highlights:	Bag two pretty lakes with one great hike.
Type of hike:	Day hike; out-and-back.
Total distance:	2.4 miles.
Difficulty:	Easy.
Best months:	July–September.
Maps:	USGS Reading Peak quad; Lassen Volcanic National Park maps by the National Park Service, Earthwalk Press, and Wilderness Press; USDAFS Lassen National Forest map.
Parking and facilities:	There are restrooms and picnic facilities at the trailhead.

Finding the trailhead: To reach the Kings Creek Picnic Area Trailhead, take the Lassen Park Road (California Highway 89) north and east from the Southwest Entrance Station for 11.5 miles to the Kings Creek Picnic Area signs. Turn right (south) onto the access road, and drive 0.1 mile to the parking area. From the Manzanita Lake Entrance Station, drive 16.5 miles south and east on the park road; the Kings Creek Picnic Area access road is on your left (south).

Key points:

0.0   Kings Creek Picnic Area Trailhead.
0.5   Pass the trail to Twin Meadows.
0.7   Arrive on the shores of Cold Boiling Lake.
1.2   Reach Crumbaugh Lake.

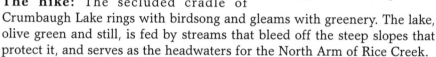

The hike: The secluded cradle of Crumbaugh Lake rings with birdsong and gleams with greenery. The lake, olive green and still, is fed by streams that bleed off the steep slopes that protect it, and serves as the headwaters for the North Arm of Rice Creek.

Obvious signs of volcanism here are limited to the lava cliffs that ring the basin; this is pure high country, replete with plentiful wildflowers throughout the hiking season and a plethora of bugs. If you hike the glorified game trail that circumnavigates the lake, be sure to keep your mouth closed, or you are likely to get your daily dose of protein via inhaled insects.

Crumbaugh Lake is reached via the same trail that leads to Cold Boiling Lake (see Hike 11). Begin at the Kings Creek Picnic Area, climb past the informational billboard, then hike down through a stunted evergreen forest and past open areas carpeted with silverleaf lupine. Go right (straight) at the intersection with the trail to Twin Meadows at 0.5 mile. Cold Boiling Lake lies 0.2 mile beyond.

At the trail intersection on the southeast shore of Cold Boiling Lake, go left (southwest) toward Crumbaugh Lake, following the sign. The trail curves south, tracing the route of the stream that drops from Cold Boiling Lake into Crumbaugh Lake. Yellow dots on the trees along the trail mark the well-maintained route.

Drop swiftly to the border of a meadow that, in early season (or longer, if it has been a heavy snow year), is pocked with standing water and shrouded in a veil of bugs. The muddy track may sport the hoof prints of deer and the waffle-stomp prints of other hiking boots. Pass a second pond/bog/meadow as you descend into a denser woodland—stay on the trail to reduce damage to fragile vegetation—then enjoy a brief flat stretch of trail alongside a narrow, grassy clearing.

An expansive view of an evergreen-crowned ridge, a stream-cut meadow, and dun mounds of sterile earth opens on your right (west) as the path continues to descend. Crumbaugh Lake lies at the foot of the barren earthworks. An overgrown and insect-infested informal trail leads around the lake to the left (southeast). There are few places to sit and contemplate the scenery on this side of the moist, grassy basin, so it is best to avoid exploration of this informal trail. The formal trail continues around the lake to the right (north); the woods creep up to the lakeshore on its southern banks, where fallen logs and stumps offer respite.

If you choose, or if you have arranged for a shuttle, you can continue on the trail, heading downhill and southwest, all the way to the Southwest Walk-in Campground. Isolated Conard Meadows lies 1.5 miles beyond Crumbaugh Lake, and Mill Creek Falls also lies downstream—and steeply downhill—2.3 miles southwest of the lake. Hikes 2 and 3, in the Southwest Entrance chapter, provide thorough descriptions of the trail between Mill Creek Falls, Conard Meadows, and Crumbaugh Lake.

Should you decide the hike to Crumbaugh Lake was enough, return as you came.

13 Twin Meadows

Highlights:	This seldom-traveled route leads through different woodland ecosystems to narrow, secluded meadows.
Type of hike:	Day hike; out-and-back.
Total distance:	4.6 miles.
Difficulty:	Moderate.
Best months:	July–September.
Maps:	USGS Reading Peak quad; Lassen Volcanic National Park maps by the National Park Service, Earthwalk Press, and Wilderness Press; USDAFS Lassen National Forest map.
Parking and facilities:	There are restrooms and picnic facilities at the trailhead.

Finding the trailhead: To reach the Kings Creek Picnic Area Trailhead, take the Lassen Park Road (California Highway 89) north and east from the Southwest Entrance Station for 11.5 miles to the Kings Creek Picnic Area signs. Turn right (south) onto the access road, and drive 0.1 mile to the parking area. From the Manzanita Lake Entrance Station, drive 16.5 miles south and east on the park road; the Kings Creek Picnic Area access road is on your left (south).

Key points:

0.0 Kings Creek Picnic Area Trailhead.
0.5 Reach the trail to Twin Meadows.
2.0 Check out the views from the rocky promontory.
2.3 Reach Twin Meadows.

The hike: The trek to Twin Meadows is one of those cases where the journey, as much as the destination, is the reward.

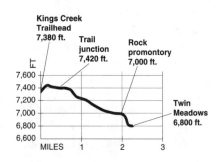

Twin Meadows

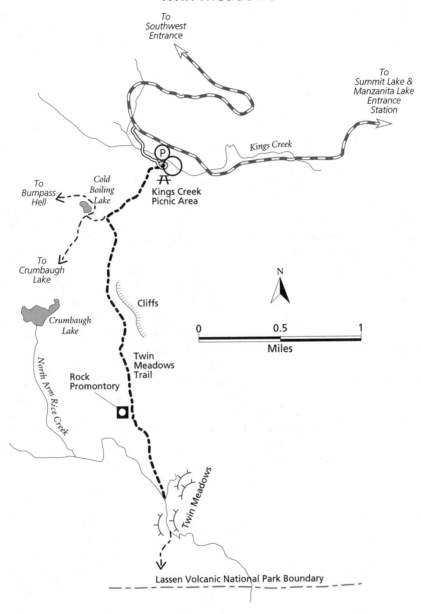

To
Southwest
Entrance

To
Summit Lake &
Manzanita Lake
Entrance
Station

P

Kings Creek

To
Bumpass
Hell

Cold
Boiling
Lake

Kings Creek
Picnic Area

To
Crumbaugh
Lake

Cliffs

N

0   0.5   1

Miles

Crumbaugh
Lake

Twin
Meadows
Trail

North Arm Rice Creek

Rock
Promontory

Twin Meadows

Lassen Volcanic National Park Boundary

The meadows themselves are lovely, their tender grasses and prolific wildflowers bordered by thick, primeval forest and guarded by armies of insects. Depending on your stamina and the strength of your insect repellent, the pests preclude a prolonged stay in the meadows, but that shouldn't deter you from this hike, which has abundant charms.

Chief among these is the trail's relative seclusion. This is one of Lassen Volcanic National Park's paths less traveled; it imparts a genuine wilderness feeling, without the uncertainty of traveling cross-country. Still, you must pay attention—because the path is not frequented by the multitudes, it is rough, and though it is marked by yellow dots on the trees, it sometimes seems as though you've wandered so far from civilization that even trail markers have been forgotten. Just above the meadows, the trail dives off a promontory with stimulating views of Mount Conard to the southwest, and the dark, wooded ridges that roll away southward.

Begin at the Kings Creek Trailhead, following the marked route that begins at the informational billboard, heading up, and then down through the stunted forest and past the meadows described in the Cold Boiling Lake hike (Hike 11). At the first trail intersection at 0.5 mile, at the edge of the big clearing above Cold Boiling Lake, take the left (south) fork, following the sign indicating that Twin Meadows lie 1.9 miles beyond.

The lonely route begins amid silverleaf lupine, which crowds the gently descending path. As the trail drops, it is siphoned through a narrow gully. Rockfall spills off the cliff to the left (east). Cross the drainage and continue downward, traversing above a seasonal streambed that is dry by late summer.

The trail leaves the drainage to circle the base of a grand, black-streaked cliff skirted with talus. The path gets rockier as it descends. At the base of a steep hill, the route zigzags through cut logs and rotting deadfall; yellow trail markers indicate the way. The trail briefly follows a dry drainage before crossing to its left (east) side and wandering out onto the sparsely wooded promontory at about the 2-mile mark. This makes a wonderful stopping place, with great views and flat rocks upon which you can picnic or meditate.

To reach the meadows, wind carefully down a steep, rocky section of trail as you drop off the promontory into the woods. Pick your way through dead and dying trees to the northern reaches of the meadow. The trail is lost amid the thick grasses, though the yellow dots still appear here and there on the trees, which are much healthier here. Explore if the bugs allow; this is a meadow in transition, marshy in spots and invaded by trees in others. After your visit, return as you came.

14 Sifford Lake

Highlights:	The small lake at trail's end sits on a picturesque rocky bench.
Type of hike:	Day hike; out-and-back.
Total distance:	4.2 miles.
Difficulty:	Moderate.
Best months:	July–September.
Maps:	USGS Reading Peak quad; Lassen Volcanic National Park maps by the National Park Service, Earthwalk Press, and Wilderness Press; USDAFS Lassen National Forest map.
Parking and facilities:	Parking is available in pullouts along the Lassen Park Road (California Highway 89). There are no other facilities available.

Finding the trailhead: The Kings Creek Falls Trailhead is located on the Lassen Park Road (California Highway 89) about 15.5 miles south and east of the Manzanita Lake Entrance Station, and 12.5 miles north and east of the Southwest Entrance Station. It is on the southeast side of the road.

Key points:

0.0   Kings Creek Falls Trailhead.
0.5   Reach the trail fork in the meadow.
1.7   Head right (west) on the trail to Sifford Lake.
2.1   Arrive on the lakeshore.

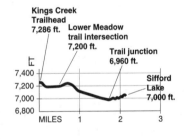

The hike: The cup of dark gray rock that cradles Sifford Lake is almost perfectly round. A smattering of evergreens shades its shoreline, but mostly the lake's shores are open, and bathed in sunlight. The rock, dacite of (you guessed it) volcanic origin, warms up nicely in the summertime, and is spread around the lake in smooth, rolling mounds that, though rather hard, invite lounging. If the day is exceptionally warm, the rocks and the sun conspire to make taking a dip in the clear, shallow waters a tempting possibility.

The trail drops to the lake over sparsely wooded benches. It's easy walking on the descent, and a bit harder on the climb up. You can also hitch this lake into a wonderful loop of the Kings Creek area, which is described in Hike 16.

The trail begins on the southeast side of the road at the Kings Creek Falls trailhead, where the sign indicates that Sifford Lake is 2.1 miles ahead. Descend through red firs to the Lower Meadow, which is watered by the narrow but vigorous Kings Creek. The meadow is large and lovely, green and sprinkled with wildflowers in spring, and glowing gold in autumn.

Sifford Lake • Kings Creek Falls
Bench Lake and Sifford Lake Loop

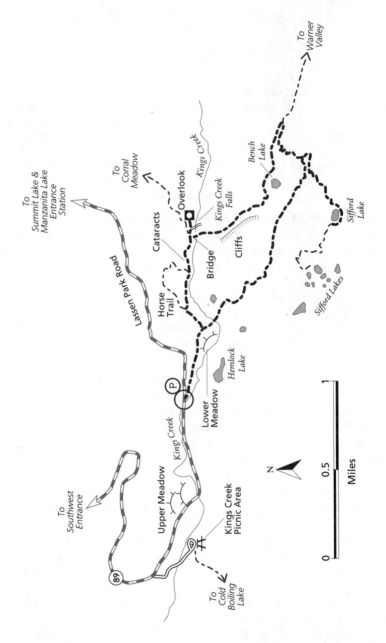

The trail forks at 0.5 mile, near the eastern edge of the meadow. The trail to Kings Creek Falls leads to the left (northeast), and Sifford Lake is 1.7 miles to the right (southeast). Go right on the trail to Sifford Lake.

The trail leads through the marshy lower reaches of the meadow, crossing Kings Creek on a log bridge. Easy climbing leads through the open forest to the vague high point of the trail, then the trail begins to descend through similar terrain.

You will drop over a number of benches as you continue. The landscape is gray and green, relatively stark, with the tops of the trees bent by the wind and sheared off by lightning. On some of the benches the rock is relatively naked, others are carpeted with thick patches of manzanita. At 1.7 miles, the trail forks, with the trail to Sifford Lake breaking off to the right (west), and the other path leading left (southeast) toward the Warner Valley.

From the trail intersection to the lake, the trail is a roller coaster, climbing through gullies with different features. The first is littered with deadfall, the second short and steep, the third much broader than the previous and thick with manzanita, and the fourth, also carpeted with manzanita, featuring the steepest pitch on the lakeside face. After the final short climb, you arrive at the lakeshore at 2.1 miles.

An informal trail leads around the peaceful lake, and to other lakes captured in depressions on the dacite benches. Explore as you wish, and return as you came, or link this with trails to Kings Creek Falls, Corral Meadow, or the Warner Valley.

15 Kings Creek Falls

See Map on Page 64

Highlights: The spectacular cataracts and falls of Kings Creek enliven this stretch of trail.

Type of hike: Day hike; out-and-back.

Total distance: 2.2 miles.

Difficulty: Moderate.

Best months: Late June–early August, when the creek is swollen with snowmelt.

Maps: USGS Reading Peak quad; Lassen Volcanic National Park maps by the National Park Service, Earthwalk Press, and Wilderness Press; USDAFS Lassen National Forest map.

Parking and facilities: Parking is available in pullouts along the Lassen Park Road (California Highway 89). There are no other facilities available.

Finding the trailhead: The trailhead is located on the Lassen Park Road (CA 89) about 15.5 miles south and east of the Manzanita Lake Entrance Station, and 12.5 miles north and east of the Southwest Entrance Station. It is on the southeast side of the road.

Kings Creek spills over its fall.

Key points:

0.0   Kings Creek Falls Trailhead.
0.5   Reach the trail intersection in the Lower Meadow.
1.1   Arrive at Kings Creek Falls.

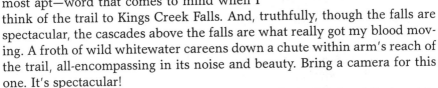

The hike: Invigorating. That's the first—and most apt—word that comes to mind when I think of the trail to Kings Creek Falls. And, truthfully, though the falls are spectacular, the cascades above the falls are what really got my blood moving. A froth of wild whitewater careens down a chute within arm's reach of the trail, all-encompassing in its noise and beauty. Bring a camera for this one. It's spectacular!

Begin by dropping from the trailhead through the brief red fir forest to the edge of the Lower Meadow. You might think that Kings Creek, which runs through the meadow, is energetic here, flowing playfully over the rocks that litter its bed, but you've seen nothing yet.

At 0.5 mile, near the east edge of the meadow, the trail forks. Go left (northeast) on the trail to Kings Creek Falls; the right (southeast) trail leads to Sifford Lake (Hike 14). The horse trail departs from the cataract trail at the next sign and trail intersection at 0.6 mile; the sign states that the cascade view is 0.1 mile ahead, and the falls are 0.5 mile ahead.

The roar of the falling creek grows louder as you approach the cascade through the woods. The overlook is off the trail to the right (south); this is the perfect place to contemplate the power and the beauty of the cascade.

Rock stairs lead down the steep pitch alongside the cataract, which becomes more vigorous as it drops. The trail is vigorous as well, plunging down beside the tumbling water. Watch your step.

Below the cataracts, the noise subsides, the pitch of the trail subsides, and the entertainment subsides as well, as forest envelopes the trail. You may wonder how the falls could top the display put on by the cascade, but "top" is the wrong word. The falls delight in an entirely different fashion.

The horse trail rejoins the trail to Kings Creek Falls at 0.9 mile. A log bridge spans the now relatively calm creek to the right (south), where a trail leads up to Bench Lake, Sifford Lake, and beyond (see Hike 16). The creek drops over the falls about 100 yards downstream from the bridge. The trail forks again before the falls, with the right (lower and streamside) fork leading to the overlook. A cable guards the steep drop, and from this high perch, you can safely observe the narrow white veil spun by the 70-foot drop of Kings Creek. Hopefully there is still film in the camera, for this is a lovely sight as well.

You can return as you came, or, if you'd like to continue, hike down to Corral Meadow or north to Summit Lake. These routes are described in Hikes 17 and 18, respectively.

16 Kings Creek Falls, Bench Lake, and Sifford Lake Loop

See Map on Page 64

Highlights: Wild cataracts, a waterfall, steep cliffs pocked with caves, a vernal pool, and a lovely lake—what more could you ask for in a hike?

Type of hike: Day hike, loop.

Total distance: 4.9 miles.

Difficulty: Moderate.

Best months: July–September.

Maps: USGS Reading Peak quad; Lassen Volcanic National Park maps by the National Park Service, Earthwalk Press, and Wilderness Press; USDAFS Lassen National Forest map.

Parking and facilities: Parking is available in pullouts along the Lassen Park Road (California Highway 89). There are no other facilities available.

Finding the trailhead: The trailhead is located on the Lassen Park Road (California Highway 89) about 15.5 miles south and east of the Manzanita Lake Entrance Station, and 12.5 miles north and east of the Southwest Entrance Station. It is on the southeast side of the road.

Key points:

0.0   Kings Creek Falls Trailhead.
0.5   Reach the trail intersection in the Lower Meadow.
1.1   Arrive at Kings Creek Falls.
1.7   Reach Bench Lake.
2.1   Drop to the trail that leads east to Warner Valley and Corral Meadow.
2.8   Climb to Sifford Lake.
4.4   Return to the Lower Meadow.

The hike: First, there is the lovely Lower Meadow. Then the wild cascades along Kings Creek. Below these, steep Kings Creek Falls. Next, yawning caves tucked in gray cliffs that hover over the trail. Beyond, shallow Bench

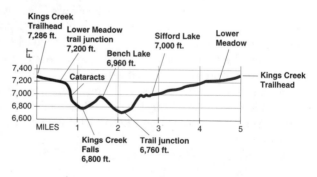

Lake in a secluded wooded bowl. Above, Sifford Lake in its perfect basin. It's almost more fun than a hiker should be allowed on a single trail loop.

I've chosen to describe this loop in a clockwise direction, beginning on the Kings Creek Falls Trail and ending with the climb from Sifford Lake. My

Cliffs line the trail between Sifford Lake to Kings Creek.

rationale: You climb on the return trip regardless, but the climb from Sifford Lake is, arguably, easier. You can hike the loop in either direction, however.

To begin, drop from the trailhead down into the Lower Meadow. Skirt the flowery meadow's northern border to the intersection with the Sifford Lake trail at 0.5 mile. Stay left (northeast) on the trail to Kings Creek Falls, which lies 0.6 mile ahead.

Before you reach the falls, you must climb down the steep trail that borders the spectacular and invigorating Kings Creek cascades. Below the cataract, you will pass the trail leading to Bench Lake and Sifford Lake, which departs to the right (south) about 50 yards before the falls overlook.

Visit the falls, then backtrack to the trail to Bench Lake, which begins by crossing a log bridge over Kings Creek. The trail climbs up and away from the creek via switchbacks through the woods, then leaves the cocoon of forest at the foot of a steep cliff of folded gray andesite. The traverse along the base of the cliffs is wonderful, with rocks that have peeled from the cliffs lying in broken chunks along the route. Caves and dark crevasses pock the cliff face, which towers more than 100 feet above the trail.

Head up along the base of the cliff through jumbled talus and trees, then climb onto the lip of the bench that is home to Bench Lake. Switchbacks drop you down to the lake, which in late season is little more than a puddle sprinkled with rocks and skirted in thin grasses. The trail skims around the north shore of the lake, then drops steeply through open woodland and scrub to the intersection with the trail to Warner Valley and Corral Meadow at 2.1 miles.

To continue the loop to Sifford Lake, turn sharply right (west) at this trail intersection; the trail leading left (southeast) heads to Warner Valley. It's a

Bench Lake evaporates to little more than a pond in late season.

steady, sometimes steep climb from here to the Kings Creek Trailhead, but you can take a break at Sifford Lake, which is 0.7 mile distant.

The climb is steep and rocky to begin, leading up and onto a bench, which is crossed to the southwest to the spur trail that leads to Sifford Lake. Bear left (west) on this trail, which leads through four swales to the lakeshore at 2.8 miles (see Hike 14 for more details). Park yourself on a patch of sun-warmed rock, catch your breath, and eat the candy bar that's been melting in your backpack, for you will need a bit of energy for the steady climbing that lies ahead.

Retrace your steps from Sifford Lake to the trail intersection, and turn left (northwest) toward the Kings Creek Trailhead. The path climbs over rocky benches carpeted with manzanita and wildflowers that flourish under a forest canopy open to sun and sky. After cresting the final bench, you will drop into the southern reaches of the Lower Meadow. Cross the log footbridge that spans Kings Creek, much calmer here than below the cataracts passed near the outset of the hike, then wander through the marshy grassland to the trail intersection with the route that leads down to Kings Creek Falls at 4.4 miles. Unless you want to do laps, turn left (northwest), and retrace your steps along the northern margin of the meadow to the trailhead.

17 Kings Creek Falls to Corral Meadow Loop

Highlights: The many faces of Kings Creek, including the cascades, the falls, and the broad sweeping stream near Corral Meadow are chief among the high points of this hike.

Type of hike: Day hike or backpack; loop.

Total distance: 10.1 miles.

Difficulty: Strenuous.

Best months: July–September.

Maps: USGS Reading Peak quad; Lassen Volcanic National Park maps by the National Park Service, Earthwalk Press, and Wilderness Press; USDAFS Lassen National Forest map.

Parking and facilities: Parking is available in pullouts along the Lassen Park Road (California Highway 89). There are no other facilities available.

Finding the trailhead: The trailhead is located on the Lassen Park Road (CA 89) about 15.5 miles south and east of the Manzanita Lake Entrance Station, and 12.5 miles north and east of the Southwest Entrance Station. It is on the southeast side of the road.

Key points:

0.0   Kings Creek Falls Trailhead.

0.5   Reach the trail intersection in the Lower Meadow.

1.1   Arrive at Kings Creek Falls.

3.3   Reach the intersection with the trail to Summit Lake.

4.4   Pass through Corral Meadow.

5.8   Turn right (north) at the trail intersection on the south side of the Flatiron Ridge.

7.5   Reach the intersection with the trail to Sifford Lake.

8.0   Take a rest at Sifford Lake.

9.6   Arrive at the Lower Meadow.

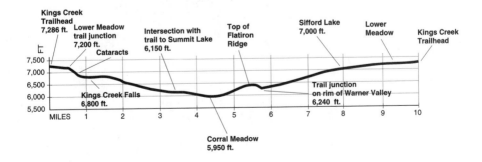

Kings Creek Falls to Corral Meadow Loop

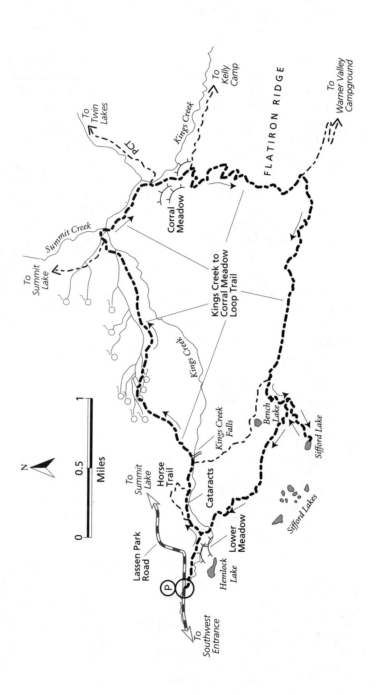

The hike: Trekking through the wilderness of Lassen Park's southern reaches can be strenuous, in terms of both distance and altitude gain and loss, but the landmarks along the loop described here more than compensate for the effort. From the cataracts and falls along Kings Creek to the fleeting beauty of Corral Meadow to the panoramic vistas on the climb along the Flatiron Ridge, you'll find plenty of satisfaction along this route.

Sections of the loop trail are described in detail in other hikes in this chapter. I'll refer you to those descriptions where applicable, and elaborate only on those sections that haven't been mentioned previously.

Begin on the trail leading to Kings Creek Falls, hiking along the northern side of Lower Meadow and staying left (northeast) at the intersection with the trail to Sifford Lake at 0.5 mile. The path plunges down alongside the Kings Creek Cascades, passes the trail that branches south to Bench Lake, and arrives at the Kings Creek Falls at 1.1 miles (see Hike 15 for details).

From the falls, the trail to Corral Meadow and Summit Lake breaks off to the left (northeast), climbing around a knob and into the drainage of the nameless creek neighboring Kings Creek to the north. From here, the route begins a long descent into the lower part of the Kings Creek drainage.

The trail traces the path of this vigorous no-name stream for a good distance. The route is in dense woodlands for the most part, with occasional small meadows and snaking riparian zones woven into the fabric of the forest. It is an easy trail to follow, and is marked with yellow dots on the trees. The stream is sometimes in sight, sometimes only within earshot, but it always makes its presence felt, either "in person" or in the form of a string of feeder streams that the trail crosses as it descends.

Near the 3-mile mark, you will reach the confluence of the feeder stream and Kings Creek. Do not cross Kings Creek—the large log that spans the creek looks inviting, but isn't on the map, so to speak. Instead, turn left (north) and cross the smaller waterway on logs and rocks. A yellow dot is tucked in the willows on the north side of the stream.

The trail wanders through a riparian zone, then a patch of woods, before arriving at the junction with the trail to Summit Lake (see Hike 18 for details) and Corral Meadow at 3.3 miles. Turn right (south) on the Corral Meadow Trail, which winds down to cross Kings Creek on logs. Follow the flat path to the confluence of Summit Creek and Kings Creek, then climb onto a hillside overlooking the now substantial waterway.

The trail leads downhill to deposit you in a clearing on the south bank of Kings Creek, which thrives on the addition of the waters of Summit Creek and the creek that drains the Grassy Swale. If you are backpacking, this is a good site to set up camp; if you are day hiking, this is the perfect place for a mid-hike rest and meal.

To continue on the loop, follow the trail south along Kings Creek to the Corral Meadow sign at 4.4 miles. Corral Meadow is a narrow, boggy strip of grassland—it appears the forest is creeping in on all sides, staking a claim to this fertile ground. The trail, now part of the Pacific Crest Trail (PCT), is a wet dirt ribbon through the grasses and wildflowers, crossing narrow rivulets via strategically scattered logs and rocks. At the next trail sign, 0.3 mile

A nameless fall feeds Kings Creek above Corral Meadow.

beyond the sign for the meadow near Kings Creek, stay right (south) on the PCT, avoiding the overgrown path that leads left (southeast) to Kelly Camp.

The PCT climbs up and away from Corral Meadow and Kings Creek onto Flatiron Ridge. Three switchbacks initiate the climb, then the route traverses through a deadfall-clogged drainage to another set of switchbacks. A few more winding curves and you crest the ridge. The trail flattens briefly, then dives down through the forest on the south side of the ridge. The pitch of the path soon mellows, and it is fairly flat to the next trail crossing at 5.8 miles, near the north rim of the Warner Valley.

The sign at this trail crossing indicates that the end of the loop, back at the Lower Meadow of Kings Creek, is 3.6 miles to the right (west and north). And it's all uphill. If you've arranged for a shuttle to pick you up at the Warner Valley Campground, you can continue on the PCT, which heads straight (left), south, and steeply downhill for 1 mile to that trailhead.

To continue the loop, turn right (west), drop through a gully cluttered with deadfall, then begin the long slog upward. The initial mile or so is in dense stands of timber; there are no views and the quiet is meditative. The trail is never torturously steep, but follows a steady incline along the northern wall of the Warner Valley.

About halfway up this section of the climb, you will break out of the forest onto a slope covered with low-growing mountain chaparral, where the views will delight. To the south are the rolling, forested slopes of Sifford Mountain; to the west are the head of the Warner Valley and the barren upper reaches of the park.

As you climb, the chaparral gives way to stony benches upon which grows a sparse forest of Jeffrey pine. The trail through this section wanders through pinemat manzanita and is marked with the ubiquitous yellow dots on the trees.

At 7.5 miles, you will reach the junction with the trails that lead right (west) to Bench Lake and left (southwest) to Sifford Lake. Take the left fork, heading toward Sifford Lake. At the next intersection, turn left (south) on the spur trail that leads to Sifford Lake, which you will reach at about the 8-mile mark. Though you can bypass this lake, I recommend that you take the side trip—it is a relatively easy roller coaster of a trail that leads to a lovely lake in a bowl of sun-warmed rock (see Hike 14 for details).

After returning from Sifford Lake, continue up and northwest on the trail to the Kings Creek Trailhead. It leads over benches shaded with open forest to the south edge of the Lower Meadow at 9.6 miles, where you will intersect with the trail leading down to Kings Creek Falls. From here, it's another 0.5 mile left (west) along the north side of the meadow to the trailhead.

18 Kings Creek Falls to Summit Lake

Highlights: This backcountry route rambles past Kings Creek Falls, then climbs through the Summit Creek drainage to picturesque Summit Lake.

Type of hike: Day hike; shuttle.

Total distance: 5 miles.

Difficulty: Moderate.

Best months: July–September.

Maps: USGS Reading Peak quad; Lassen Volcanic National Park maps by the National Park Service, Earthwalk Press, and Wilderness Press; USDAFS Lassen National Forest map.

Parking and facilities: Parking is available in pullouts along the Lassen Park Road (California Highway 89). There are no other facilities available. At Summit Lake endpoint, you will find abundant amenities, including restrooms, picnic areas, and a ranger station.

Finding the trailhead: The trailhead is located on the Lassen Park Road (CA 89) about 15.5 miles south and east of the Manzanita Lake Entrance Station, and 12.5 miles north and east of the Southwest Entrance Station. It is on the southeast side of the road.

Key points:
- 0.0   Kings Creek Falls Trailhead.
- 0.5   Reach the intersection with the trail to Sifford Lake in the Lower Meadow.
- 1.1   Arrive at Kings Creek Falls.
- 3.3   Reach the intersection with the trail to Summit Lake.
- 4.3   Leave the little creek behind.
- 5.0   Arrive at Summit Lake.

The hike: Kings Creek Falls, with all its vigor and noise, enlivens your senses at the outset of this hike, but by the time you reach Summit Lake, after hiking for nearly four miles along serene streams clothed in colorful riparian vegetation, you feel marvelously mellow.

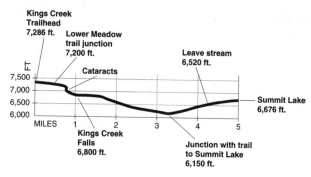

As with the Kings Creek to Corral Meadow Loop (Hike 17), this trek takes you along sections of trail described in detail previously in this chapter. I will refer you to those hike descriptions for the sake of brevity. It is possible to hike this trail in reverse—from Summit Lake to the Kings Creek

Kings Creek Falls to Summit Lake

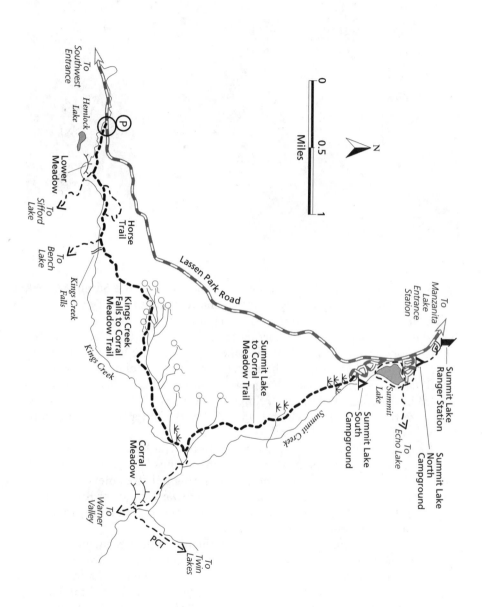

Hikers head up the trail from Corral Meadow to Summit Lake.

trailhead—but I found the climbing more moderate in the Summit Creek drainage. I don't know about you, but I tend to choose the easy way up.

The trail begins as the others in this chapter, dropping from the trailhead into the Lower Meadow, and skirting the north side of the meadow to the intersection with the trail to Sifford Lake at 0.5 mile. Go left (northeast) on the trail to Kings Creek Falls, which drops precipitously alongside the Kings Creek cascades, then passes the intersection with the trail to Bench and Sifford Lakes. At 1.1 miles, reach Kings Creek Falls. Visit the falls overlook, then take the upper trail, which leads left (north) and away from the falls toward Summit Lake and Corral Meadow.

The route climbs around a knob and into the cradle of a no-name creek that drains the heavily forested swale north of Kings Creek. A long descent through the dense woodlands, and across spring-fed streamlets lined with small meadows and riparian zones, drops you toward the lower Kings Creek drainage. Though it sees relatively little traffic, the footpath is easy to follow and marked with yellow dots on the trees.

Near the 3-mile mark, you reach the confluence of the stream you've been following and Kings Creek. Do not cross Kings Creek; instead, turn left (north) and cross the smaller waterway on logs and rocks. A yellow dot in the willows on the north side of the stream confirms you are on the right track.

The trail continues to its junction with the trail to Summit Lake and Corral Meadow (see Hike 17 for details) at 3.3 miles. Turn left (north) on the trail to Summit Lake, which lies 1.7 miles ahead.

Summit Creek rumbles out of sight to your right (east) as you begin the steady but not brutal climb toward the lake. The trail flattens as it crosses a tributary stream into a thicket of willow and alder, then continues its ascent with the lively streamlet on the east side of the route.

You cross the stream again via a split log bridge, then continue upward with the waterway on the south side of the trail. Climb onto a bench littered with pinemat manzanita; the trail curves in a more northwesterly direction and crosses a narrow meadow. Beyond, at about 4.3 miles, the friendly little stream disappears.

You won't miss a liquid companion for long, however. Climb up and over the next bench, and the trail approaches a second tinkling creek—another tributary feeding Summit Creek. This one is bordered by a phalanx of alder standing 7 feet high in places. Cross the stream, then switchback north into the woods, arcing up along the path of the ephemeral waterway. The gradual ascent leads through a forest of huge firs, then drops into a steep gully, climbing out on a traverse along its northern flank.

As you approach Summit Lake, you pass through three lovely meadows thick with wildflowers in spring and early summer, and separated from one another by narrow strips of evergreens. The trail ends on the E loop of the Summit Lake South Campground, adjacent to site 10. The main trailhead, with an informational billboard, lies north on the paved loop road; the Summit Lake Ranger Station lies about 0.5 mile north (see Hike 19). Arrange to have your shuttle provider pack a picnic lunch or barbecue to share on the shores of lovely Summit Lake, where you can enjoy great views of Lassen Peak as you cool your feet in the calming waters.

Or, if you must, return as you came.

Summit Lake

If you seek family fun a bit farther afield than busy Manzanita Lake, Summit Lake is the ideal choice. This pretty lake, at an elevation of nearly 6,700 feet, lies in the midst of a red fir forest that shelters its campgrounds and picnic sites from the summer sun. From the lake's eastern shore, the snowy heights of Lassen Peak dominate the horizon, with Reading Peak spilling to the southwest. To the north, flat-topped Hat Mountain shelters the lake, its forested flanks serving as the gateway to the backcountry.

Summit Lake is perhaps Lassen Park's friendliest lake to swimmers, its calm waters cool and inviting when the sun burns strongly. Those not willing to dive in often take to the water on inflatable rafts and in canoes (no motorized watercraft are permitted); others choose to wade in the shallows, fishing rods in hand, visions of catching the "big one" circling in their heads.

The backcountry north of Summit Lake is dotted with other lakes—Echo, Upper and Lower Twin, Little and Big Bear, Silver, Feather, and others. These lakes are reached via a well-used trail that forms a nice loop for either a day hike or a backpacking journey, or that can be broken down into shorter, out-and-back hikes. Both the short hikes and the loop are described in this chapter. You can follow these descriptions, or use a good trail map to customize your hike. As with nearly all trails in the park, this one offers links to other popular destinations, with the area around Snag Lake being the closest.

Backcountry camping is permitted near most of these lakes, with the exception of Echo Lake. Please adhere to backcountry regulations, which are delineated in the introduction and also in Lassen Volcanic National Park literature. There are no potable water sources along the trails; either pack in all the water you will need, or treat water from the lakes by boiling it, filtering it, or treating it with chemicals.

Given Summit Lake's many attractions, its two campgrounds fill quickly in the summer. The Summit Lake North Campground offers 46 sites and costs $14 per night. The Summit Lake South Campground has 48 sites and costs $12 per night. Amenities include restrooms, developed campsites with fire rings and bearproof food storage cabinets, and ranger-led programs offered in the amphitheater. Stays at Summit Lake are limited to 7 days per year. All sites are available on a first come, first served basis.

To reach Summit Lake from the Manzanita Lake Entrance Station, follow the Lassen Park Road (California Highway 89) south and east for about 12 miles. The turnoff to the Summit Lake Ranger Station and trailhead is 0.1 mile before (west of) the turnoff for the campgrounds. The lake, campgrounds, and ranger station are on the left (north) side of the Lassen Park Road. To reach the trailhead from the Southwest Entrance Station, follow the Lassen Park Road for about 16 miles to the Summit Lake campgrounds and the Summit Lake Ranger station.

19 Summit Lake

Highlights:	This pleasant, short hike features gorgeous views of Lassen Peak and a rustic amphitheater.
Type of hike:	Lollipop loop.
Total distance:	1.7 miles.
Difficulty:	Easy.
Best months:	Late May–October.
Maps:	USGS Reading Peak quad; Lassen Volcanic National Park maps by the National Park Service, Earthwalk Press, and Wilderness Press; USDAFS Lassen National Forest map.
Special considerations:	The route along the western shore of the lake follows informal paths through shoreline grasses. You can't get lost, but you might pick a path that dead-ends at the lakeshore. No worries—take a breather, then pick another path and continue around the lake.
Parking and facilities:	There are abundant facilities in the Summit Lake area, including campgrounds, restrooms, water sources, a ranger station, and picnic facilities.

Finding the trailhead: To reach the trailhead at the Summit Lake Ranger Station from the Manzanita Lake Entrance Station, follow the Lassen Park Road (California Highway 89) south and east for 12 miles to the turnoff, which is on the left (north) side of the road. The parking area is 0.1 mile north of the pavement. From the Southwest Entrance Station, follow the Lassen Park Road for about 16 miles to the turnoff for the Summit Lake Ranger Station.

Lassen Peak forms the backdrop for Summit Lake.

Summit Lake

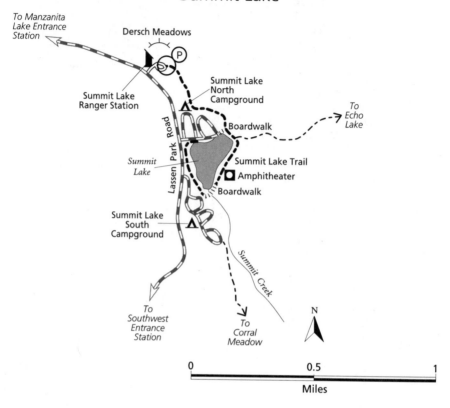

Key points:

- 0.0   Summit Lake Ranger Station Trailhead.
- 0.4   Arrive at the lakeshore.
- 0.5   Reach the intersection with the trail to Echo Lake.
- 0.7   Visit the amphitheater.
- 0.8   Pass the Summit Lake South Campground.
- 1.3   Return to the turnoff to the trailhead.

The hike: Perhaps it's early morning: The summer sun hasn't reached its apex, breakfast lies heavy in your belly, and you feel the need to stretch your legs before rigging up the fishing gear or climbing into the boat. Or perhaps it's midday: You have just arrived in the park, and want to walk off the stiffness of the car. Or perhaps it's evening: The sun, which has not quite settled below the western horizon, paints Lassen Peak with alpenglow, and you want a nice walk before you settle at the campfire, cup of tea in hand. Regardless of the motivation, the short loop trail around Summit Lake is easy and inviting.

If you are camping on the lake, you can jump on the loop at any point. For those without a campsite, the trail is described here beginning at the Summit Lake Ranger Station Trailhead. Pass the informational kiosk and walk across the boardwalk that leads east through the first of several small, marshy swales toward the lake. Roll through the shallow boggy gullies—one with round log stepping stones that help keep you on track—to the intersection with an informal trail that leads into the Summit Lake North Campground at 0.2 mile.

Stay left (northward), and hike over the next hummock; you can see the camp through the trees. Drop past a small pond to the intersection with the lakeside loop at 0.4 mile. Go left (northeast) to circle the lake in a clockwise direction.

At 0.5 mile, you will reach the intersection with the trail that leads left (northeast) to Echo Lake and into the backcountry. Stay right (south) on the lakeside path; there is a sign for the amphitheater at this point. The views of Lassen Peak, rising above the trees, are wonderful from the north shore of the lake.

At the trail intersection at 0.7 mile, go left (up and east) to visit the amphitheater, or right (down and east) to continue around the lake. The amphitheater is small and rustic, with bare wooden benches, but it has a remarkable setting, with commanding views of the volcano and the lake spread at its feet.

Back on the lakeside trail, you will reach the boardwalk across the outlet stream near the Summit Lake South Campground's C Loop at 0.8 mile. The formal trail ends here: You can return as you came, or wander along the often soggy informal trails that hug the lake's east shore to the picnic area on the west side of the lake. Stay lakeside as you pass through the picnic area to pick up the boardwalk that leads back to the intersection with the trail to the Summit Lake Ranger Station at 1.3 miles. From here, retrace your steps to the trailhead.

20 Echo Lake

Highlights:	A pleasant trail leads to an inviting backcountry lake.
Type of hike:	Out-and-back.
Total distance:	4.4 miles.
Difficulty:	Moderate.
Best months:	July–October.
Maps:	USGS Reading Peak quad; Lassen Volcanic National Park maps by the National Park Service, Earthwalk Press, and Wilderness Press; Lassen National Forest map.
Parking and facilities:	There are abundant facilities in the Summit Lake area, including campgrounds, restrooms, water sources, a ranger station, and picnic facilities.

Echo Lake

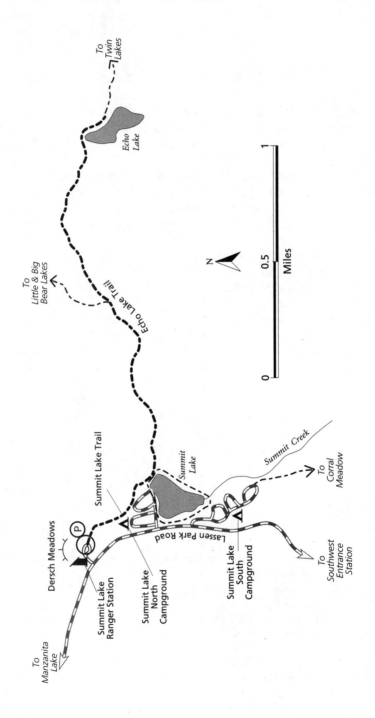

Finding the trailhead: To reach the trailhead at the Summit Lake Ranger Station from the Manzanita Lake Entrance Station, follow the Lassen Park Road (California Highway 89) south and east for 12 miles to the turnoff, which is on the left (north) side of the road. The parking area is 0.1 mile north of the pavement. From the Southwest Entrance Station, follow the Lassen Park Road for about 16 miles to the turnoff for the Summit Lake Ranger Station.

Key points:

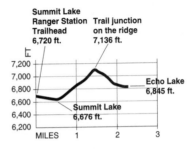

0.0 Summit Lake Ranger Station Trailhead.
0.4 Arrive at Summit Lake.
0.5 Reach the intersection with the trail to Echo Lake.
1.4 Reach the second trail intersection on the ridge.
2.2 Arrive at Echo Lake.

The hike: Echo Lake is the first in a series of lovely backcountry lakes reached via the trail that leads northeast from the developed areas around Summit Lake. While this little tarn is a relatively easy day hike from the trailhead or the Summit Lake campgrounds, it also can serve as the first stop in a longer day hike—or overnight trip—into the northern backcountry of the national park.

The waters of Echo Lake are clear and blue, fading to green in the shallows. Thick forest drops to the waterline and hugs the walls of the shallow basin. Narrow strips of rocky shoreline offer respite in the sun, and the still waters are perfect for cooling tired feet before carrying on to the Twin Lakes or beyond. Some folks hike up in their swimsuits, with the goal of taking a brisk plunge before heading back to camp at Summit Lake or another of the park's campgrounds. There is no camping permitted at Echo Lake.

The trail is straightforward. It begins at the Summit Lake Ranger Station Trailhead, crossing the boardwalk and rolling through a series of shallow drainages before linking up with the Summit Lake Trail (Hike 19) at 0.4 mile. Go left (east) on the trail around Summit Lake to the next trail junction at 0.5 mile, where you break to the left (northeast), and climb away from the lake under the shade of nicely spaced evergreens.

The forest opens as you climb, and pinemat manzanita carpets the floor of the woodland. Glance southwest over your shoulder for spectacular views of Lassen Peak, which you enjoy more easily on the descent.

After a steady climb along a broad ridge, views of the park's open eastward backcountry. Ascend a switchback, then the trail flattens along the ridgetop. At 1.4 miles, you reach a trail intersection. The trail to the left (north) leads to Little and Big Bear Lakes; stay right (east) on the trail to Echo Lake, which lies 0.8 mile ahead.

A gentle, ascending traverse along a ridgeline that sweeps east from the flanks of Hat Mountain leads through massive trees to a descent that begins easily, running down the east-facing slope of the ridge. The brief downhill pitch is followed by a flat passage through the woods; Echo Lake flits in and out of view, screened by the trees.

A final short hop down some quick switchbacks, and you are on Echo Lake's secluded shores. Tarry here, swimming, picnicking, and enjoying, then continue on to another backcountry destination, or return as you came.

21   Upper and Lower Twin Lakes

Highlights:	The Twin Lakes lie at the absolute center of the park, serving both as a delightful destination and a hub from which you can reach every corner of the park.
Type of hike:	Day hike or backpack; lollipop loop.
Total distance:	7.2 miles to Upper Twin Lake; 9 miles with a circuit of Lower Twin Lake.
Difficulty:	Moderate.
Best months:	Late June–October.
Maps:	USGS Reading Peak, West Prospect Peak, and Prospect Peak quads; Lassen Volcanic National Park maps by the National Park Service, Earthwalk Press, and Wilderness Press; USDAFS Lassen National Forest map.
Special considerations:	If you choose to camp at Lower Twin Lake, be sure to obey backcountry camping regulations by obtaining a permit and by setting up camp at least 100 feet from any water source or trail. An inclusive description of backcountry regulations is listed in the introduction.
Parking and facilities:	There are abundant facilities in the Summit Lake area, including campgrounds, restrooms, water sources, a ranger station, and picnic facilities.

Finding the trailhead: To reach the trailhead at the Summit Lake Ranger Station from the Manzanita Lake Entrance Station, follow the Lassen Park Road (California Highway 89) south and east for 12 miles to the turnoff, which is on the left (north) side of the road. The parking area is 0.1 mile north of the highway. From the Southwest Entrance Station, follow the Lassen Park Road for about 16 miles to the turnoff for the Summit Lake Ranger Station.

Key points:

0.0   Summit Lake Ranger Station Trailhead.
0.5   Reach the intersection with the trail to Echo Lake.
1.4   Pass the second trail intersection on the ridge.
2.2   Arrive at Echo Lake.
2.7   Begin to descend through a steep drainage.
3.6   Reach Upper Twin Lake.
4.0   Arrive at Lower Twin Lake.
5.1   Complete the circuit of Lower Twin Lake.

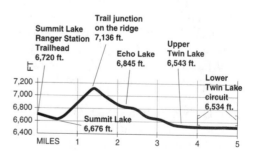

Upper and Lower Twin Lakes

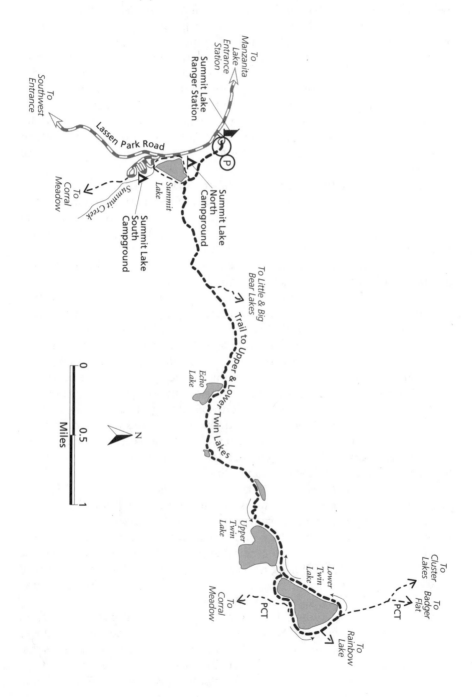

The hike: These fraternal twins are connected by more than the narrow umbilical cord of the stream that links them. They are alike in setting as well. Each is rather large, and pleasantly blue, with a shoreline trail that introduces the hiker to the nuances of its shape. Each sports a net of sun-bleached logs along its northeast shore, offering a rather obvious clue to the direction of the prevailing winds in the heart of Lassen Volcanic National Park.

But, as with many sets of twins, these two lakes are also profoundly different. Upper Twin is quieter and smaller, with a more remote feel. Lower Twin Lake is larger, and, if you'll pardon the anthropomorphism, a bit more gregarious. A trail encircles it, offering links to other lakes and areas of the backcountry, as well as to the Pacific Crest Trail. It is a hub, you are likely to encounter hikers from Butte Lake, Juniper Lake, or farther afield at some point along the circuit.

The trail begins at the Summit Lake Ranger Station Trailhead. Roll through several shallow gullies before linking up with the trail around Summit Lake at 0.4 mile. Go left (east) on the Summit Lake trail to the next trail intersection at 0.5 mile; a trail sign directs you left (northeast) toward Echo Lake, Twin Lakes, and other destinations in Lassen's backcountry.

The climb away from Summit Lake is steady. Negotiate a switchback, then the trail flattens along a ridgetop. At 1.4 miles, you will reach a trail intersection; the trail to Echo Lake and the Twin Lakes heads right (east), and the trail to Little and Big Bear Lakes leads left (north). Go right, toward Echo Lake.

After a short climb, the trail descends to Echo Lake at 2.2 miles. This is a good place to rest and snack. To continue to Twin Lakes, follow the trail left (clockwise) around the northeastern shore of Echo Lake. At the northeast corner of the lake (an Echo Lake sign marks the spot), the trail heads left and up (east), out of the basin. Yellow dots on the trees mark the route.

The trail becomes a bit rougher as it drops into a gully at 2.7 miles. At the base of the first downhill pitch of the drainage, the trail skirts a small green pond. Beyond, the path descends again, then flattens in the belly of the drainage. Pass a nameless lake on your left (north), this one long and shallow. The trail traverses above its shoreline.

A short climb leads away from the no-name lake, then the trail follows switchbacks down through the forest to the edge of the Twin Lakes basin. Upper Twin Lake comes into view through the trees. Cross a seasonal stream, which is usually dry by mid-July, and arrive on the lakeshore at 3.6 miles.

At the trail sign, veer left (clockwise) around the lake. The path hugs the shoreline for a stretch, offering unobstructed views of blue water rumpled by whatever breeze stirs the alpine air. A raft of bleached driftwood marks the arc of Upper Twin Lake's northeast corner.

As it leaves Upper Twin Lake, the trail borders the narrow outlet stream that connects the two lakes. Follow the stream down to the shore of Lower Twin Lake at 4 miles, which is big, blue, and iridescent with dragonflies that feed, thankfully, on mosquitoes. Fairfield Peak rises to the northeast, its burnished cinders nourishing a healthy cloak of pine and fir. A trail sign at this point indicates that, from here, you can hike to the Cinder Cone, to Horseshoe Lake, or to Snag Lake.

A streamside trail leads around Upper Twin Lake.

The lake circuit trail is described in a counterclockwise direction. Most of the landmarks are trail intersections, and you follow the Pacific Crest Trail (PCT) for a little more than half a mile as you trace the eastern shore of the lake. To begin the circuit, go right (east) from the trail intersection, crossing the inlet/outlet stream. Red diamonds on the trees mark the route. At 4.3 miles, you will reach the next trail junction. Swan Lake, Horseshoe Lake, and Corral Meadow lie to the right (south). Keep left (northeast), staying adjacent to the lakeshore on the PCT; this trail connects with trails to Cinder Cone and other points in the northeastern portion of the park.

At about 4.5 miles, you will reach another trail intersection, where signs indicate that the trail to the right (northeast), leads to Rainbow Lake, Snag Lake, and Butte Lake. Stay left (north), follow the signs toward the Cluster Lakes and Badger Flat. About 0.1 mile beyond, at the northern border of the lake, the circuit trail breaks off of the PCT, veering to the left (west) and crossing the lake's natural dike. A logjam of bleached deadfall abuts the dike, which is amply shaded with evergreens and offers yet another perfect picnicking opportunity. If you plan to spend the night here, you can find nice campsites along the eastern and northern shores of Lower Twin Lake. Be sure to pick a site well away from the water and trails.

The circuit trail continues around the lake until it intersects the route by which you came, adjacent to the inlet/outlet stream. From here, retrace your steps to the trailhead.

22 Rainbow Lake

Highlights: This small lake sits in its own secluded basin on the southern flanks of Fairfield Peak.

Type of hike: Day hike or backpack; out-and-back.

Total distance: 10 miles.

Difficulty: Moderate.

Best months: July–October.

Maps: USGS Reading Peak, West Prospect Peak, and Prospect Peak quads; Lassen Volcanic National Park maps by the National Park Service, Earthwalk Press, and Wilderness Press; USDAFS Lassen National Forest map.

Special considerations: If you camp at Rainbow Lake or Lower Twin Lake, please obey backcountry camping regulations by obtaining a permit and by setting up camp at least 100 feet from any water source or trail. An inclusive description of backcountry regulations is listed in the introduction.

Parking and facilities: There are abundant facilities in the Summit Lake area, including campgrounds, restrooms, water sources, a ranger station, and picnic facilities.

Finding the trailhead: To reach the trailhead at the Summit Lake Ranger Station from the Manzanita Lake Entrance Station, follow the Lassen Park Road (California Highway 89) south and east for 12 miles to the turnoff, which is on the left (north) side of the road. The parking area is 0.1 mile north of the pavement. From the Southwest Entrance Station, follow the Lassen Park Road for about 16 miles to the turnoff for the Summit Lake Ranger Station.

Key points:

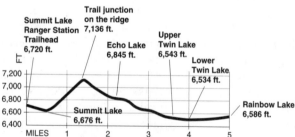

0.0 Summit Lake Ranger Station Trailhead.

0.5 Reach the intersection with the trail to Echo Lake.

1.4 Pass the second trail intersection on the ridge.

2.2 Arrive at Echo Lake.

2.7 Begin a descent through a steep drainage.

3.6 Reach Upper Twin Lake.

4.0 Arrive at Lower Twin Lake.

4.5 Reach the intersection with the trail to Rainbow Lake.

5.0 Arrive at Rainbow Lake.

Rainbow Lake

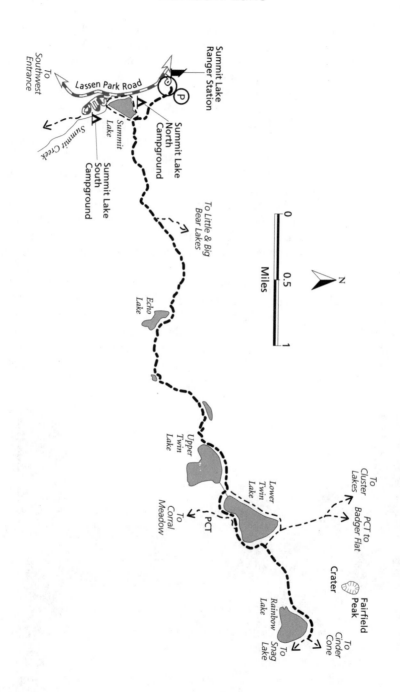

The hike: It's not the prettiest, or the biggest, or the deepest lake in Lassen Volcanic National Park, but Rainbow Lake has an intangible and very inviting ambiance. Perhaps its special to me because I was able to rest and refuel on its pleasant, secluded shores on several occasions, undisturbed by pests of any kind, including the sometimes ubiquitous mosquito. You might call it the mother of Lassen's lakes, not overwhelming in any way, but always there, always comfortable, always welcoming.

The lake is located in the heart of the backcountry, making an ideal stopover for trekkers taking off from either Summit Lake or Butte Lake. The hike to the lake is described here as a side trip from the trek to neighboring Twin Lakes, but it also is an integral part of a delightful loop from the Butte Lake area (see Hike 43 in the Butte Lake chapter).

The bulk of this trail mirrors the Twin Lakes hike. I will summarize those portions of the hike here; refer to Hike 21 for more details.

The trail begins at the Summit Lake Ranger Station Trailhead. Roll through several gullies to the intersection with the trail around Summit Lake at 0.4 mile. Go left (east) on the Summit Lake trail to the next intersection at 0.5 mile; a trail sign directs you left (northeast) on the trail to Echo Lake and the Twin Lakes.

A steady climb and a switchback lead onto a ridgetop. At the trail intersection at 1.4 miles, go right (east) on the trail to Echo Lake (the trail to Little and Big Bear Lakes leads left and north).

The trail drops to Echo Lake at 2.2 miles. Continue to Twin Lakes by following the footpath clockwise around the northeast shore of Echo Lake. At the northeast corner of the lake, the trail heads left and up (east), out of the basin. Yellow dots on the trees mark the route.

Rainbow Lake lies in the heart of Lassen's backcountry.

The trail descends through a drainage at 2.7 miles, passing a small, green pond, then a nameless lake. A short climb leads away from the no-name lake, then the trail follows switchbacks down into the Twin Lakes basin. Cross a seasonal stream, usually dry by mid-July, to Upper Twin Lake at 3.6 miles.

Hike left (clockwise) on the shoreline path. As the trail leaves the northeast corner of Upper Twin Lake, it borders the narrow outlet stream that connects it to Lower Twin Lake. Follow the stream to the shore of Lower Twin Lake at 4 miles.

At the trail sign on the west shore of Lower Twin Lake, turn right (southeast) on a counterclockwise circuit of the lake. At 4.3 miles, you will reach the junction with the Pacific Crest Trail. Go left (northeast) on the PCT. At 4.5 miles, on the east shore of Lower Twin Lake, you reach the intersection with the trail that leads right (northeast) to Rainbow Lake, Snag Lake, and Butte Lake.

Turn right on this trail, climbing through an open woodland sprinkled with wildflower meadows and scented with sage and pine. The trail flattens atop a shallow rise, then slopes gently downward, with the azure waters of Rainbow Lake shimmering through a lacy screen of trees.

At 4.6 miles, you reach the trail sign that confirms you have arrived at Rainbow Lake. A soft mat of marsh grasses lines its shore, and the surrounding woodlands offer inviting campsites. Enjoy your stay at the lake, whether for an hour or several days, then either return as you came, or tie this trail into another to make a longer loop or shuttle hike.

23 Big and Little Bear Lakes

Highlights:	This hike arcs around the backside of Hat Mountain to a charming pair of secluded lakes.
Type of hike:	Day hike or overnight trip; out-and-back.
Total distance:	8.4 miles.
Difficulty:	Moderate.
Best months:	July–October.
Maps:	USGS Reading Peak and West Prospect Peak quads; Lassen Volcanic National Park maps by the National Park Service, Earthwalk Press, and Wilderness Press; USDAFS Lassen National Forest map.
Special considerations:	If you camp at either of the Bear Lakes, please obey backcountry camping regulations by securing a permit and by setting up camp at least 100 feet from any water source or trail. An inclusive description of backcountry regulations is listed in the introduction.
Parking and facilities:	There are abundant facilities in the Summit Lake area, including campgrounds, restrooms, water sources, a ranger station, and picnic facilities.

Big and Little Bear Lakes

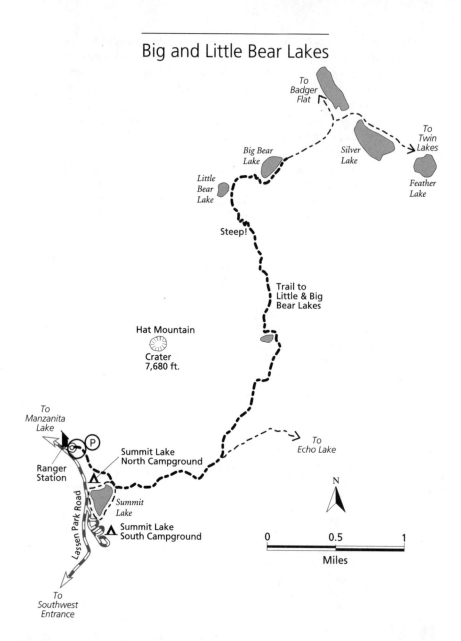

Finding the trailhead: To reach the trailhead at the Summit Lake Ranger Station from the Manzanita Lake Entrance Station, follow the Lassen Park Road (California Highway 89) south and east for 12 miles to the turnoff, which is on the left (north) side of the road. The parking area is 0.1 mile north of the pavement. From the Southwest Entrance Station, follow the Lassen Park Road for about 16 miles to the turnoff for the Summit Lake Ranger Station.

Key points:

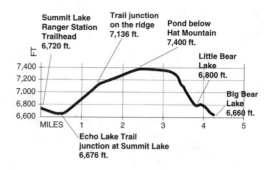

The hike: Most folks heading off into the backcountry north of Summit Lake hike to Echo Lake and the Twin Lakes. These are wonderful destinations, but if you want to take the path less traveled, one with a bit more mystery and certainly fewer human distractions, venture to the Bear Lakes.

Big and Little Bear Lakes, captured in shallow basins on the northwest flank of a broad ridge that sweeps off the eastern side of Hat Mountain, are both relatively small. What they lack in size, however, they more than make up for in the clarity of their waters, their classical settings, and the enticing sense of remoteness that surrounds them. Make them the destination of a day hike, or tie them in to the Cluster Lakes Loop (Hike 24).

The trail begins at the Summit Lake Ranger Station Trailhead. Roll through several marshy gullies to the intersection with the trail that leads around Summit Lake at 0.4 mile. Go left (east) on the Summit Lake Trail to the next trail intersection at 0.5 mile; a sign directs you left (northeast) toward Echo Lake and the Twin Lakes. The trail climbs steadily, and rounds a switchback, before reaching the crest of a ridge. At the ridgetop trail intersection at 1.4 miles, go left (north) on the trail to Little and Big Bear Lakes. The trail to Echo Lake and Twin Lakes is to the right (east).

The traversing ascent to the apex of the broad, flat-topped ridge below the east face of Hat Mountain is not terribly steep, but it is steady. Views of Lassen Peak are behind you, to the south and west, and are easier to enjoy on the return trip. The woodland, however, is wonderfully open, with birdsong emanating from bush and tree, and pinemat manzanita filling in the blank spots between lumps and clumps of mottled gray andesite.

The incline moderates after 0.5 mile, as you begin to traverse the rolling top of the ridge. It's a solitary and spectacular landscape, with swales devoid of vegetation in their bellies, but lined with stands of evergreens and thickets of manzanita and wildflowers.

A narrow tarn lies in a depression in the lee of Hat Mountain near the crest of the climb at 2.4 miles. Beyond the lakelet, the trail climbs in and out of shallow gullies for a quarter of a mile or so, then begins a roller coaster ride down and north toward the Bear Lakes basins. Near the northern limit of the mesa, the trail winds through a gully, then through a narrow gap. A tiny pond on the right (east) marks the end of the traverse and the beginning of the rather steep descent to Little Bear Lake.

Deadfall clutters the shores of Big Bear Lake.

There are lovely views of the deep, wooded ravine to the west of the trail, with Lassen Peak visible over the top of the forested ridge, but leave these views for the climb out, as this descent demands your focus. Switchbacks make the decline more bearable, but watch your knees on the way down (and your lungs on the way back up).

You then drop into a sun-dappled evergreen forest, its floor barren of all greenery, the perfect setting for one of the prettiest little lakes in Lassen's backcountry. Little Bear Lake, at 3.7 miles, is bottle green and so clear that the grasses clinging to its sandy bottom are set off in sharp relief. When breezes aren't wrinkling the face of the lake, you can see how deadfall, fuzzy with rot, has created stunning horizontal architecture beneath the lake's surface.

The trail skirts the eastern shore of the lake, then begins a short but rather steep descent to Big Bear Lake, at 4.2 miles. This good-sized lake, while not the end of the trail, is the final destination for this route. Remarkably clear, you can see every detail of the logs that have fallen into its shallows as well, and a pile of silvered driftwood has accumulated along the north shore. Though the shoreline is heavily forested, there are plenty of places to sit, rest, eat, and contemplate. Late in the season, you may want to cool off by dipping into the lake's still waters. Enjoy.

Either return as you came, or continue on a clockwise journey along the Cluster Lakes Loop, which is described in Hike 24—though in the opposite direction. Not to worry: the trails are all clearly marked, and while landmarks may present different faces, they are still recognizable.

24   Cluster Lakes Loop

Highlights:	Lakes, lakes, and more lakes. Big and small, deep and shallow, bottle green and reflective blue, it's a virtual bonanza of lakes!
Type of hike:	Day hike or backpack; loop.
Total distance:	12.1 miles.
Difficulty:	Moderate.
Best months:	July–October.
Maps:	USGS Reading Peak, Prospect Peak, and West Prospect Peak quads; Lassen Volcanic National Park maps by the National Park Service, Earthwalk Press, and Wilderness Press; USDAFS Lassen National Forest map.
Special considerations:	If you camp near any of the lakes along this popular route, please obey backcountry camping regulations by obtaining permits and by setting up camp at least 100 feet from any water source or trail. An inclusive description of backcountry regulations is listed in the introduction. No camping is permitted at Echo Lake.
Parking and facilities:	There are abundant facilities in the Summit Lake area, including campgrounds, restrooms, water sources, a ranger station, and picnic facilities.

Finding the trailhead: To reach the Summit Lake Ranger Station Trailhead from the Manzanita Lake Entrance Station, follow the Lassen Park Road (California Highway 89) south and east for 12 miles to the turnoff, which is on the left (north) side of the road. The parking area is 0.1 mile north of the highway. From the Southwest Entrance Station, follow the Lassen Park Road for about 16 miles to the turnoff for the Summit Lake Ranger Station.

Key points:

0.0	Summit Lake Ranger Station Trailhead.
0.5	Reach the intersection with the trail to Echo Lake.
1.4	Pass the second trail intersection on the ridge.
2.2	Arrive at Echo Lake.
3.6	Reach Upper Twin Lake.
4.0	Arrive at Lower Twin Lake.
4.6	Branch off left (west) on the trail to Feather and Silver Lakes.
5.3	Reach Feather Lake.
6.4	At the trail junction, go left (southwest) toward the Bear Lakes.
6.9	Arrive at Big Bear Lake.
7.4	Reach Little Bear Lake.
12.1	Return to the Summit Lake Ranger Station Trailhead.

The hike: The Cluster Lakes number nearly a dozen. Not all have names, and some are no larger than ponds, but they all have great charm. Silver Lake is the largest, its cool waters spreading south from the trail toward the wooded mesa that guards the eastern flanks of Hat Mountain; its sister,

Cluster Lakes Loop

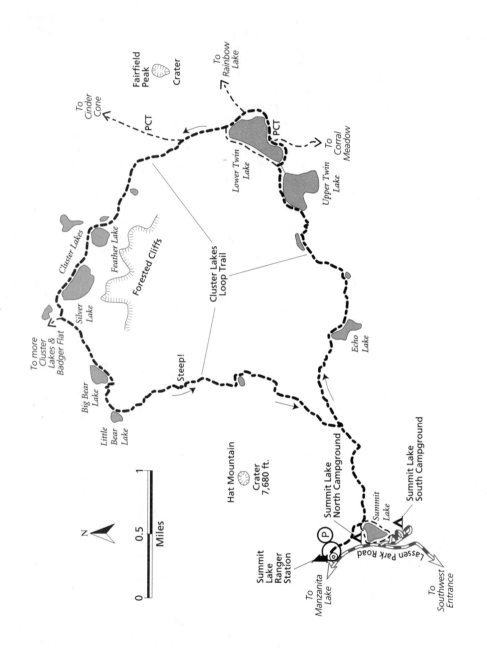

To Cinder Cone

Fairfield Peak

Crater

To Rainbow Lake

PCT

PCT

Lower Twin Lake

Upper Twin Lake

To Corral Meadow

Cluster Lakes

Feather Lake

Forested Cliffs

Cluster Lakes Loop Trail

Silver Lake

To more Cluster Lakes & Badger Flat

Big Bear Lake

Little Bear Lake

Steep!

Echo Lake

Hat Mountain

Crater 7,680 ft.

N

0   0.5   1

Miles

Summit Lake North Campground

Summit Lake South Campground

Summit Lake

Summit Lake Ranger Station

P

Lassen Park Road

To Manzanita Lake

To Southwest Entrance

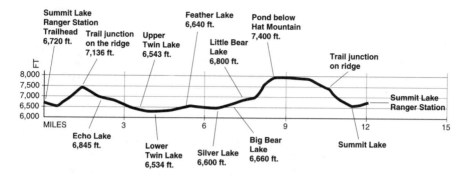

Feather Lake, also lies at the foot of this broad, flat-topped ridge. Tie these two in with Summit Lake, the Twin Lakes, Echo Lake, and the Bear Lakes, and you've got a loop that skirts so many bodies of water you'll feel down-right soggy by the time you return to the trailhead.

This loop can be a long day hike or a backpack. Several trails connecting to other areas of the park intersect the route at Lower Twin Lake, so if you choose, you can branch off to another destination or trailhead. Much of this trail has already been described thoroughly in this chapter (see Hikes 20–23); for more details of what you see along a specific section of the route, refer to the pertinent hike descriptions. The loop is described here in a counterclockwise direction, but you can go either way. It is well marked with both trail signs and the ubiquitous yellow or red dots on the trees.

The trail begins at the Summit Lake Ranger Station Trailhead. Roll through several boggy gullies to the intersection with the trail that leads around Summit Lake at 0.4 mile. Go left (east) on the Summit Lake Trail to the next trail intersection at 0.5 mile; a sign directs you left (northeast) toward Echo Lake and the Twin Lakes. The trail climbs steadily, and rounds a switchback, before reaching the crest of a ridge. At the ridgetop trail intersection at 1.4 miles, go right (east) on the trail to Echo Lake and the Twin Lakes (the trail to Little and Big Bear Lakes leads left and north).

The trail drops through the woods to Echo Lake at 2.2 miles. Follow the trail clockwise around the northeast shore of Echo Lake. At the northeast corner of the lake, the trail to the Twin Lakes heads left and up (east), out of the Echo Lake basin.

Beyond Echo Lake, the trail descends through a drainage, passing a small pond on the south side of the trail, then a nameless lake on the north side. A short climb leads away from the narrow no-name lake, then the trail follows switchbacks down to the floor of the Twin Lakes basin. Cross a seasonal stream, usually dry by midsummer, to the shore of Upper Twin Lake at 3.6 miles.

Hike left (clockwise) on the shoreline path to the northeast corner of Upper Twin Lake. The route follows the narrow outlet stream that connects Upper Twin Lake with its lower twin. You stand beside Lower Twin Lake at 4 miles.

At the trail sign on the west shore of Lower Twin Lake, turn right (southeast) on a counterclockwise circuit of the lake. At about 4.3 miles, you reach the junction with the Pacific Crest Trail junction. Go left (northeast) on the PCT; the right-hand trail leads south to Swan Lake and Corral Meadow. At about 4.5 miles, on the east shore of Lower Twin Lake, you reach the intersection with the trail that leads right (northeast) to Rainbow Lake, Snag Lake, and Butte Lake. Stay left again, continuing north to the north shore of the lake.

A circuit trail of Lower Twin Lake breaks left (west) from the PCT to cross the lake's natural dam. To continue on the Cluster Lakes Loop, stay right (north) on the PCT. A small backcountry ranger cabin (off limits to hikers) sits in the woods on the right (east) side of the trail; continue north on the broad path. At 4.6 miles, you arrive at the intersection with the trail that heads left (west) to Feather and Silver Lakes. The PCT continues north to Badger Flat, then out of the park and on to Canada.

Red diamonds on the trees mark this section of trail, which follows a small stream as it descends easily through dense stands of timber. A yellow dot marks a tree at the stream crossing, then the red and yellow markers intermingle. The path meanders gently upward and away from the stream as it traverses the shady, northeast-facing slope, then it arcs westward and the upward pitch moderates. The trail passes several ponds that precede the larger lakes that lie ahead.

Though the climb is never arduous, it is steady and unbroken until the trail reaches Feather Lake at 5.3 miles. You will circle the wooded northern edge of this lake, passing a sign confirming its identity, and passing (or taking advantage of) several clearings along the shore that present perfect picnicking or resting opportunities. A tree-dotted, gray-rock rampart hovers over the lake's south side, an interesting break in the otherwise seamless forest.

Feather Lake is one of the Cluster Lakes.

Climb out of the Feather Lake basin, cross a windblown ridge, and then drop in on Silver Lake. The setting is similar to that of Feather Lake, peaceful and remote. Gazing up over the tops of the trees and beyond the forested, northwest-facing slope of Hat Mountain, you can see the snowy heights of Lassen Peak, which has been well hidden by the trees since the initial climb away from Summit Lake.

The footpath traces the north shore of Silver Lake, passing its sign, then leaves the lake behind as it reenters the forest. Drop down through two seasonal streams, dry by late season, to a trail intersection at 6.4 miles.

You can turn right (north) here to visit the two nameless lakes that lie along the path to Badger Flat, which is 2.6 miles north near the border of the park. The Cluster Lakes Loop continues by taking the left-hand (southwest) path toward the Bear Lakes.

This section of the loop begins with a gentle climb through open woodlands to Big Bear Lake at 6.9 miles. The trail skirts the east shore of the lake; at the south corner, begin to climb up and south toward Little Bear Lake. This is the first serious ascent since you climbed away from Summit Lake, and is a harbinger of things to come—you've come many miles since the hike began, so pace yourself on the hills that follow.

You top out in the brightly lit forest that frames Little Bear Lake at 7.4 miles. This lake is just as clear as its neighbor, muted green with grasses clinging to its sandy bottom and breezes rippling its surface. Pass it by on the east shore, then begin the final leg of the loop.

Another stiff climb leads out of the Little Bear Lake basin. Switchbacks mitigate the ascent, and the views become more and more gratifying as you gain altitude, with Lassen just visible over the crest of the forested ridge to the west of the trail.

A tiny pond marks the top of the climb. The footpath meanders through a small, lonely gap, wanders through a winding ridgetop gully, and rolls through a swale scoured of vegetation. You will reenter the woods when the trail begins to slope gently downhill. Pass a small lake on the right (east) of the path; a brief uphill section of trail leads to a roller-coaster traverse of the flat-topped ridge that spills north and east from Hat Mountain. After a mile or so, the trail begins to drop in earnest, falling south off the ridge to its junction with the trail to Summit Lake. From here, retrace your steps to the trailhead at the Summit Lake Ranger Station, which is at the 12.1-mile mark.

25 Summit Lake to Corral Meadow

Highlights: Hike down along the Summit Creek drainage to Kings Creek and lush Corral Meadow.
Type of hike: Day hike; out-and-back.
Total distance: 4.8 miles.
Difficulty: Moderate.
Best months: July–October.
Maps: USGS Reading Peak quad; Lassen Volcanic National Park maps by the National Park Service, Earthwalk Press, and Wilderness Press; USDAFS Lassen National Forest map.
Parking and facilities: There are abundant facilities in the Summit Lake area, including campgrounds, restrooms, water sources, a ranger station, and picnic facilities.

Finding the trailhead: To reach the Summit Lake South Campground from the Manzanita Lake Entrance Station, follow the Lassen Park Road (California Highway 89) south and east for 12.2 miles, passing the Summit Lake Ranger Station. Turn left (east) into the campground and park near the campground information kiosk or in the picnic area. If there is no parking in either of these locations, you may have to begin at the Summit Lake Ranger Station, which is 0.2 mile north on the Lassen Park Road. To reach the campground from the Southwest Entrance Station, follow the Lassen Park Road for about 15.8 miles to the turnoff for the Summit Lake South Campground or for 16 miles to the ranger station.

Key points:

0.0   Summit Lake South Campground Trailhead.

1.7   Reach the intersection with the trail that leads up to the Kings Creek Falls area.

2.4   Arrive at Corral Meadow.

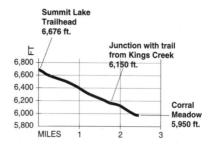

The hike: Deep green serenity and solitude—with every step you take down from Summit Lake toward Corral Meadow, you'll find yourself more profoundly meshed with both. The other trails departing from the Summit Lake area, leading to Echo and Twin Lakes and beyond, see far more traffic than this one, and this is a good thing for those of us who thrive on singular communion with nature.

The trail begins in the Summit Lake South Campground. Depending on the availability of parking, you may be starting from the campground or from the Summit Lake Ranger Station; regardless, you must follow the paved camp road to the southernmost point of the campground's E Loop. The trail begins at campsite 10, heading south and gently downhill into a small chain of meadows thick with grasses and wildflowers. Narrow bands of trees

Summit Lake to Corral Meadow

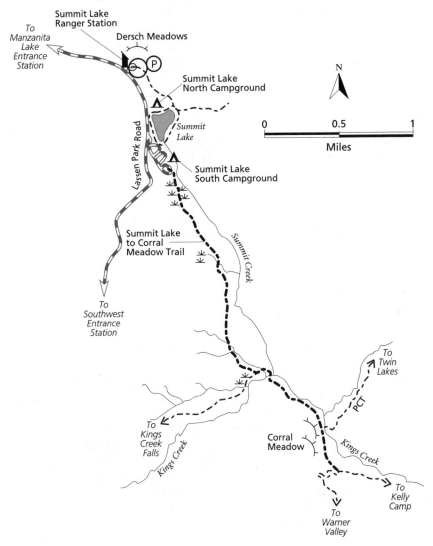

separate one meadow from the next—or perhaps it's more accurate to say the evergreens interrupt the flow of a bigger meadow. The infant Summit Creek waters the lushness; this is as close as you will get to the creek until you near its confluence with Kings Creek above Corral Meadow. Though the route traces the Summit Creek drainage, and though it parallels and crosses several tributary creeks as it descends, Summit Creek proper rests in the bed of the drainage that is east of the trail.

Leave the meadow and any sign of water behind as you hike into the forest, then descend to a rather substantial gully. Traverse down the north face into the bottom of the ravine, then climb out and into a dense forest of red firs. Beyond the gully, the route continues gently downhill, rolling over benches to a nameless stream, the first in a series that you will either flank or cross as you descend toward Corral Meadow. Follow the stream to an easy crossing in a thicket of riparian shrubs and grasses.

Leave the first stream behind as the trail continues its descent, crossing another forested bench and dropping to the edge of the second stream. This waterway will be your companion for the next 0.5 mile or so. Follow the stream south and east through a narrow meadow to an easy crossing; the stream is now on the east side of the trail, chattering playfully and watering a strip of verdant grass and foliage that winds through the much darker green of the forest. Cross yet another tributary stream via a small split-log bridge. Now, as you approach the bottom of the trail, you can hear the more substantial rumble of Summit Creek, which remains out of sight to your left (east).

At 1.7 miles, you reach the intersection with the trails that lead right (southwest) to the Kings Creek Falls area, and left (southeast) to Corral Meadow. Go left toward the meadow. A shuttle hike between Kings Creek Falls and Summit Lake is described in Hike 18 in the Kings Creek chapter.

The trail to Corral Meadow crosses the tributary stream that has been your cheery companion once more before making a more substantial crossing of Kings Creek near its confluence with Summit Creek. The path then parallels Kings Creek, which lies in the bottom of the valley to the northeast. The trail climbs onto a hillside that offers a birds-eye view of the creek, then drops quickly to deposit you on the bare earth of a clearing on the creek's south bank. A sign indicates that Corral Meadow lies just south of this clearing.

Former park naturalist Paul Schulz reports, in his booklet *Lassen's Place Names,* that a Frenchman named George La Pie once built a corral for his livestock on this site. Today no sign remains of any manmade structure—indeed, it seems like the meadow itself may not be around for much longer. Though the meadow grasses are thick and seemingly impenetrable, the forest is creeping in on all sides, gradually staking its claim in the natural succession of the wildlands. Bugs and moisture preclude the meadow as a nice place to take a mid-hike rest and snack, but the clearing at the edge of Kings Creek is a wonderful spot for such pleasures.

Unless you plan to link this with another trail as a shuttle or loop, return as you came.

Emigrant Pass and Hat Creek

Just before midnight on May 19, 1915, as part of an eruptive cycle that had kept Lassen Peak in the local and national headlines for a year, a huge mudflow swept down off the mountain. Triggered when heat from within the volcano melted the snowpack on the mountain's surface, the mudflow raged down the Lost Creek and Hat Creek drainages, taking out everything in its path, and devastating several homesteads.

Benjamin F. Loomis, who chronicled Lassen Peak's eruption both in memorable pictures and in a booklet entitled *Eruptions of Lassen Peak,* (see Appendix C, Further Reading) surveyed the scene after the flood. "It is no exaggeration to say that the volume of water and mud in the two creeks must have been equal to that carried in the Sacramento River . . . at flood tide or high water mark," Loomis wrote.

The mudflow was followed by a second major event—this one a huge eruption of steam and ash known as the "Great Hot Blast," on May 22, 1915. The blast completed the damage done by the mud, decimating the forest and leaving in its wake a moonscape. The blast also littered the peak's lower slopes with super-heated boulders, including the 30-ton Hot Rock, which stayed warm for up to a week after the eruption.

These cataclysmic events forever altered the landscape on Lassen Peak's northeast slope, which is now known as the Devastated Area. Today, evergreens are reclaiming the Devastated Area, but it is still clear that a force more awesome than most of us will witness in our lifetimes shaped the landscape.

The Emigrant Pass and Hat Creek trailhead lies on the eastern edge of the floodplain. Two trails depart from this trailhead, one leading south to Paradise Meadow and beyond, the other leading north along the Nobles Emigrant Trail to the park's northern boundary area. The Devastated Area Interpretive Trail offers a quick and dirty on-the-ground overview of the forces that shaped the surrounding terrain. This short chapter includes descriptions of these trails.

There are no amenities outside of roadside parking areas at the Hat Creek trailhead, and no potable water sources. If you must drink from trailside streams, be sure to treat the water first. There is a large parking area at Emigrant Pass, where the Devastated Area Interpretive Trail is located, along with restrooms.

To reach Emigrant Pass and the Devastated Area Interpretive Trail from the Manzanita Lake Entrance Station, follow the Lassen Park Road (California Highway 89) east and south for about 9 miles to the parking area, which is on the left (east) side of the road. The parking lot is 19 miles north and east of the Southwest Entrance Station. The Hat Creek Trailhead is located about 9.5 miles south and east of the Manzanita Lake Entrance Station, and 18.5 miles north and east of the Southwest Entrance Station.

26 Paradise Meadow

Highlights: Paradise Meadow is the premier meadow of the park, thick with wildflowers and watered by a meandering stream.

Type of hike: Day hike; out-and-back.

Total distance: 2.8 miles.

Difficulty: Moderate.

Best months: July–August.

Maps: USGS West Prospect Peak and Reading Peak quads; Lassen Volcanic National Park maps by the National Park Service, Earthwalk Press, and Wilderness Press; USDAFS Lassen National Forest map.

Parking and facilities: There are no facilities other than a small roadside parking area at the trailhead. The nearest restrooms are 0.5 mile north of the Hat Creek parking area at the Devastated Area Interpretive Trailhead. Complete amenities are available at Manzanita Lake.

Finding the trailhead: From the Manzanita Lake Entrance Station, follow the Lassen Park Road (California Highway 89) south and east for 9 miles to the parking area, which is on the left (north) side of the highway. From the Southwest Entrance Station, the parking area is 19 miles north and east on the Lassen Park Road.

Key points:

0.0   Hat Creek Trailhead.

1.4   Arrive at Paradise Meadow.

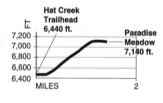

The hike: What's in a name? You look on a map and see a lake called Sapphire, or a ridge called Sawtooth, and you pretty much know what you're going to find when you get there. The lake will be blue, and the ridge will be jagged. But Paradise Meadow? Paradise?

The truth is, this meadow is extraordinary. I've done a lot of hiking in my day, and seen a lot of meadows, but this one took my breath away. Set in a steep-walled cirque, a clearly glacial feature in an otherwise very volcanic environment, the meadow is so soft and lush that it purrs. In midsummer, the wildflowers bloom in profusion, painting purple, white, and yellow streaks amid the vivid greenery. By late August, the flowers have begun to fade, but the grasses are tinged with autumnal gold, and shimmer richly when the wind combs through them.

Do I tend toward hyperbole? Perhaps. You'll just have to see for yourself.

The hike begins on the south side of the park road; from the parking area, cross the highway carefully to reach the trailhead proper. The path is wide and flat to begin with, nicely shaded, with Lassen Peak looming above and Hat Creek rollicking in its bed on the west side. The site of Hat Lake also lies to the right (west) of the trail.

Paradise Meadow • Hat Lake to Terrace Lake

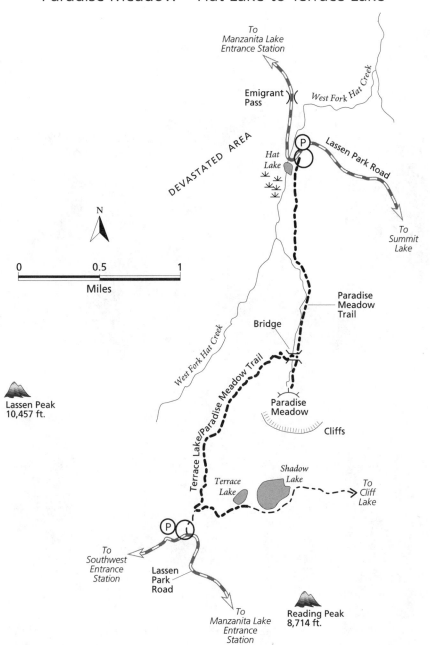

To
Manzanita Lake
Entrance Station

Emigrant
Pass

West Fork Hat Creek

DEVASTATED AREA

Hat
Lake

P

Lassen Park Road

To
Summit
Lake

N

0   0.5   1
Miles

Paradise
Meadow
Trail

Bridge

West Fork Hat Creek

Terrace Lake/Paradise Meadow Trail

Paradise
Meadow

Cliffs

Lassen Peak
10,457 ft.

Shadow
Lake

Terrace
Lake

To
Cliff
Lake

P

To
Southwest
Entrance
Station

Lassen
Park
Road

To
Manzanita Lake
Entrance
Station

Reading Peak
8,714 ft.

Hikers enjoy Paradise Meadow.

The route begins to climb shortly, leading through dips that may hold water in early season, and lined with a thick, unruly hedge of willow, mule ear, and other riparian plants. The trail is marked with yellow dots on the trees.

At about the 0.5-mile mark, you will climb into a narrowing ravine that cradles a tributary of the West Fork of Hat Creek. Stream crossings are made via small footbridges, until the path settles in on the south side of a sweet cataract.

Cross another tributary stream, then the trail steepens abruptly, with the cataract growing larger and louder as the pitch of the path increases. The trees thin and the walls of the ravine open as the stream tumbles over a set of short, frothy falls. Here, thankfully, the angle of the climb becomes almost flat.

Paintbrush, clover, penstemon, lupine, gentian—and a trail sign—mark the grassy expanse that spreads from the trail at 1.4 miles as Paradise Meadow. The trail forks, with the right-hand (west) path leading across the bridge that spans the creek toward Terrace Lake (Hike 27), and the left-hand (south) path trickling to an end in the meadow.

The stream loses its steam as it meanders through the grasses, becoming a thick-banked snake that can be straddled or waded through easily. At the head of the meadow, talus lines the base of the cliff that forms the southern horizon, creating a dark contrast to the light of the meadow. Bring the kids, bring the grandparents, and bring a picnic. And don't forget the bug juice!

If you decide to venture no farther, then return as you came.

27 Hat Lake to Terrace Lake

See Map on Page 107

Highlights: Climb past a tumbling cataract to a spectacular meadow, then up to a small lake poised at the edge of a high basin.
Type of hike: Day hike; out-and-back or shuttle.
Total distance: 5.6 miles.
Difficulty: Strenuous.
Best months: July–September.
Maps: USGS West Prospect Peak and Reading Peak quads; Lassen Volcanic National Park maps by the National Park Service, Earthwalk Press, and Wilderness Press; USDAFS Lassen National Forest map.
Parking and facilities: There are no facilities other than a small parking area at the trailhead. The nearest restrooms are located 0.5 mile north of the Hat Creek parking area at the Devastated Area Interpretive Trailhead. Complete amenities are available at Manzanita Lake.

Finding the trailhead: From the Manzanita Lake Entrance Station, follow the Lassen Park Road (California Highway 89) south and east for 9 miles to the parking area, which is on the left (north) side of the highway. From the Southwest Entrance Station, the parking area is 19 miles north and east on the Lassen Park Road.

Key points:

0.0 Hat Creek Trailhead.
1.4 Arrive at Paradise Meadow.
2.7 Reach the trail intersection.
2.8 Rest on the shores of Terrace Lake.

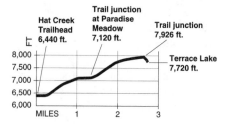

The hike: It's a stiff climb, but this trail leads to two of the prettiest places in Lassen Volcanic National Park's high country. Paradise Meadow, a glorious spill of lush grass and colorful wildflowers, lies a bit below the halfway point of the ascent, and is a wonderful place to rest and regroup. From the meadow, steep climbing leads onto the rolling benches of Lassen's upper reaches, where little Terrace Lake rests at the cusp of a shallow bowl.

The trail begins on the flats alongside the west fork of Hat Creek, but begins to climb almost immediately, passing first through dense riparian flora, then into a shady evergreen forest. The route is marked with yellow dots on the trees.

By the 0.5-mile mark, the trail is climbing through a narrowing ravine that cradles a tributary of the West Fork of Hat Creek. Small footbridges span this tributary and others that follow, all of which feed a tumbling nameless cataract that parallels the trail.

As the trail grows steeper, the cataract grows more energetic. But the pitch of the trail moderates as you approach Paradise Meadow, passing a short waterfall shaded by a thinning forest. At 1.4 miles, you stand amid the grass and wildflowers of the meadow, at the intersection with the trail that leads right (west) over the split log bridge toward Terrace Lake.

If you've the time and inclination, head left (south) into the meadow; what you'll see in the meadow is described in detail in Hike 26. To continue to Terrace Lake, cross the bridge, and begin to climb steeply out of the cirque that cradles the meadow. This section of the ascent can be boggy even in late season, but offers wonderful views to the northeast of the Prospect Peak and West Prospect Peak.

Follow switchbacks up into widely spaced trees; again, yellow dots mark the route. The grade lessens, but still ascends once you climb atop a bench overlooking the meadow. The terrain has morphed into that more typical of the high country: The hemlocks and pines have stooped to the winds and winter snows, and shallow swales wear a thin layer of silverleaf lupine, or nothing at all. The path continues to flatten, with the steeper slopes of the east face of Lassen Peak tantalizingly close.

Roll up and over a series of benches, following the path as it loops in and out of the swales and through stands of timber. Rock cairns join the yellow dots in marking the trail as it snakes through more open sections.

Broad switchbacks lead up to the junction with the trail to Terrace Lake at 2.7 miles. Turn sharply left (east) on the trail to Terrace Lake; if you go right (up and southwest), you will reach the Terrace Lake Trailhead on the Lassen Park Road, which is the end of the line if you've arranged a shuttle.

The trail to Terrace Lake dives into a ravine, which bottoms out in a meadow that spreads from the shores of the shallow lake on the east to a spill of talus on the west. The lake, clear and inviting, sits at the edge of its basin like a child perched on the edge of his seat, straining to see something in the distance. It's a lovely spot at which to end a day's hiking. Unless you choose to take the option described below, return as you came.

Option: If you've arranged for a shuttle, you can combine this trail with the trail that leads from Terrace Lake down to Summit Lake, which will allow you to visit Shadow Lake and Cliff Lake on your descent. The total distance from Terrace Lake to the Summit Lake Ranger Station is 3.7 miles. For a complete description of the descending trail, see Hike 10 in the Lake Helen chapter.

28 Nobles Emigrant Trail to Badger Flat

Highlights:	This is a portion of a trail that was used by emigrants to northern California in the mid-1800s.
Type of hike:	Day hike or backpack; out-and-back.
Total distance:	12.2 miles.
Difficulty:	Moderate.
Best months:	June–October.
Maps:	USGS West Prospect Peak quad; Lassen Volcanic National Park maps by the National Park Service, Earthwalk Press, and Wilderness Press; USDAFS Lassen National Forest map.
Special considerations:	If you choose to camp at Badger Flat, or at another location along this stretch of the Nobles Emigrant Trail, be sure to abide by the park's backcountry regulations. Secure a backcountry permit, and set up camp at least 100 feet from all water sources and trails. If you get water from Hat Creek or the stream that waters Badger Flat, purify it by boiling, filtering, or chemically treating it.
Parking and facilities:	There are no facilities other than a small parking area at the trailhead. The nearest restrooms are located 0.5 mile north of the Hat Creek parking area at the Devastated Area Interpretive Trailhead. Complete amenities are available at Manzanita Lake.

Finding the trailhead: From the Manzanita Lake Entrance Station, follow the Lassen Park Road (California Highway 89) south and east for 9 miles to

Nobles Emigrant Trail to Badger Flat

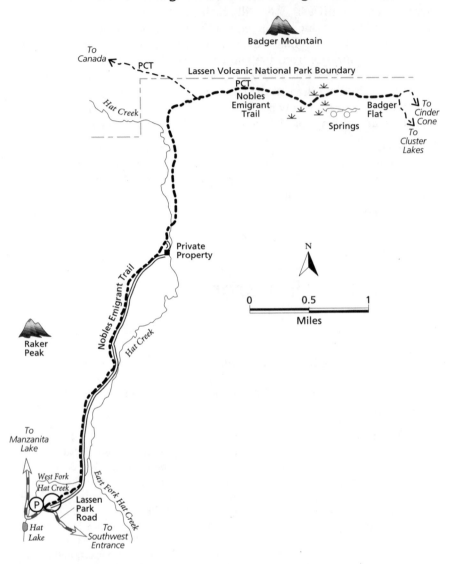

the parking area, which is on the left (north) side of the highway. From the Southwest Entrance Station, the parking area is 19 miles north and east.

Key points:

- 0.0   Hat Creek Trailhead.
- 0.5   Cross Hat Creek.
- 3.0   Pass private property and cross Hat Creek a second time.
- 4.0   Reach the intersection with the Pacific Crest Trail.
- 6.1   Arrive at Badger Flat.

The hike: The Nobles Emigrant Trail traverses most of the northern reaches of Lassen Volcanic Park, and though most of the historic path is eas-

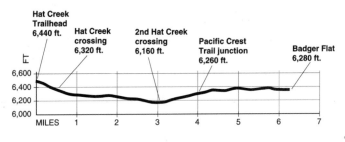

ily accessible and makes for enjoyable day hiking or backpacking, some sections are more inviting than others. The trail from Hat Creek to Badger Pass is one of those enjoyable sections, a delightful hike that traces a century-old migration route into California, as well as delves into little-visited regions of the park.

The entirety of the trail—or the portions that are still passable—is described in detail in Chapter 11 of this guide. This portion, though magnificent as part of the whole, provides an opportunity to sample the trail without more than a daylong or overnight commitment.

Begin at the Hat Creek Trailhead. Pass the gate on the north side of Lassen Park Road, and head north on the gravel road. The roadbed ensures easy hiking for the first three miles or so, and is spiced with two interesting crossings of Hat Creek.

The first creek crossing comes at about the half-mile mark. You have two options: rock-hop across the waterway, or try the tightrope log crossing that lies downstream. Whichever method you choose, when you get to the opposite bank, you will be on Hat Creek's west side.

The trail/road weaves through a shady woodland thick with lodgepole pines and continues north, gradually descending, with Raker Peak sloping up on the west side and Hat Creek on the east. When you reach a clearing at about the 1-mile mark, turn around and enjoy a great view of Lassen Peak to the southwest. You won't have another shot of it that's this good until you reach Badger Flat.

As you approach the 3-mile mark, you encounter some signs of civilization. The cluster of old buildings at this point is on private property, and seems incongruous in the wilderness—even more so on the return trip, after you've seriously sampled seclusion. Continue north on the roadway.

At 3 miles, you must cross Hat Creek again. And again, there are two possibilities: a fallen tree or a logjam that forms a haphazard bridge. Choose one, then proceed across the creek with care. The trail sign at this point indicates that Badger Flat is three miles distant, and that Butte Lake or the Cluster Lakes can also be reached via the route, if you desire.

The trail follows the creek for a stretch beyond the creek crossing. The roadway disintegrates to doubletrack, a refreshing reminder that this path was once a wagon trail weaving through a wilderness of pine and fir. At about the 4-mile mark, the wagon trail climbs eastward and away from Hat Creek to its junction with the Pacific Crest Trail (PCT). The PCT, which traverses the park from north to south, heads left (northwest) to cross the park's northern boundary near this point, and merges with the Nobles Emigrant Trail as it heads right (east) toward Badger Flat.

The trail rolls easily through more dense forest as it cruises toward Badger Flat. The seclusion and ease of the hiking allows for contemplation of the hardships, and beauty, that must have been encountered along the trail by intrepid travelers in the nineteenth century.

After about 1.5 miles, the forest disintegrates into an area of stark deadfall, a landscape of mature evergreens that bear the dark signs of the lightning-sparked fire that ravaged them in 1984. The clearing of the canopy, however, renders open views southwest to the barren heights of Lassen Peak.

At 6.1 miles, you will arrive at Badger Flat, an open and lovely expanse of meadow from which you can catch sight of Lassen Peak. Consider this an endpoint, though a trail intersection at the eastern end of the meadow points to other destinations within the park. You can continue south to the Cluster Lakes and Summit Lake, or hike eastward toward the Cinder Cone and Butte Lake. Or, you can return as you came.

29 Devastated Area Interpretive Trail

Highlights:	Short and sweet, this trail features interpretation of the forces that shaped the northeastern slopes of Lassen Peak.
Type of hike:	Day hike; loop.
Total distance:	0.4 mile.
Difficulty:	Easy.
Best months:	June–October.
Maps:	USGS West Prospect Peak quad; Lassen Volcanic National Park maps by the National Park Service, Earthwalk Press, and Wilderness Press; USDAFS Lassen National Forest map.
Special considerations:	This trail is paved and wheelchair accessible.
Parking and facilities:	There is ample parking at the trailhead, as well as restrooms and benches.

Finding the trailhead: From the Manzanita Lake Entrance Station, follow the Lassen Park Road (California Highway 89) east and south for 8.5 miles to the Emigrant Pass parking area, which is on the left (east) side of the road. The parking lot is 19.5 miles north and east of the Southwest Entrance Station.

Key points:

0.0 Devastated Area Interpretive Trail Trailhead.
0.4 Complete the loop.

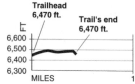

Devastated Area Interpretive Trail

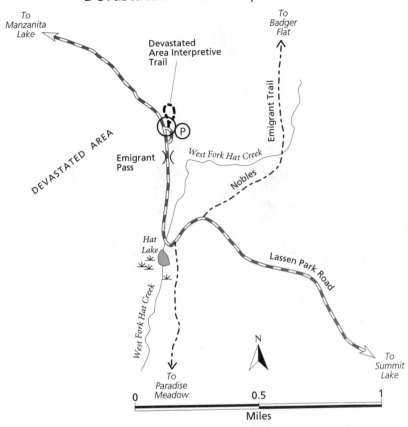

The hike: Like the proverbial nutshell, the Devastated Area Interpretive Trail holds a tasty little nugget of Lassen Volcanic National Park within its limited confines. Picture-perfect views of Lassen Peak and interpretive signs that describe volcanism's effect on the surrounding terrain make this a perfect choice for families, those unable or unwilling to take longer treks, or those who are short on time.

The trail begins at the hiker sign in front of the restrooms on the east side of the parking area. After about 25 feet, the

Hikers read interpretive plaques along the Devastated Area Interpretive Trail.

Lassen Peak and Crescent Crater as seen from the Devastated Area.

pavement forks; the right (east) path leads to the restrooms, and the left (northeast) to the first interpretive marker, which describes that panorama of volcanoes before you, as well as the Chaos Jumbles.

The path wanders very gently upward and north through pink and gray lava rocks to a Y intersection. You can hike in either direction, but I describe the trail here in a clockwise direction. Take the left-hand trail to the next interpretive sign, which describes how boulders were moved during the 1915 eruption of the peak. The third sign discusses the "Great Hot Blast" that blew from the peak, and the fourth describes different types of dacite and the forces that color the rock. And above all rises Lassen Peak, architect and wreaker of havoc, now calm and benevolent.

Beyond the fourth sign, the trail veers eastward, and circles back on itself. The next signs, discussing the Loomis Hot Rock, plant succession, and the dynamics of avalanches, mudflows, and pyroclastic flows, follow quickly. The black boulders that lie scattered among the fledgling trees are part of a dacite dome that was blasted out of the peak in the eruptions of late May 1915.

The last two signs provide further insight into the area's geology, then the trail makes a quick, easy switchback that lands you at the first trail intersection. From here, retrace your steps to the trailhead.

Manzanita Lake

Manzanita Lake is the heart of Lassen Volcanic National Park. Though park administration—the brains, if you will—is headquartered in Mineral, most visitors get their introduction to Lassen at Manzanita Lake. Manzanita Lake is what leaves a lasting impression.

And a spectacular impression it is. The lake itself, dammed by the rubble of the eruptive forces that dominate its surroundings, is peaceful and calm below a turbulent horizon. A walk along its shores in early morning encapsulates the contradiction: The lapping of glistening water against the still grasses along the bank is meditative, and the jumbled pink hulks of the Chaos Crags and Lassen Peak, which rise above, are provocative and slightly enervating. The forest of Jeffrey pines that envelopes the lake is elegant and emanates permanence; the barren summits of the peaks are equally elegant, but generate instead an impression of flux. To be soothed by water and challenged by mountains seems to me a basic human instinct, and that instinctual understanding is confirmed at Manzanita Lake.

Accommodations at Manzanita Lake are generous. The Manzanita Lake Campground offers 179 campsites, including sites for recreational vehicles up to 35 feet long, for $14 per night. Sites are available on a first-come, first-served basis; the campground fills up quickly on holiday weekends during the summer months.

In the vicinity of the campground, there are facilities for fishing, picnicking, swimming, and hiking. The Manzanita Lake Camper Store carries all the necessities—and some very cool unnecessary items, like clothing with wonderful Lassen logos and other park souvenirs. A laundry facility and showers are also available at the camper store.

The Loomis Museum, a charming little stone structure near the intersection of the Lassen Park Road and the campground access road, is the park's educational hub. Both the museum and the neighboring Loomis Ranger House once served as the summer home and studio of Lassen photographer B. F. Loomis. The museum boasts wonderful geologic and natural exhibits, including spectacular photos taken by Loomis of the 1914–15 eruptions of Lassen Peak. A number of informative books and pamphlets about the park's natural and human history are sold here, and knowledgeable park rangers and staff are available daily from 9 A.M. to 5 P.M. during the summer season. Wilderness permits and horse permits are also available. The neighboring seismic station is a quaint reminder of the area's continuing volatility.

If you are camping at Manzanita Lake, be sure to take in an interpretive program at the park's amphitheater. Programs on geology, wildlife, human history, and other subjects are presented on a regular schedule here, as well as at the Loomis Museum and other locations throughout the park during the summer. Check at the museum or on campground bulletin boards for schedules of these ranger-led programs.

And then, of course, there is the hiking. Six delightful trails begin in the vicinity of Manzanita Lake, delving into very different ecosystems. Pick one or do them all; each is guaranteed to delight.

30 Reflection Lake

Highlights:	This short, lakeside trail offers stunning views of the Chaos Crags and Lassen Peak.
Type of hike:	Day hike; loop.
Total distance:	1 mile.
Difficulty:	Easy.
Best months:	May–October.
Maps:	USGS Manzanita Lake quad; Lassen Volcanic National Park maps by the National Park Service, Earthwalk Press, and Wilderness Press.
Parking and facilities:	Parking is available in the Loomis Museum/visitor center parking lot, but this fills quickly on summer weekends and holidays, in which case you may have to park on the road to the Manzanita Lake Campground. Water and restrooms are available outside the Loomis Museum.
Special considerations:	While not as popular as the Manzanita Lake Trail, Reflection Lake is heavily used. Tread lightly.

Lassen Peak and Chaos Crags rise above Reflection Lake.

Reflection Lake • Lily Pond Nature Trail
Manzanita Lake Trail

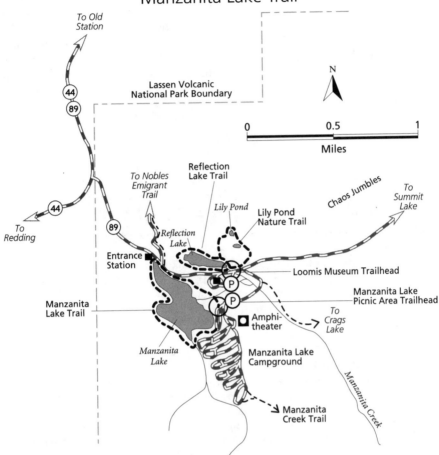

Finding the trailhead: From the Manzanita Lake Entrance Station, follow the Lassen Park Road (California Highway 89) east for 0.5 mile to the parking area for the Loomis Museum/visitor center. Park in the lot. From the front porch of the Loomis Museum, drop down the paved path on the west side of the building, then cross the road to the trailhead.

Key points:

  0.0   Lily Pond Trailhead.
  0.5   Reach the west end of the lake.

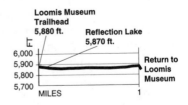

The hike: On a calm summer morning, it becomes abundantly clear how Reflection Lake earned its name. From openings in the woods on the western shore of the lake, Chaos Crags and Lassen Peak dominate both the skyline and the glassy mirror of the water. Bring a camera: the photo opportunities are grand.

The trail begins at the Lily Pond Trailhead; at the first trail intersection, go left (straight and north) into the woods, and at the second intersection, stay left, heading north, and then west along the lakeshore.

The trail wanders at the woodland's edge around the placid pool. You will reach the west shore at about 0.5 mile, where views invite contemplation, and photo ops abound. Continue around the lake to the south shore; the trail empties into a pullout alongside the park access road (California Highway 89). Veer left (north) toward the lake onto a small, grassy promontory, then head back right (south) to a footbridge over an outlet stream that flows into a culvert with a stone facade. Continue east along the faint roadside path, hugging the lakeshore, to the trailhead. Turn right (south) to cross the road and return to the Loomis Museum.

31 Lily Pond Nature Trail

See Map on Page 119

Highlights: This short nature walk skirts a small lake covered in water lilies and the edge of the Chaos Jumbles, and boasts wonderful interpretation of the natural features of the area.

Type of hike: Day hike; loop.

Total distance: 1 mile.

Difficulty: Easy.

Best months: May–October.

Maps: USGS Manzanita Lake quad; Lassen Volcanic National Park maps by the National Park Service, Earthwalk Press, and Wilderness Press; Lily Pond Nature Trail leaflet (available at the trailhead).

Parking and facilities: Parking is available in the Loomis Museum/visitor center parking lot, but this fills quickly on summer weekends and holidays, in which case you may have to park farther afield on the road to the Manzanita Lake Campground. Water and restrooms are available outside the Loomis Museum.

Special considerations: The Lily Pond Nature Trail receives fairly heavy traffic. Walk with consideration.

Finding the trailhead: From the Manzanita Lake Entrance Station, follow the Lassen Park Road (California Highway 89) east for 0.5 mile to the parking area for the Loomis Museum/visitor center. Park in the lot. From the front porch of the Loomis Museum, drop down the paved path on the west side of the building, then cross the road to the trailhead.

Key points:
  0.0   Lily Pond Nature Trail Trailhead.
  0.5   Reach the lily pond.
  1.0   Return to the trailhead.

The hike: Do you have a tendency to call every evergreen tree you see a pine? Are you convinced you will never be able to tell a Jeffrey pine from a ponderosa, much less a sugar pine or a lodgepole pine? Take heart, for there is hope—though you may have to do laps on the Lily Pond Nature Trail to get it all straight.

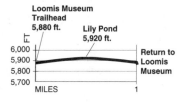

This pleasant little loop, perfect for small ones, begins in the mixed forest bordering Reflection Lake. An interpretive brochure available at the trailhead corresponds to numbered posts along the route, and many of these posts mark different species of trees. Once the botany lesson ends, the geology lesson begins, as you enter the Chaos Jumbles, the remnants of an avalanche from the Chaos Crags that occurred about 300 years ago.

From the trailhead, walk down to the first trail intersection, just beyond the box holding the interpretive brochures, and go left (straight and north). Curve around Reflection Lake to the next intersection, marked with a Lily Pond Trail sign. Go right (north), following the arrow.

Meander through the woods, pausing to learn about the ecosystem at the numbered signposts, to a couple of log footbridges that lead through a marshy area at the head of a small meadow. Just beyond, at about 0.5 mile, lies the lily pond, with its blooms brilliantly yellow amid the verdant forest in early summer. Pass the skinny incense cedar and continue on the rockier trail. A grassy depression to the right (west) holds water in early season; a hairpin turn in the path takes you back into the open woodland. The pink rock, called dacite, is part of the Chaos Jumbles. Dacite towers above in the form of the Chaos Crags, and composes the surface upon which you walk.

Pass marker 30 and cross a park service road to the final interpretive marker. Drop through the woods to the first trail intersection, and go left (south), back up to the Loomis Museum and parking area.

32 Chaos Crags and Crags Lake

Highlights: Tiny Crags Lake lies in an exposed basin below the unstable slopes of the Chaos Crags.
Type of hike: Day hike; out-and-back.
Total distance: 4 miles.
Difficulty: Moderate.
Best months: June–early October.
Maps: USGS Manzanita Lake quad; Lassen Volcanic National Park maps by the National Park Service, Earthwalk Press, and Wilderness Press; USDAFS Lassen National Forest map.
Parking and facilities: There is limited parking at the trailhead, and no other facilities. You can find water and restrooms at the Loomis Museum, located 0.1 mile north on the Lassen Park Road (California Highway 89), and at the Manzanita Lake picnic area, located 0.3 mile south on the Manzanita Lake Campground access road.
Special considerations: Though this hike is not especially long, it involves stiff climbing and uneven footing, and ends in a location exposed to wind and rockfall. Be sure to wear adequate footwear, bring extra clothing, and stay on the trail.

Finding the trailhead: From the Manzanita Lake Entrance Station, follow the Lassen Park Road (California Highway 89), for 0.5 mile to the turnoff for Manzanita Lake campground. Turn right (south) onto the campground road and follow it for 0.1 mile to the trailhead, which is on the left (east) side of the road.

Key points:
0.0   Trailhead.
1.9   Reach the open ridge above Crags Lake.
2.0   Drop into the Crags Lake basin.

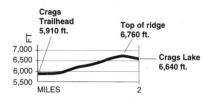

The hike: The crater at the end of this splendid hike now cradles a small lake, but it once was the fulcrum of a cataclysm that forever changed the surrounding landscape, and resulted in the formation of the Chaos Jumbles. About 300 hundred years ago, a portion of the Chaos Crags, plug dome volcanoes like Lassen Peak, let loose a massive avalanche of rock. The landslide scarred the landscape to the north and east of the Manzanita Lake area, and its debris makes up the dam of the lake itself.

The hike's setting is as spectacular as the violence that created it. The trail begins in an open woodland dominated by sweet-smelling Jeffrey pine and the roar of Manzanita Creek. The forest thins as you climb higher, until you break out of the trees on an exposed ridge sweeping down from the barren Chaos Crags. A brief, but steep drop lands you beside the tiny, shallow

Chaos Crags and Crags Lake

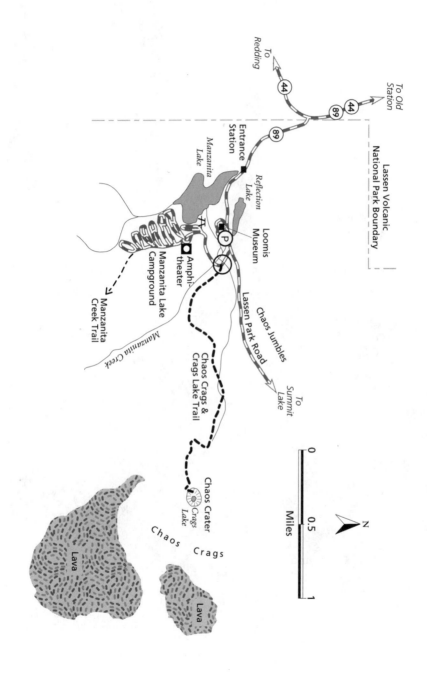

Crag Lake lies below Chaos Crags.

lake, with its sparse trimming of pine and manzanita. Standing on the lake's shores, you can hear the nearly constant clatter of rockfall, as the loose dacite of the crags continues to seek its angle of repose.

From the trailhead, the path climbs gently through the open pine forest alongside Manzanita Creek. The creek grows louder, and the trees grow more dense, as you ascend. Yellow dots on the trees mark the route. Crest a small hill, and the creek sounds fade. Follow a much smaller stream into the mixed woodlands that have taken root on the volcanic debris, which runs in low ridges from the Crags down to Manzanita Lake.

After 0.2 mile, cross a footbridge spanning the stream, climb out of the creek drainage, and the trail flattens. The path swings through a broad, dry gully, then meanders upward on a ridge between two swales. Two steep switchbacks lead up to a traverse along another small ridge, where the trees drip with lichen the color of pea soup.

Climb two more broad switchbacks, and the forest thins; through the living trees and the silvering snags, you can snatch views of the pink cliffs of the Chaos Crags. Pinemat manzanita carpets the forest floor, thriving in a seemingly inhospitable area.

At 1.9 miles, the traversing climb ends atop the ridge separating Crags Lake from the drainages leading into Manzanita Creek. The views are best from here, sweeping up the scree slopes to the summits of the Crags, northwest to Table Mountain, and southwest across the forested ridges sweeping down toward the northern Sacramento Valley.

A steep, ankle-twisting path leads down to the lake at 2 miles. In a good snow year, the lake sparkles in icy blue contrast to its pink rock basin. Toward the end of the hiking season, particularly when the snowfall has not been heavy, the lake dries up, and the pinging of the ubiquitous rockfall ends not with a splash but a clunk.

After enjoying the lake, return as you came.

33 Manzanita Lake Trail

See Map on Page 119

Highlights: A pleasant romp around a popular mountain lake.
Type of hike: Day hike; loop.
Total distance: 1.5 miles.
Best months: May–October.
Maps: USGS Manzanita Lake quad; Lassen Volcanic National Park maps by the National Park Service, Earthwalk Press, and Wilderness Press; USDAFS Lassen National Forest map.
Difficulty: Easy.
Parking and facilities: The parking lot is next to the Manzanita Lake Picnic Area, which has restrooms. It is also very close to the Manzanita Lake Camper Store, where food and drink are sold.
Special considerations: Because of its proximity to the campground and entrance station, this trail sees a lot of traffic. Tread lightly.

Finding the trailhead: You can hop onto this loop trail from a variety of points, including from the campground, but the best parking is in the picnic area near the Manzanita Lake Camper Store. From the Manzanita Lake Entrance Station, drive east on the Lassen Park Road (California Highway 89) for 0.5 mile, past the Loomis Museum, and turn right (south) on the access road for the Manzanita Lake Campground. Drive 0.5 mile south on campground road to the picnic area. The marked trail starts at the south end of the parking lot, just beyond the turnaround area (no parking is allowed here).

Key points:

0.0 Manzanita Lake Trailhead.
0.5 Reach the west end of the lake near the park's entrance station.
1.0 Pass the Loomis Museum.

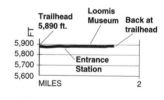

The hike: This pleasant and well-used trail affords a delightful romp among the Jeffrey pines and willows that surround Manzanita Lake. From the trail, which never wanders far from the shoreline, you can watch ducks, geese, and a number of fishermen and paddlers in small boats ply the serene green surface of the water. Lassen Peak and the Chaos Crags, looming above the lake to the southeast, provide early morning shade, and glow an otherworldly pink in the light of the setting sun.

The trail, which is easy to follow, is described in a clockwise circuit, starting on the east shore of the lake south of the picnic area. Pass some sun-bleached snags peeking out of the lake's surface; the campground lies just south of the path, screened by the trees. The trail leapfrogs the shallow inlet stream; beyond, it is bordered by green-leafed manzanita on the woodland side, and willows on the lake side.

A wonderful trail circles Manzanita Lake.

Fly fishermen wade in the shallows at the west end of the lake, which is reached at about the 0.5-mile mark. At openings in the trees, you can see the Chaos Crags and Lassen Peak to the south. A wooden footbridge spans Manzanita Creek at the lake's outlet; the park's entrance station, wedged between the two lanes of California Highway 89, is just to the north.

The trail parallels the park road as it circles the north shore of the lake. The route gradually divorces itself from the road, passing behind the Loomis Museum and visitor center at about 1 mile. Cross the bridge over Manzanita Creek and follow the silvery stream through the open woodlands back to lakeside. Skirt the lake back to your car or the trailhead.

Option: You can reach this trail from any of the campsites by hiking to the west side of the loop roads, where you will reach the small inlet stream. Cross the stream and follow it down to the Manzanita Lake Trail.

34 Manzanita Creek Trail

Highlights:	A hike into the upper Manzanita Creek basin features backside views of Lassen Peak and Loomis Peak.
Type of hike:	Day hike; out-and-back.
Total distance:	7 miles.
Difficulty:	Moderate.
Best months:	June–early October.
Maps:	USGS Manzanita Lake and Lassen Peak quads; Lassen Volcanic National Park maps by the National Park Service, Earthwalk Press, and Wilderness Press; USDAFS Lassen National Forest map.
Parking and facilities:	There is extremely limited parking at the trailhead, which is north of campsite 30 in Loop F (the tent loop) of the Manzanita Lake Campground. A gate marks the spot. The nearest water sources and restrooms are located on the west side of the tent loop.

Finding the trailhead: From the Manzanita Lake Entrance Station, follow the Lassen Park Road (California Highway 89) for 0.5 mile to the turnoff for Manzanita Lake campground. Turn right (south) onto the campground road and follow it for 0.9 mile to the trailhead. If there is no parking at the trailhead, return to the Manzanita Lake Camper Store parking area, and walk 0.4 mile to the trailhead.

Key points:

0.0 Manzanita Creek Trailhead.
2.0 The trail flattens before entering the upper portion of the drainage.
3.5 The footpath peters out in the marshy meadow.

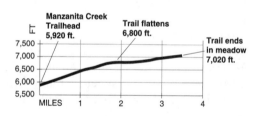

The hike: Manzanita Lake is a busy place, but you can escape its relative hustle and bustle by hiking into the upper reaches of the Manzanita Creek drainage on this relatively unused route.

The Manzanita Creek Trail has a meditative beginning, in a quiet woodland where footfalls are muffled by a sandy cushion on the forest floor. Toward its terminus, however, it takes on a different persona—one active and vibrant. The headwalls of the valley in which Manzanita Creek is born are steep and imposing. On the north is Lassen Peak, the Crescent Cliff dominating its lower reaches. Scanning southward, Eagle Peak, Vulcan's Castle, and sprawling Loomis Peak reach for the heavens, their pink summits harboring cups and creases of glittering snow late into the summer season.

The trailhead is on the north side of campsite 30 in the F Loop of the Manzanita Lake Campground. A chain is slung across the trail at its intersection with the loop road; pass around the chain and walk southeast on the broad gravel track. After about 200 yards, the trail merges with a dirt road

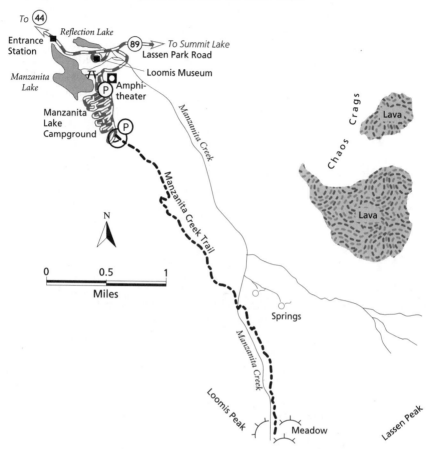

Manzanita Creek Trail

To (44)

Reflection Lake

Entrance
Station

(89) → To Summit Lake
Lassen Park Road

Loomis Museum

*Manzanita
Lake*

Amphi-
theater

P

Manzanita
Lake
Campground

P

N

0   0.5   1
Miles

Manzanita Creek

Manzanita Creek Trail

C h a o s   C r a g s

Lava

Lava

Springs

Manzanita Creek

Loomis Peak

Lassen Peak

Meadow

that leads back right (west) into the campground; go left (southeast) on the trail. Yellow dots on the trees mark the route.

There is no sign of the creek at this point, but plenty of manzanita on the forest floor. The sandy, very obvious trail climbs gently through the firs and pines. At about the 1-mile mark, broad switchbacks lead onto the crest of a low ridge separating two wooded swales. Once on the ridge, the trail's pitch steepens.

The looming pink slopes behind the trees are the west-facing flanks of the Chaos Crags; the trail proceeds upward in their shadow. Once atop the next swale, it's Lassen Peak that looms ahead, with views of its heights becoming more and more stunning as you climb.

Pass through a small, lovely meadow, redolent with the scent of herbs and pines, at about the 2-mile mark. Glancing to the north, you will be treated to unobstructed views of the Chaos Crags. Like wind through the trees, the sounds of Manzanita Creek drift down to the trail from the left (north). The path loops away from the water before doubling back and crossing the stream via a culvert and an earthen bridge. Once on the north side of the stream, the trail continues east toward the foot of Lassen.

At about 3 miles, a broad switchback leads up onto a bench, then the trail begins to descend, with the forest closing in on its edges. Pass into the narrow valley that cradles the headwaters of Manzanita Creek, traversing its west-facing slope and enjoying intermittent views of the rocky summits to the south, most notably that of Loomis Peak.

The traverse ends in the valley floor, where a marshy meadow separates the trail from the creek, which flows to the right (west) of the footpath. A dense stand of fir obliterates views for a short distance, then the trail pops out into the meadow again, crossing a streamlet feeding Manzanita Creek.

A tangle of young firs that have been bent and twisted by heavy winter snow crowds the trail, which becomes narrower and rougher as you climb. Finally, the path is swallowed by the meadow near the headwall of the valley. The roar of the falls on the right (west) side of the valley is concentrated in the upper meadow. If the bugs aren't too bothersome, this is a nice place to check out the panorama presented by Eagle Peak, Vulcan's Castle, and Loomis Peak. Return as you came.

35 Nobles Emigrant Trail—Nobles Pass to Summertown

Highlights:	This peaceful, seldom-traveled route follows the track left by pioneers to the area, and includes fleeting glimpses of Lassen Peak and the Chaos Crags.
Type of hike:	Day hike; shuttle (or out-and-back).
Total distance:	3.5 miles.
Difficulty:	Moderate.
Best months:	May–late October.
Maps:	USGS Manzanita Lake quad; Lassen Volcanic National Park maps by the National Park Service, Earthwalk Press, and Wilderness Press; USDAFS Lassen National Forest map.
Parking and facilities:	There is a large pullout/parking area at the Nobles Pass trailhead. The nearest parking lot and restroom at the Summertown end of the trail are at the Loomis Museum.

Finding the trailhead: The Summertown trailhead is located on the north side of the Manzanita Lake Entrance station. The closest parking is at Loomis Museum, located 0.5 mile east on the Lassen Park Road (California Highway 89). Backtrack to the trailhead on the portion of the Manzanita Lake Trail that parallels the park road. To reach the Nobles Pass Trailhead, follow the park road east from the Manzanita Lake Entrance Station for 3 miles to Sunflower Flat. The parking area is on the right (south) side of the road. A plaque mounted on a stone commemorates the Emigrant Trail. The trail is

Nobles Emigrant Trail—Nobles Pass to Summertown

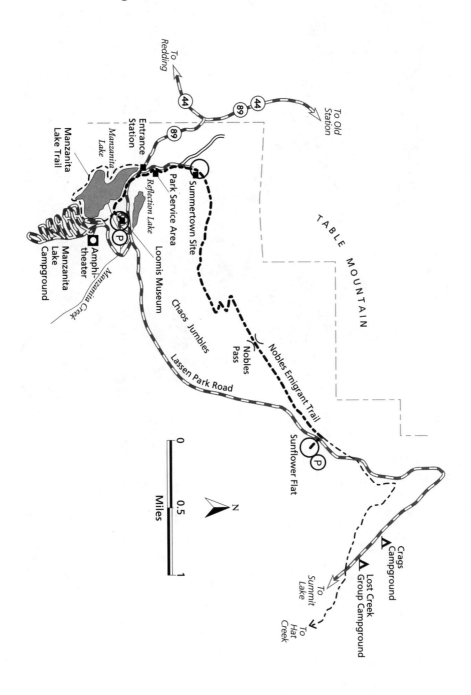

Hikers on the Nobles Emigrant Trail in the Chaos Jumbles.

on the north side of the road and can be reached either by hiking straight north through the woods to the obvious doubletrack, or by hiking east along the road for 0.2 mile to a small rock cairn that marks where the trail crosses the park road.

Key points:

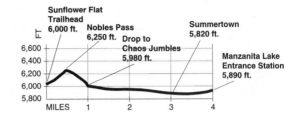

- 0.0 Sunflower Flat Trailhead.
- 0.5 Crest the summit of Nobles Pass.
- 1.0 Walk between the Chaos Jumbles and the base of Table Mountain.
- 3.0 Reach Summertown trailhead.

The hike: Imagine yourself a pioneer. You are headed for California, where you plan to strike it rich in a gold mine, or farm a patch of land in the northern Sacramento River valley, which has been touted as one of the most fertile valleys on Earth. You've crossed the Mississippi, endured the endless monotony of the Great Plains, struggled over the Rocky Mountains, and survived the high desert of the Great Basin. There is one last mountain range to be crossed, and you stand amid dense woodlands on the crest of that range's divide. You stand on Nobles Pass in what will one day become Lassen Volcanic National Park. Take a deep breath—it's all downhill from here.

To Summertown, that is. For the modern hiker, the Nobles Emigrant Trail presents a nice, easy stroll on a slice of history. The doubletrack was originally set by the wheels of wagons, and slips through corridors in the trees that were cleared by the hearty souls of bygone days.

The landscape covered by this section of the Nobles Emigrant Trail has been profoundly impacted by a centuries-old avalanche of rock that spilled from the slopes of the Chaos Crags. Rocky hummocks of pink dacite dominate the terrain, and the trail, shaded by Jeffrey and sugar pines, follows the route of least resistance through the maze. You can hike this route in either direction, as an out-and-back proposition or as a shuttle. It is described here as a shuttle hike heading downhill from Nobles Pass.

Beginning at Sunflower Flat, carefully cross the park road to its north side, and strike off through the woods for a little more than 100 yards to the obvious doubletrack trail, which parallels the highway. Turn left (west), and head uphill through a corridor of trees to the pass, which is at about the 0.5-mile mark.

From the pass, you'll drop almost directly into the Chaos Jumbles, with its widely spaced overcoat of Jeffrey pines. As you descend on the path, which is marked by yellow triangles with red trim, you can look left (southeast) to where Lassen Peak and the Chaos Crags peek over the dusky summits of the rubble hummocks.

Switchbacks lead down into easier terrain, with the trail tracing broad curves through the evergreen parkland until it settles into a sheltered depression between the northern edge of the Chaos Jumbles and the southern flank of Table Mountain at about 1 mile.

Continue gently down and west, passing through a gully clogged with deadfall. Above and to the right (north), dark talus spills down the slopes of Table Mountain, contrasting with the pinks and pale grays of the Jumbles.

At about 3 miles, you begin to see the first signs of civilization. A pile of pipes, a trail sign, and overhead wires appear along the trail. The doubletrack ends in a large clearing, where you can scout the scant remains of Summertown: Broken foundations, shattered ceramics, and shards of glass litter the forest floor.

If you are hiking out-and-back, this is the place to turn around. If you have planned a shuttle, pick up the gravel road that leads west, then southwest. Trail markers line the road, which quickly becomes asphalt littered with pine needles. The roadway bends south; stick to the pavement, ignoring gravel roads that branch off left and right. At the top of the rise, pass through a park maintenance area. The Lassen Park Road is about 0.1 mile beyond. A gate blocks access to the road, which is directly opposite the entrance station and the northwestern shores of Manzanita Lake.

Butte Lake

There are few places within Lassen Volcanic National Park that can rival Lassen Peak, Bumpass Hell, and the Chaos Crags in terms of dramatic landscapes. But the Butte Lake area does just that, with a collection of geologic formations of raw and otherworldly beauty.

The centerpiece of this portion of the park is the slumbering Cinder Cone, a perfectly symmetrical, 750-foot-high volcano. Nearly devoid of vegetation, stark, and new-looking, eruptions from this vent are responsible for the creation of many of the other noteworthy features that surround it. Volcanic rock dominates the landscape, in all forms, from the fine grains that surface trails in the area to the chunky barriers that dam Snag Lake and frame Butte Lake.

The Fantastic Lava Beds, blocks of black basalt that range north and east of the Cinder Cone, were expelled from the base of the volcano in eruptions that ended in the mid-1800s. Piled to heights of 200 feet and more, these lava beds separate Snag Lake from Butte Lake, and create a formidable eastern rampart for the section of the Nobles Emigrant Trail that passes through this area.

The Painted Dunes, spreading south and east from the Cinder Cone, are lava beds covered with a veneer of volcanic ash that took on a swirling pattern of muted hues—umber and sienna, brown and orange, pale red and dusky gray—as they were oxidized by heat and steam. Surrounding the Cinder Cone, the dunes, and the lava beds, spread in a broad arc around the base of Prospect Peak, is a rolling plain of smooth cinders, acres of vegetation-free land that appears to have been blanketed in a fresh coat of soot-colored snow.

Rising above all this is Prospect Peak, a long-defunct shield volcano that is as different from the Cinder Cone as dough is from toast. It was created by flows of viscous lava like those belched from Hawaiian volcanoes, and is now almost completely blanketed in a dense forest. Its summit offers the best views in the area, ranging from Lassen Peak in the southwest to, on clear days, Mount Shasta in the northwest.

Forming a quiet contrast to their earth-shattering brethren are the two major lakes of the area. Butte Lake, jade-green and milky with minerals leached from the lava beds, serves as trailhead for all of the hikes listed in this chapter. Snag Lake, separated from Butte by the formidable lava beds, is stained an opaque turquoise by the same minerals, and bordered on its western shores by a striking forest of silvered snags.

The campground at Butte Lake seldom fills, even during holiday weekends in the summertime, and offers a wonderful alternative to the hustle and bustle of Manzanita Lake and Summit Lake. There are at least 45 sites available throughout the summer, with 101 available by late summer. The cost is $10 per night. Each site has a fire pit, table, and bear-proof food storage cabinet; the campground amenities include toilets and garbage collection. There was no potable water available at the campground at the time of this writing, but plans called for water to be available by the summer of 2001 or 2002. Boil, filter, or chemically purify water before drinking from lakes and streams in the area. Check at the ranger station, which is manned most of the summer, for details. Aside from hiking, swimming and non-motorized boating are available at Butte Lake.

Most of the destinations in this area of the park are open to overnight camping. Be sure to obtain a permit before any backpacking excursion. Park regulations require that all backcountry camps be established at least 100 feet from water sources and trails. Complete backcountry camping regulations are listed in this guide's introduction.

To reach Butte Lake from the Manzanita Lake Entrance Station, backtrack west along California Highway 89 from the entrance station for 0.5 mile to the intersection of CA 44 and CA 89. Turn right (north) on CA 44/89, and follow the merged highway for 13.6 miles to Old Station, where CA 44 makes a sharp right (east) turn, breaking away from CA 89. Continue on CA 44 for another 11 miles to a right (south) turn onto the well-signed road to Butte Lake. The gravel road leads for about 7 miles to the campground and picnic area.

36 Bathtub Lake Loop

Highlights:	The trail leads to a sun-warmed lake frequented by swimmers, then to Butte Creek and Butte Lake.
Type of hike:	Day hike; out-and-back or loop.
Total distance:	0.8 mile to Bathtub Lake and back, or 2.3 miles for the loop.
Difficulty:	Easy.
Best months:	Late July–early September.
Maps:	USGS Prospect Peak quad; Lassen Volcanic National Park maps by the National Park Service, Earthwalk Press, and Wilderness Press; USDAFS Lassen National Forest map.
Parking and facilities:	Sites in the Butte Lake Campground are equipped with tables, fire pits, and bear-proof food cabinets. Restrooms are available at both the campground and the picnic area. There is ample trailhead parking available at the picnic area for those not camping in the area. At the time of this writing, there was no potable water source at the lake, but the park plans to have water available for the 2001 or 2002 summer season.

Finding the trailhead: To reach the Butte Lake Trailhead from the Manzanita Lake Entrance Station, backtrack west from the entrance station for 0.5 mile to the intersection of California Highways 44 and 89. Turn right (north) on the merged highway, and follow it for 13.6 miles to Old Station, where CA 44 makes a sharp right (east) turn. Continue on CA 44 for another 11 miles to a right (south) turn onto the signed road to Butte Lake. The gravel

Bathtub Lake Loop

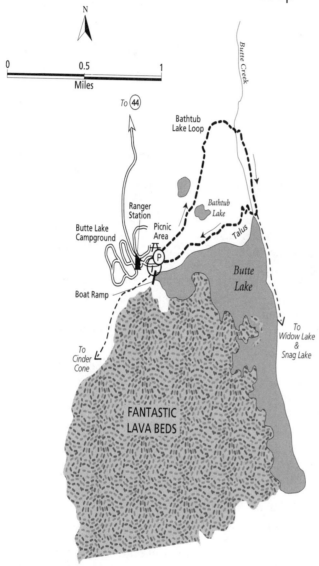

road leads about 7 miles to the campground and picnic area. The trailhead is on the north side of the picnic area parking lot.

Key points:

0.0	Butte Lake Trailhead.
0.4	Arrive at Bathtub Lake.
1.0	Cross Butte Creek.
1.5	Arrive at Butte Lake and cross the creek a second time.
2.3	Reach the Butte Lake Trailhead.

The hike: A friendlier lake would be hard to find. Bathtub Lake, small, cupped in a little tree-lined basin, and warmed by the sun, is the perfect destination for families with small children. It offers rock-throwing, wading, swimming, and fishing, all within a short walk from the Butte Lake Campground and picnic area. A neighboring tarn, separated from its more popular neighbor by a forested hummock, is more peaceful and contemplative.

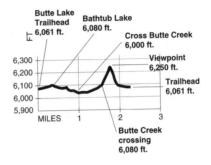

Most hikers are content to walk to Bathtub Lake and back, but those wishing to wander a bit farther afield will enjoy the little-used loop trail that continues north of Bathtub Lake to Butte Creek, then circles back to finish along the shores of Butte Lake. A creek crossing over a makeshift driftwood dam, and a rather steep climb to a promontory with great views of Butte Lake and the Fantastic Lava Beds, add challenge to the hike.

The trail begins on the north side of the Butte Lake picnic area parking lot, and is marked with a sign. The broad, sandy, cinder path begins by climbing rather steeply away from Butte Lake. At the top of the hill, you will pass among trees bearing the black scars of a controlled burn that was conducted in the area in 1998.

Climb over a short hump, and the trail drops gently, curving around a fallen tree above Bathtub Lake, which is on the right (east) side of the trail at 0.4 mile. This small, dark lake sports a collar of reeds on its southeast shore, and rocks on which you can climb or rest. Many hikers make this their final destination, but if you continue on the trail, you will trace the north shore of the lake, climb over a hummock, then descend to another little lake. Smaller and more peaceful than Bathtub Lake, this tarn is tucked between hills on the left (north) side of the trail.

But there is more. To complete the Bathtub Lake Loop, you can continue north past the second lake; the trail is marked with red dots on the trees. Grand Jeffrey pines, both standing and fallen, line the narrowing track, which climbs out of the hollow holding the second lake. A big mound of talus rises on the right (east) side of the trail.

The path drops into another hollow on the north side of the talus slope, then curves to the east. At about 1 mile, the route dips down a switchback to Butte Creek, Butte Lake's outlet stream. Verdant grasses and fragrant herbs line its banks, and a pair of bridges—one plank and one hewn log—span the stream. Climb through the underbrush on the east side of the water course.

The path rides up and over a hummock into a dry swale, and heads south through the woods toward Butte Lake, paralleling the rock-jumbled bed of Butte Creek. A steep slope of talus spills to the creek on its west side.

Proceed to a trail intersection at the northern tip of Butte Lake. To complete the loop, you must go right (west), across the driftwood dam that serves as a bridge across Butte Creek at the mouth of the lake. If you want to follow the trail along the east shore of Butte Lake to Widow Lake (Hike 37) or Snag Lake (Hike 40), continue straight (left).

Pick your way through the tangle of fallen silvered snags to the west side of Butte Creek, and rejoin the trail, which climbs over the steep talus slope. At the top of the rise, you'll be treated to wonderful views of Butte Lake, the Fantastic Lava Beds, and the Cinder Cone. On the west side of the talus ridge, the trail's surface becomes sandy with cinders. Drop down switchbacks through widely spaced pines, and follow the broad path back along the north shore of Butte Lake to the picnic area and trailhead.

37 Widow Lake

Highlights:	This seldom-visited lake sits in a high basin near the eastern boundary of the park.
Type of hike:	Day hike or overnight trip; out-and-back.
Total distance:	7.2 miles.
Difficulty:	Strenuous.
Best months:	Late June–October.
Maps:	USGS Prospect Peak quad; Lassen Volcanic National Park maps by the National Park Service, Earthwalk Press, and Wilderness Press; USDAFS Lassen National Forest map.
Parking and facilities:	Sites in the Butte Lake Campground are equipped with pit toilets, fire pits, and bear-proof food cabinets. There is ample parking at the picnic area, where the trailheads are located, for those not camping in the area. At the time of this writing, there was no potable water source at the lake, but the park plans to have water available for the 2001 or 2002 summer season.

Finding the trailhead: To reach the Butte Lake Trailhead from the Manzanita Lake Entrance Station, backtrack west from the entrance station on the Lassen Park Road (California Highway 89) for 0.5 mile to the intersection of CA 44 and CA 89. Turn right (north) on the merged highway, and follow it for 13.6 miles to Old Station, where CA 44 makes a sharp right (east) turn. Continue on CA 44 for another 11 miles to a right (south) turn onto the signed road to Butte Lake. The gravel road leads for about 7 miles to the campground and picnic area. The trailhead is on the east side of the picnic area parking lot.

Key points:
0.0   Butte Lake Trailhead.
0.5   Drop down and across Butte Creek to the trail intersection.
2.2   Reach the head of Butte Lake and the trail to Widow Lake.
3.6   Arrive on the shores of Widow Lake.

Widow Lake

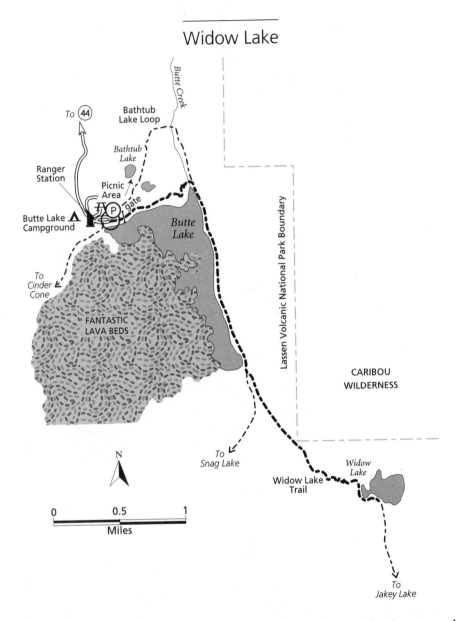

The hike: Isolation. Two trails lead to Widow Lake, but neither is easy, and both are seldom traveled. Traveling north from Jakey Lake (Hike 46), you must hike for miles through viewless forest on a path faded with disuse and sometimes completely obscured by deadfall and underbrush. The trail that leads southeast from Butte Lake, which is described here, includes a pitch steep enough to slow even the hardiest hiker to a crawl.

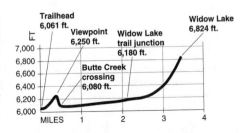

The difficulty of the two access trails, coupled with the lake's proximity to more easily reached destinations in the Butte Lake area, conspire to make Widow Lake a locale of profound isolation.

Tucked in the northeast corner of the park, Widow Lake is divided by a narrow grassy isthmus, and water lilies flourish in the shallow pool that has been carved off the lake's main body. Black Butte rises above the lake's eastern shore, but dense forests on all sides permit only fleeting views of the Cinder Cone, and, if the day is clear, Lassen Peak on the descent.

The trail begins on the east side of the Butte Lake picnic area parking lot, where a sign lists the many destinations that can be reached via this trail and others that branch off it.

The footworn path leads east through the cinders and Jeffrey pines along the north shore of the lake. Switchbacks climb to the summit of the steep knob overlooking Butte Lake and the Fantastic Lava Beds, then switchbacks lead down to the driftwood bridge that spans Butte Creek. Carefully cross to the east side of the creek, where a trail sign indicates the horse trail going left (north) along Butte Creek (this is also part of the Bathtub Lake Loop). To reach Widow Lake, go right (south) along the lakeshore.

The lakeside path is mostly overhung with evergreens, with Butte Lake a thinning strip of blue between the forest and the dark rock of the lava beds. At about the 1-mile mark, the trail threads through an open area between a talus field and the shoreline, then plunges back into the mixed evergreen woodland. The nature of the forest changes as you approach the head of Butte Lake, however; quaking aspens, a relatively rare occurrence in the park, thrive here, rustling even in the gentlest breezes.

At 2.2 miles, you will reach a trail intersection. The path to Widow Lake, obviously the one less traveled, breaks off to the left (southeast), with the other path leading right (southwest) to Snag Lake and beyond (see Hike 40 for a description of the Butte and Snag Lakes Loop).

Though the path isn't well used, it's clear and marked with yellow dots on the trees. It follows the drainage carved by Widow Lake's outlet stream, a seasonal creek that is usually dry by late summer. You will cross the stream several times as you climb—at one point, you hike right through the rocky streambed. The farther you go, the steeper it gets.

At about the 3-mile mark, you will enter an area scarred by fire in 1987. The bed of the stream is littered with deadwood, but it appears as though the forest took a stand against the flames, with the creekbed as a battle line, and won. Blackened trees stand south of the waterway, but the woods on the north side are fine and green.

As you continue up, the creek corridor widens, and meadowland creeps in, thick with fern, mullein, dense grasses, and wildflowers. Skirt the south side of the meadow, which is boggy in early season, then cross to its left (north) side and keep climbing.

You will cross the stream yet another time, then the trail will take you into a steep, shady ravine. The stream falls away swiftly as you gain altitude on the switchbacking path that leads up the south side of the ravine, and swatches of talus spill down from the head of the gully into the creekbed

A narrow isthmus splits Widow Lake.

below. The quick switchbacks hardly mitigate the climb, though the incline eases as the trail traces the southern edge of the talus slope.

In fact, the route doesn't mellow until it and the talus slope bend to the north, then arc southeast to the small pool on the west side of Widow Lake at 3.6 miles. An opening in the trees that have taken root on the otherwise grassy isthmus allows you to look past the lilies to the main body of Widow Lake as you circle the western shoreline.

The trail swings around to the lake's south shore, then departs to the south on the cross-country route to the Red Cinder Cone and Jakey Lake. Unless you plan to follow this route, return as you came.

38 Prospect Peak

Highlights: The panorama from the top of Prospect Peak includes Lassen Peak, Mount Harkness, the upper Sacramento Valley, and, on a clear day, Mount Shasta.
Type of hike: Day hike; out-and-back.
Total distance: 6.6 miles.
Difficulty: Strenuous.
Best months: Late June–September.
Maps: USGS Prospect Peak quad; Lassen Volcanic National Park maps by the National Park Service, Earthwalk Press, and Wilderness Press; USDAFS Lassen National Forest map.
Special considerations: The summit of Prospect Peak, at 8,338 feet, is high enough to induce symptoms of altitude sickness, including headache, nausea, and fatigue. If any of these symptoms manifest, descend immediately. Also, there is no water available on this hike. Be sure to carry an ample supply.
Parking and facilities: Sites in the Butte Lake Campground are equipped with pit toilets, fire pits, and bear-proof food cabinets. There is ample parking at the picnic area, where the trailheads are located. At the time of this writing, there was no potable water source at the lake, but the park plans to have water available for the 2001 or 2002 summer season.

Finding the trailhead: To reach the Butte Lake Trailhead from the Manzanita Lake Entrance Station, backtrack west from the entrance station on the Lassen Park Road (California Highway 89) for 0.5 mile to the intersection of CA 44 and CA 89. Turn right (north) on the merged highway, and follow it for 13.6 miles to Old Station, where CA 44 makes a sharp right (east) turn. Continue on CA 44 for another 11 miles to a right (south) turn onto the signed road to Butte Lake. The gravel road leads for about 7 miles to the campground and picnic area. The trailhead is on the southwest side of the boat ramp.

Key points:

0.0   Butte Lake Trailhead.
0.5   Reach the Prospect Peak trail intersection.
3.3   Arrive on the summit.

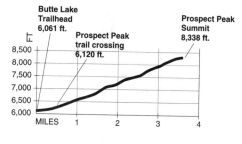

The hike: You probably know that old hiking cliché: The top is just over the next rise (or next hill, or around the next bend). Every experienced hiker knows this is *never* true. The hike to the top of Prospect Peak is emphatic proof of the point.

Prospect Peak

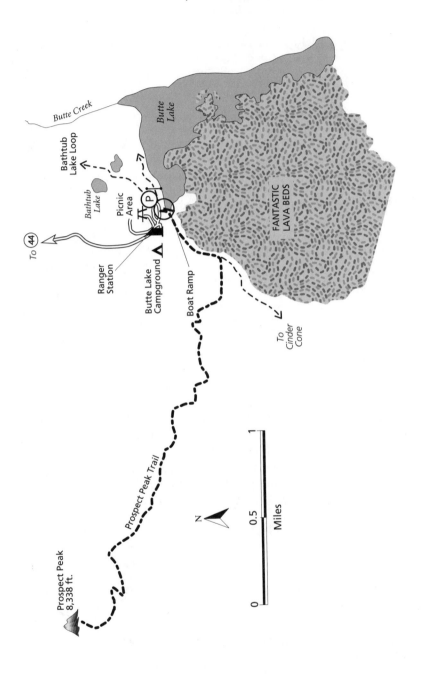

Butte Creek

Butte Lake

Bathtub Lake Loop

Bathtub Lake

Picnic Area

To 44

Ranger Station

Butte Lake Campground

Boat Ramp

FANTASTIC LAVA BEDS

To Cinder Cone

Prospect Peak Trail

Prospect Peak 8,338 ft.

N

Miles

0   0.5   1

It's not the most flattering description for a hike, but the route up Prospect Peak, a long-defunct shield volcano, is a meditative slog. The regularly spaced 200-foot contour intervals that can be seen on topographic maps of the area are almost visible on the ground; they rise for nearly 2,000 feet through dense woods that don't allow for views until you are within spitting distance of the summit.

This is not to say that the hike isn't worthwhile. The spell woven in the woods is peaceful to the point of being hypnotic. The muted greens and browns of the terrain are broken only by the vivid red of snow plant thriving in some spots on the forest floor. And the views from the top are superlative, with Lassen Peak dominating the southwestern horizon, and, on clear days, Mount Shasta visible across the Great Valley to the northwest.

The route begins on the Cinder Cone Trail/Nobles Emigrant Trail. Though comprised of cinders, the trail's surface feels like sand underfoot, and can make for deceptively strenuous hiking. The Fantastic Lava Beds rise close to the route on the left (east) and an open forest of Jeffrey pine is on the right (west).

After 0.5 mile, you arrive at a trail fork; take the right (west) trail, past the sign that indicates the summit of East Prospect Peak is 2.8 miles ahead. The trail, which is padded with a thick carpet of pine needles, begins to climb immediately. Red dots on the trees keep you on track, though the path is fairly easy to discern. The incline of the path fluctuates between nearly flat and more steeply pitched as it meanders up the east-facing slope of the mountain. The dots on the trees change from red to yellow, the Cinder Cone flickers in and out of view through the trees. Set a rhythm and go with it.

The nature of the forest changes as you gain altitude, fading from one dominated by Jeffrey pines to one dominated by red firs, with occasional mats of manzanita taking hold in clearings. At about the 2-mile mark, pass a circular gully filled with a jumble of talus on the right (north) side of the trail. More piles of talus spice the trail above. Continue rolling upward.

At about the 2.5-mile mark, the trees thin perceptibly, with more sun filtering to the forest floor, feeding a more diverse understory. The trail bumps against a spill of gray and tawny talus; keep this talus field on your right (north), following the yellow dots. A sharp right bend in the trail (watch for the dot) takes you around another talus field; the trail is narrow and twisting, switching back and forth among talus fields.

Though the change in the scenery is encouraging, the summit remains elusive—just when you think you are getting somewhere, the mountain rolls away, swathed in its mantle of trees. A long, ascending traverse leads to the south face of the mountain, then the trail switchbacks to the north. The forest obscures views, but you can make out the lava beds, Butte Lake, and green hills rolling to the north, east, and south. The matrix of the trail changes as well, becoming light brown and supporting a cover of meadow grasses. Mount another switchback; as you head back south, the vistas finally open; Snag Lake appears, then Lassen Peak. The trail lazily circles the summit area through trees and scrub clipped by snow and wind, climbing onto the rim of the volcano's shallow crater. The crater slopes gently in on itself,

Lassen Peak from the summit of Prospect Peak.

with scattered pines and firs taking root in its coarse soil. Wind westward along the rim to its northwest side, where you'll find the USGS benchmark, which disagrees with the map, stating 8,340 feet rather than 8,338—what's a couple of feet after you've ascended a couple of thousand? A ring of rocks marks the location of the tin can that holds the register. Inside, you find that the summit is a lonely place, especially when compared with busy Lassen Peak. But the vistas are inspiring, and the solitude refreshing. Directly west rises West Prospect Peak with its road and heliport structure; behind it are the twin summits of Badger Mountain. On clear days, you can see northwest to Mount Shasta. To the south are the Chaos Crags and Lassen Peak. Views to the south and east, best enjoyed on the descent, are of Snag Lake, Butte Lake, and the Cinder Cone.

Return as you came.

39   Cinder Cone Nature Trail

Highlights: This remarkable trail leads to the rim of the Cinder Cone. And if that's not enough of a thrill for you, you can climb down into the crater itself.

Type of hike: Day hike; lollipop loop or out-and-back.

Total distance: 5 miles.

Difficulty: Strenuous.

Best months: June–October.

Maps: USGS Prospect Peak quad; Lassen Volcanic National Park maps by the National Park Service, Earthwalk Press, and Wilderness Press; USDAFS Lassen National Forest map.

Special considerations: Though the distance is hardly daunting, the surface of this trail, loose and sandy in the lower reaches and loose and rocky on the Cinder Cone itself, makes for challenging walking. In addition, there is little shade, and no water can be obtained along the trail. The combination of tough walking and exposure to the sun and wind can be withering. Take plenty of water, and take your time.

Parking and facilities: Sites in the Butte Lake Campground are equipped with pit toilets, fire pits, and bear-proof food cabinets. There is ample parking available at the picnic area for those not camping in the area. At the time of this writing, there was no potable water source at the lake, but the park plans to have water available for the 2001 or 2002 summer season.

Finding the trailhead: To reach the Butte Lake Trailhead from the Manzanita Lake Entrance Station, backtrack west from the entrance station on the Lassen Park Road (California Highway 89) for 0.5 mile to the intersection of CA 44 and CA 89. Turn right (north) on the merged highway, and follow it for 13.6 miles to Old Station, where CA 44 makes a sharp right (east) turn. Continue on CA 44 for another 11 miles to a right (south) turn onto the signed road to Butte Lake. The gravel road leads for about 7 miles to the campground and picnic area. The trailhead is on the southwest side of the boat ramp.

Key points:

0.0   Butte Lake Trailhead.

1.2   Reach the trail intersection at the base of the Cinder Cone.

2.0   Arrive on the rim of the volcano.

3.6   Finish the circuit trail at the initial trail junction.

5.0   Return to the Butte Lake Trailhead.

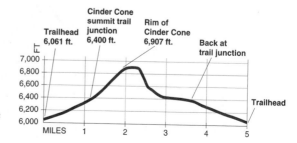

147

Cinder Cone Nature Trail

To (44)

Ranger
Station

Bathtub Lake

Butte Lake
Campground

Boat Ramp

To
*Prospect
Peak*

*Butte
Lake*

Cold
Spring

N

0	0.5	1

Miles

Cinder Cone
Nature Trail

Nobles–Emigrant Trail

Cinder
Cone

Painted
Dunes

*To
Badger
Flat*

Vernal
pool

Cinder
fields

FANTASTIC LAVA BEDS

*To
Widow
Lake*

Butte to Snag Lakes Loop Trail

*To
Rainbow
Lake*

Panther
Spring

*Snag
Lake*

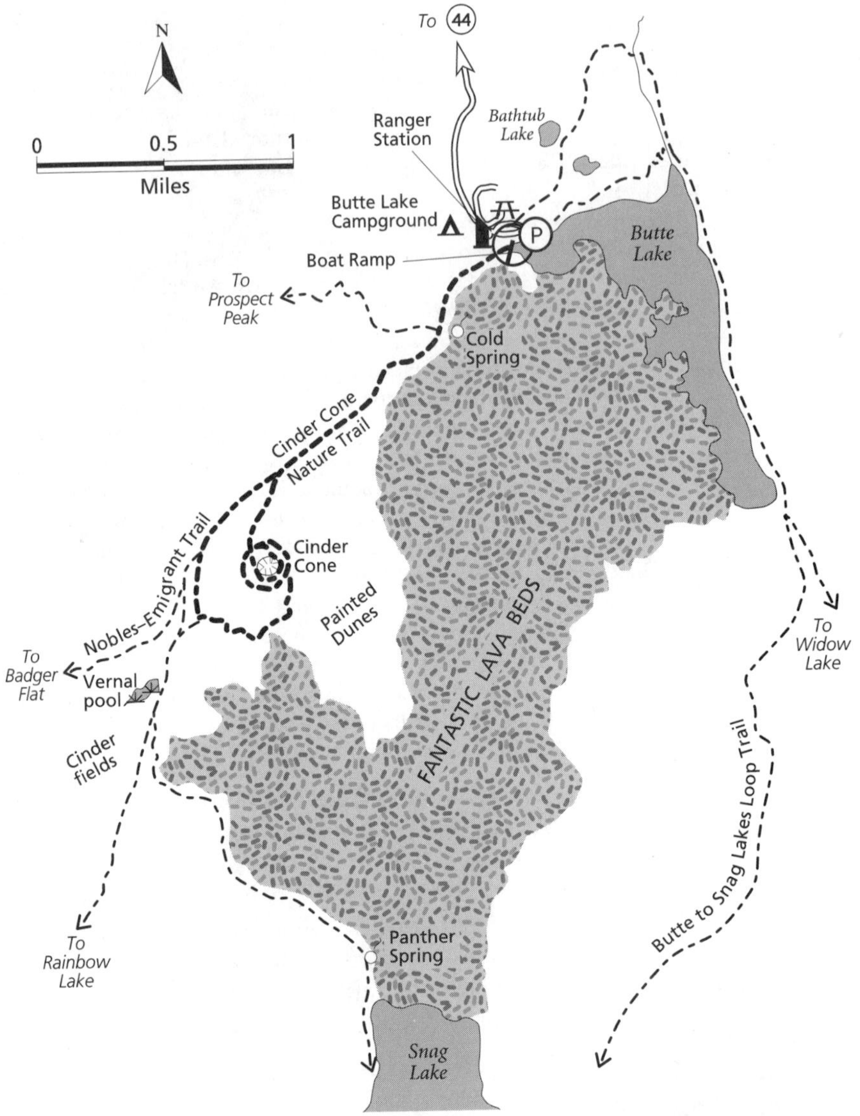

The hike: If Lassen Peak is the heart of Lassen Volcanic National Park, then the Cinder Cone is its navel. It even resembles a navel—a brown outie plunked in the belly of a grand volcanic basin that sprawls at the foot of Prospect Peak. But while Lassen Peak is the focus of the park, the vital force that underlies it pulsing in nearby hot springs and mudpots, the Cinder Cone remains out of the mainstream, tucked away in a corner of the park, quiet but never forgotten. It may be less majestic, but the Cinder Cone is closely related to Lassen Peak, for the same powerful forces have created both, and also produced the remarkable landscapes that surround them.

Geologists believe the Cinder Cone began to take shape in the mid-sixteenth century. A series of eruptions, spewing lava, cinders, and ash, built up the distinctive cone, and a different type of volcanic flow, coming from the base of the cone, created the neighboring Fantastic Lava Beds. It's a fascinating story, wonderfully explained in a recently revised interpretive pamphlet that is keyed to posts along the trail. The pamphlet is available at the trailhead.

The trail is very popular, and sees a lot of traffic. Please respect the terrain by remaining on the trail. Random footprints in the cinders don't erode quickly, leaving unsightly scars on the otherwise smooth slopes of the cone and surrounding dunes.

The trail begins on the southwest side of the Butte Lake picnic area parking lot, next to the boat ramp. You are also on the Nobles Emigrant Trail, used in the 1850s and 1860s by emigrants traveling from Nevada and points farther east to California's upper Sacramento Valley.

The sandy trail gradually climbs as it wanders through a woodland dominated by Jeffrey pine and bordered on the east by the angular basalt blocks of the Fantastic Lava Beds. Like the tailings of a volcanic mine, these massive lava beds dominate the landscape.

At about 0.5 mile, the trail to the summit of Prospect Peak (Hike 38) breaks off to the right (west). Continue south on the Cinder Cone Nature Trail/Nobles Emigrant Trail to where a spur trail leads left (east) to the Cold Spring, then return to the main trail and continue south toward the Cinder Cone.

As you gently climb, the steep, symmetrical slope of the cone comes into view. It grows in dominance as you continue through the woodland, with the widely spaced trees filtering sunlight onto the fine black cinders that carpet the forest floor.

As the trail grows steeper and the Cinder Cone looms larger, you can see the scar of the trail that leads to its rim. You gain 750 feet in less than a mile as you climb from the trail fork at 1.2 miles to the summit. Gather your strength in the shade of a stately Jeffrey pine that shadows the trail junction. To make the ascent, go left (south) on the summit trail. The right-hand trail also leads south, to Snag Lake and other destinations, but bypasses the top of the cone.

You might feel like you are taking one step forward and two steps back as you ascend. Persevere and enjoy the views as you climb—Lassen Peak comes into view as you circle toward the south face of the cone. The cinders grow coarser as you ascend, testament to the fact that the bigger, heavier cinders fell closer to the volcano's vent, while the lighter, smaller cinders were carried farther away.

At 2 miles, you've reached the rim of the volcano. The views are great in all directions—the spreading green slopes of Prospect Peak to the west, Lassen Peak and its neighbors to the southwest, Snag Lake to the south, and the lava beds and the Painted Dunes to the east. The trail leads around each of two distinct rims on the crater, and a separate spur trail leads down into the maw of the crater itself. Explore and enjoy.

The steep Cinder Cone Trail leads to fantastic views.

When you are ready to return, you can either retrace your steps to the trailhead, or descend the south face of the mountain, and circle the base of the Cinder Cone to the intersection with the Nobles Emigrant Trail. To take the latter route, circle the outer rim of the cone, which overlooks the lava beds and the swirling browns and oranges of the Painted Dunes to the east. The obvious descending trail follows a steep pitch down the east face toward the foot of the volcano.

In contrast to the ascent, one step forward on the descent equals three steps. Big, fun steps! It isn't long before you find yourself at the base of the mountain, on a trail that is wedged between the rough cinders and the rolling hillocks of the Painted Dunes. Circle right (west) around the base of the cone to the point where the trail splits: you can stay right (west) on the main trail, or take the left (southwest) spur down to the vent of a lava flow that occurred in 1851. The spur loops you back to the main trail, which continues its circumnavigation of the base of the Cinder Cone.

By the time you climb to the base of the west face of the Cinder Cone, you have returned to the Nobles Emigrant Trail. Follow the trail right (north) to the trail intersection on the north side of the cone at the big pine tree, and then retrace your steps to the Butte Lake Trailhead.

40 Butte and Snag Lakes Loop

Highlights: This trail circles the two lakes of the area, passing through the cinder beds adjacent to the Fantastic Lava Beds and the Painted Dunes.
Type of hike: Day hike or backpack; loop.
Total distance: 10.5 miles.
Difficulty: Strenuous.
Best months: Late June–October.
Maps: USGS Prospect Peak and Mount Harkness quads; Lassen Volcanic National Park maps by the National Park Service, Earthwalk Press, and Wilderness Press; USDAFS Lassen National Forest map.
Special considerations: If you choose to make a backcountry camp along this trail, be sure to abide by park regulations by securing a backcountry permit and setting up camp at least 100 feet from lakes, other water sources, and trails.
Parking and facilities: Sites in the Butte Lake Campground are equipped with pit toilets, fire pits, and bear-proof food cabinets. There is ample parking at the picnic area, where the trailheads are located. At the time of this writing, there was no potable water source at the lake, but the park plans to have water available for the 2001 or 2002 summer season.

Finding the trailhead: To reach the Butte Lake Trailhead from the Manzanita Lake Entrance Station, backtrack west from the entrance station on the Lassen Park Road (California Highway 89) for 0.5 mile to the intersection of CA 44 and CA 89. Turn right (north) on the merged highway, and follow it for 13.6 miles to Old Station, where CA 44 makes a sharp right (east) turn. Continue on CA 44 for another 11 miles to a right (south) turn onto the signed road to Butte Lake. The gravel road leads for about 7 miles to the campground and picnic area. The trailhead is on the east side of the picnic area.

Key points:

0.0 Butte Lake Trailhead.
0.5 Drop down and across Butte Creek to the trail intersection.
2.2 Reach the head of Butte Lake and the junction with the trail to Widow Lake.

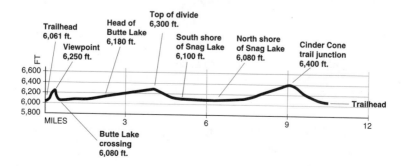

Butte and Snag Lakes Loop

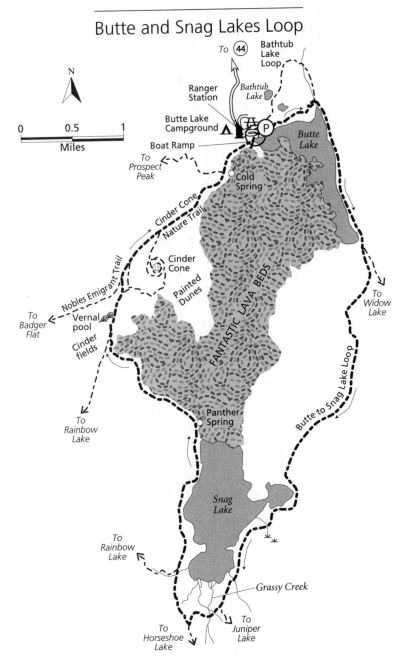

- 5.0   Arrive on the south shore of Snag Lake.
- 6.3   Reach the beach on the north shore of Snag Lake.
- 9.1   Pass the last trail intersection near the Cinder Cone.
- 10.5   Arrive back at the Butte Lake Trailhead.

The hike: The Fantastic Lava Beds divide Butte Lake from Snag Lake, and define the ambiance of both. A dark and unusual presence, the lava beds on the Butte Lake side appear utterly devoid of life, a tumbled mass of new black rock. On the Snag Lake side, signs of the fertility that will blossom once the lava beds have broken down begin to appear. Solitary evergreens have somehow found purchase atop the mound of jagged rock, harbingers of the forest to come.

This trail circumnavigates both lakes. As it is described here, the trail leads first south along the long arm of Butte Lake, then circles back north along the west shore of Snag Lake, and finishes by passing the Cinder Cone and descending back to the Butte Lake Trailhead. But, as with all loops, this one can be done in either direction. Regardless of whether you travel clockwise or counterclockwise, you can break the hike up by camping in the open woodlands that bound Snag Lake.

The trail begins on the east side of the Butte Lake picnic area. A trail sign lists the mileages to several destinations that can be reached via this trail, including Snag Lake at 5 miles.

The trail, a swath of footprints laid down by hikers as they passed through the cinders, leads east along the north shore of the lake. Climb switchbacks to the top of a knob that overlooks Butte Lake and the Fantastic Lava Beds. More switchbacks careen down to a clutter of driftwood that forms a makeshift bridge over Butte Creek. Cross to the east side of the creek, where a sign indicates the horse trail (part of the Bathtub Loop Trail) going left (north). Stay right (south), following the narrow trail that runs along the east shore of Butte Lake.

The lakeside path is shaded by evergreens, tracing the narrowing blue arm of Butte Lake as it reaches southward. The lava beds spill into the lake on the west, and the rolling slopes of Prospect Peak rise beyond them. At about the 1-mile mark, the trail passes through an opening in the forest at the foot of a small talus field, where you can enjoy better views of the westward vistas, then heads back into the woodland. Near the head of Butte Lake, you pass through a stand of quaking aspen, with paddle-like leaves that shimmy and crackle in the slightest winds.

At 2.2 miles, you reach the intersection with the Widow Lake Trail (Hike 37). Stay right (southwest) on the path to Snag Lake.

Red dots on trees mark the route through the open, fire-damaged forest that predominates between Butte Lake and Snag Lake. The trail seems flat at times, but steadily gains altitude, climbing about 300 feet before topping out on a forested knoll. As it approaches this crest, the trail follows the path of a seasonal stream, passing through meadowy patches and crossing the drainage a couple of times as it proceeds. The gentle climb gives you plenty of opportunity to observe how randomly fire can touch a forest; the trees on one side of the path may be completely consumed, while on the other side of the trail, less than 10 feet away, the forest thrives.

The trail flattens amid stands of living and dead trees at about 3.5 miles, then the equally gentle descent to the shores of Snag Lake begins. As you near the water, aspen trees edge into the evergreens. At about the 5-mile mark, the trail arcs sharply southward and Snag Lake is visible through the trees on the right (west) side of the path.

Snag Lake is surrounded on the west by snags and on the east by lava beds.

The trail rolls through alternating aspen and meadow as it traces the east shore of Snag Lake. At openings in the trees, you can look northwest across the lake's sandy beaches and turquoise surface to the Fantastic Lava Beds, with the Cinder Cone and Prospect Peak visible above and beyond. At about the 6-mile mark, you will pass a sandy peninsula that juts into the lake—a perfect location to sit for a while, empty the cinders out of your shoes, have a bite to eat, and, if you are backpacking, scout a campsite.

Continuing south along the lakeshore, you will cross an inlet stream via a makeshift "bridge" of downed trees, then curve around the southern shore of the lake to the intersection with the trail that leads south to Cameron Meadow and Juniper Lake. Stay right (west) on the loop route, which arcs through open woodland and a marshy area littered with funky boardwalks of fallen logs to Grassy Creek. A wooden pier juts into the rocky creekbed but doesn't reach to the opposite shore; you'll have to cross logs to do that. There is no trail marker on the opposite bank, but it is easy to locate the trail, which curves east and uphill to a second trail intersection. Choose the path that leads right (north); a trail sign indicates that Butte Lake via the Cinder Cone is 5.7 miles distant. Horseshoe Lake and Juniper Lake lie to the south, along the trail that leads up Grassy Creek (see Hike 47).

Trees between the two trail junctions have screened Snag Lake, but as you begin to head north, you can see the water through the thinning trees on the right (east) side of the trail. Climb behind a bluff, then continue traversing the slope above the lake to another trail intersection. The trail to the left (west) leads to Rainbow Lake and beyond. Stay straight (north), continuing along Snag Lake's west shore.

The trees, both green and dead, grow thinner as you move northward, until the living disappear, leaving in their absence a surreal landscape of silvery standing snags. The lake's name actually refers to snags that lie beneath the water's surface, but those on the ground add to the appropriateness of the moniker.

The trail weaves through this eerily beautiful landscape. The creaking of the standing dead as they shudder in the wind can be enervating, drawing your eyes away from the path to scan for trees that look like they might topple over. If you've ever wanted to ponder that old conundrum—"If a tree falls in the forest, does anybody hear?"—this is the place to do it. But if you linger, bring a hard hat.

Yellow dots help you stay on the route, which remains within about 50 yards of the lakeshore. As you approach the lake's northern edge, the Fantastic Lava Beds, a formidable dam, loom larger and larger, and the fledgling hopes of a new forest, tender and vividly green, begin to sprout amid the deadfall.

Traverse a wooded knob as the trail climbs about 100 yards above the lake; fallen trees make for exciting trail negotiations. The path drops off the knob onto a lovely beach in the shadow of the lava beds at about 6.3 miles. The beach offers a breathtaking view southeast across the lake toward Mount Hoffman. Panther Spring, tucked into the lava rocks, lies north of the beach.

The trail curves west away from the lake, and now you are in the realm of the lava beds, a great red and black jumble that blocks the horizon on the right (east) side of the trail. It's inhospitable terrain, but a scattering of lone pines make do, clinging to chunks of basalt. The trail of crushed cinder makes for exhausting, if straightforward, walking.

Slog up one of several short hills, then ski down through a drainage that is dry by late summer. At the crest of the next hill, the smooth sides of the Cinder Cone come into view. Continue along the perimeter of the lava beds as the trail breaks away from the woodland and into open fields of cinders, with the streaked browns, golds, and oranges of the Painted Dunes covering the jagged edges of the lava flow. Pass a buttress of red rock, a silvered snag, and then a trail sign asking that you remain on the trail while among the cinder fields.

The trail swings more directly northward to the first of several trail intersections as you approach the Cinder Cone. At the first, continue straight (right/north) toward the cone, dipping through a swale with a sparse mat of low-growing herbs in its bed. Less than 0.5 mile farther, pass a rock cairn or duck at a Y intersection; stay left (north) here, unless you want to climb the Cinder Cone. About 200 yards beyond, at the base of the cone, you will reach the third trail junction. Again, remain to the left (north); the right trail also leads up the volcano. The next junction is with the Nobles Emigrant Trail, which departs to the left (west). Stay right (north) and walk another 0.5 mile to the last trail intersection, with the main route to the summit of the Cinder Cone at 9.1 miles. From here, you will follow the merged Cinder Cone Trail and Nobles Emigrant Trail back to the Butte Lake Trailhead at 10.5 miles. A more detailed description of this last leg of the trail is in Hike 39.

41   Rainbow and Snag Lakes Loop

Highlights:	This tour cruises past the Cinder Cone before climbing to secluded Rainbow Lake, then drops by Snag Lake and the Fantastic Lava Beds on its way back to the Cinder Cone and Butte Lake.
Type of hike:	Day hike or backpack; lollipop loop.
Total distance:	12 miles.
Difficulty:	Strenuous.
Best months:	July–October.
Maps:	USGS Prospect Peak quad; Lassen Volcanic National Park maps by the National Park Service, Earthwalk Press, and Wilderness Press; USDAFS Lassen National Forest map.
Special considerations:	If you choose to make a backcountry camp along this trail, be sure to abide by park regulations, including securing a backcountry permit and setting up camp at least 100 feet from all water sources and trails.
Parking and facilities:	Sites in the Butte Lake Campground are equipped with pit toilets, fire pits, and bear-proof food cabinets. There is ample trailhead parking in the picnic area parking lot. At the time of this writing, there was no potable water source at the lake, but the park plans to have water available for the 2001 or 2002 summer season.

Finding the trailhead: To reach the Butte Lake Trailhead from the Manzanita Lake Entrance Station, backtrack west from the entrance station on the Lassen Park Road (California Highway 89) for 0.5 mile to the intersection of CA 44 and CA 89. Turn right (north) on the merged highway, and follow it for 13.6 miles to Old Station, where CA 44 makes a sharp right (east) turn. Continue on CA 44 for another 11 miles to a right (south) turn onto the road to Butte Lake. The gravel road leads for about 7 miles to the campground and picnic area. The trailhead is on the southwest side of the boat ramp.

Key points:

0.0   Butte Lake Trailhead.
1.2   Reach the intersection with the trail that leads to the summit of the Cinder Cone.

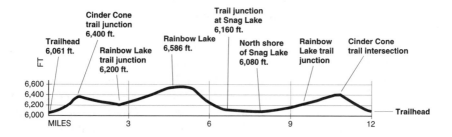

Rainbow and Snag Lakes Loop

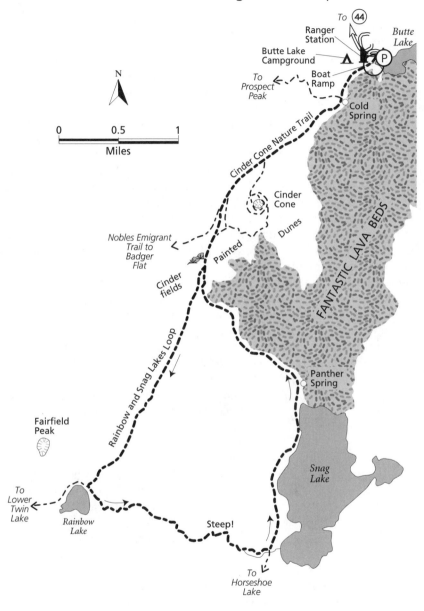

2.7   Take the trail that climbs to Rainbow Lake.
4.8   Arrive at Rainbow Lake.
6.7   Reach the trail intersection on the west side of Snag Lake.
7.9   Rest on the beach at the north end of Snag Lake.
9.4   Return to the intersection with the trail that leads to Rainbow Lake.
12.0   Arrive back at the Butte Lake Trailhead.

The hike: Unique volcanic formations, a historic trail used by emigrants to California in the mid-nineteenth century, a secluded lake in the heart of Lassen's north country—all this and more lies along the loop that links Butte Lake, Rainbow Lake, and Snag Lake.

Most of this trail is described in detail in other hikes in this chapter, so I've limited extensive descriptions of those portions of the trail for the sake of brevity. Take your time on the trail, enjoy the spectacular vistas, and savor the blessings of backcountry travel. Should you decide to camp along the route, either at Rainbow Lake or Snag Lake, be sure to abide by the park's backcountry rules, which are detailed in the introduction to this guide.

The first part of the trail, which does double duty as the Cinder Cone Trail and the Nobles Emigrant Trail, sees a good number of hikers. Remain on the trail, as the footprints left by people straying from the main route leave permanent scars on the otherwise smooth cinder landscape surrounding the Cinder Cone, the Painted Dunes, and the Fantastic Lava Beds.

The trail begins on the southwest side of the Butte Lake picnic area parking lot, next to the boat ramp. The cinder trail gradually climbs as it wanders through a woodland of Jeffrey pine, with the Fantastic Lava Beds guarding the east side of the trail.

The trail to the summit of Prospect Peak leads to the right (west) at 0.5 mile. Continue south on the Cinder Cone Trail/Nobles Emigrant Trail. The symmetrical slopes of the Cinder Cone appear as you climb to the intersection with the trail that leads to its summit at the 1.2-mile mark.

The volcano presents itself as an opportunity for a rewarding side trip both now, at the outset of the loop, and at the end of the loop. If you choose to add this to the hike, the climb is detailed in Hike 39. To continue on the loop trail to Rainbow Lake, stay right (south) on the Nobles Emigrant Trail, which leads for 0.5 mile to the next trail intersection. Here, stay straight (south); the emigrant trail continues right (west). A trail sign indicates that you are on the trail that leads to Snag Lake and Rainbow Lake.

Three more trail intersections follow within the next mile. The first leads left (southeast) to the summit of the Cinder Cone; stay right (south) on the trail toward Snag Lake. Another trail about 200 yards farther also leads left (southeast) to the summit of the cone. Again, stay right (south).

At the trail junction at 2.7 miles, stay right (southwest) on the trail to Rainbow Lake, which lies 2.1 miles distant, according to the trail sign. The other fork is the trail to Snag Lake, which you return on. You can do the loop in this direction (clockwise) as well, but the trail between Rainbow Lake and Snag Lake is steep and better tackled heading downhill. Thus, the loop is described here in a counterclockwise direction.

The path leads up through the cinder fields, with the Painted Dunes spreading east and south into the Fantastic Lava Beds. Jeffrey pines begin to shade the trail as you leave the open area; if you look behind you, to the north, the Cinder Cone dominates the views. Enjoy the vista, because it's the last you'll see of this impressive volcano until near trail's end.

The path proceeds steadily uphill, skirting islands of cinders devoid of vegetation as it climbs through the trees. As the forest thickens, and fades from Jeffrey pines to stands of lodgepole pines and firs, deadfall occasionally clutters the trail. The path grows steeper as it ascends. You cross an intermittent stream, then the pitch of the trail moderates as you climb onto open benches that drop south from the base of Fairfield Peak.

You climb gently from one bench to the next, with Fairfield Peak the dominant landmark on the western horizon. The swales between the lips of the benches are broad and sunny, and sparkle with pinemat manzanita and wildflowers; stands of red fir separate one swale from the next. This type of terrain dominates until you reach the border of the Rainbow Lake basin, where the climbing ends and you drop swiftly to the northeast shore of the peaceful lake. Set almost perfectly in the center of the park, Rainbow sees less traffic than the Twin Lakes, its neighbors to the southwest, and is the perfect spot for a backcountry camp or a midday meal.

The trail from the Cinder Cone dead ends on the path that runs west to east from Lower Twin Lake to Snag Lake. A trail sign marks the spot. To continue the loop, turn left (east) on the trail to Snag Lake. Climb out of the Rainbow Lake basin onto more benchlands shaded by red firs—this time, however, instead of climbing through the terrain, you will be descending.

The drop steepens abruptly as it drops toward Snag Lake along the drainage of a seasonal stream, descending nearly 600 feet in the span of a mile. Toward the bottom of the drop, Snag Lake can be glimpsed through the evergreens that crowd the trail. At 6.7 miles, the trail from Rainbow Lake ends on the path that traces the western shore of Snag Lake. Turn left (north) on this trail; if you go right (south), you will meet the trail that leads south up the Grassy Creek drainage to Horseshoe and Juniper Lakes.

The Cinder Cone and Painted Dunes viewed from the trail from Rainbow Lake.

The mostly healthy stands of timber that have shaded the trail since you left the cinder fields gradually disappear as the trail skims the shoreline of Snag Lake, until only silvery standing snags jut from the earth like the grizzled stubble on an old man's chin. The trail weaves through the standing dead. Yellow dots mark the route, which remains within about 50 yards of the lakeshore.

Living forest gradually reestablishes itself as you near the north shore of the lake, where the Fantastic Lava Beds rear up as an impressive black dam. Climb up and over a wooded knob, then the trail drops onto a beach on the lake's north shore at 7.9 miles, just south of Panther Spring.

The crushed-cinder trail continues northwest, wedged between the open forest and the western edge of the lava beds. After climbing over several mounds of cinder, where the footing makes it abundantly clear that going down is much easier than going up, the trail arcs north into the Painted Dunes, and the Cinder Cone comes into view. As you cross the open cinder fields, you will pass a silvered snag, and a trail sign asking you to remain on the trail.

At 9.4 miles, you reach the intersection with the trail that leads to Rainbow Lake, and the lollipop part of the loop is complete. Make your way through the string of trail intersections that crowd the southwestern base of the Cinder Cone, then retrace your steps along the Cinder Cone Trail/Nobles Emigrant Trail to the Butte Lake Trailhead at 12 miles.

Juniper Lake

Nothing quite compares to a large lake when it comes to showcasing the influence of weather on both the wilderness and the hiker traveling in that wilderness. Completely open to the heavens, Juniper Lake is the perfect stage. When the sun is bright and high, glistening on the lake's breeze-rumpled surface and warming the beaches along its shore, the natural world couldn't be more gentle and serene. When storm clouds gather over the high peaks, and a maelstrom of rain and wind-whipped white caps marches across the lake, that same natural world becomes inhospitable, and most of us would quickly forsake its shores for a comfy couch in a home warmed by a crackling fire.

The sprawling lapis expanse of Juniper Lake dominates a high basin in the southeastern portion of Lassen Volcanic National Park. The largest lake in the park, it lies at the foot of Mount Harkness, a defunct shield volcano that flows across the park's southern boundary. The lake is hemmed in on all sides by a thick, mixed evergreen forest dominated by the stately red fir, and is home base for most of the trails in the area. From the trailhead on its south shore, you can climb Mount Harkness or embark on a circumambulation of the lake. The Crystal Lake Trailhead lies along the lake's east shore, and from its north shore, trails lead to Inspiration Point, Horseshoe Lake, Jakey Lake, and down the Grassy Creek drainage to Snag Lake.

Accommodations at Juniper Lake are rustic, which adds to its charm. The campground offers 18 campsites for $10 per night, on a first come, first served basis. The campsites are simple, including only fire rings and picnic tables; other campground amenities include toilets and garbage collection. In addition to hiking, you can swim, ride horses, and use non-motorized boats on the lake.

At the north end of the lake, you find a picnic area with tables and restrooms—and the best beach in the park—as well as a corral. There are two ranger stations in this area, one near the north-end trailheads, and one on the east shore of Horseshoe Lake. Check with park officials at the Manzanita Lake or Southwest Entrance Stations to determine whether the Juniper or Horseshoe Lake ranger stations will be open during your visit.

To reach Juniper Lake from the Southwest Entrance Station, follow California 89 south to its junction with California 36. Turn left (east) on CA 36, and follow the merged highways east to the town of Chester. Turn left (north) on the Feather River Road, and go 0.7 mile to the first road fork. Turn right (north) on the Juniper Lake Road (Plumas County 318) at the fork (the left fork leads to the Drakesbad area). Follow the Juniper Lake Road, which is well signed, for 11.7 miles to the Juniper Lake Campground, and 13.4 miles to the end of the road at the Juniper Lake Picnic Area. The access road is paved for its first 5.5 miles, then becomes rough dirt that is not suitable for trailers.

42   Mount Harkness

<table>
<tr><td align="right">Highlights:</td><td>A hike to the top of one of the friendliest mountains in the park leads to great panoramic vistas from the lookout tower.</td></tr>
<tr><td align="right">Type of hike:</td><td>Day hike; loop.</td></tr>
<tr><td align="right">Total distance:</td><td>5.6 miles.</td></tr>
<tr><td align="right">Difficulty:</td><td>Strenuous.</td></tr>
<tr><td align="right">Best months:</td><td>July–late September.</td></tr>
<tr><td align="right">Maps:</td><td>USGS Mount Harkness quad; Lassen Volcanic National Park maps by the National Park Service, Earthwalk Press, and Wilderness Press; USDAFS Lassen National Forest map.</td></tr>
<tr><td align="right">Special considerations:</td><td>The summit of Mount Harkness is more than 8,000 feet high, and those not acclimatized may experience symptoms of altitude sickness, including headache, nausea, and fatigue. Should any of these symptoms manifest, retreat immediately to a lower altitude. No water is available on the trail on the mountain. If you choose to drink from Juniper Lake, be sure to purify the water by boiling, filtering, or chemically treating it.</td></tr>
<tr><td align="right">Parking and facilities:</td><td>There is a small parking lot at the trailhead. Toilets are available in the Juniper Lake Campground, and a picnic area lies at the northern tip of Juniper Lake, 1.7 miles north of the campground.</td></tr>
</table>

Finding the trailhead: From the town of Chester on California 36, take the Feather River Road north for 0.7 mile to where the road forks. Go right (north) on the Juniper Lake Road (Plumas County 318) at the fork. Follow this road for 11.7 miles to the Juniper Lake Campground; the pavement ends after 5.5 miles and you pass the park entrance signs at 9 miles. Turn left (west) into the campground. After less than 0.1 mile, pull into the trailhead parking area on the right (north).

Key points:

0.0   Juniper Lake Campground Trailhead.
1.9   Arrive on the summit of Mount Harkness.
3.8   Reach the trail junction at the western base of Mount Harkness.
5.6   Complete the loop back in the Juniper Lake Campground.

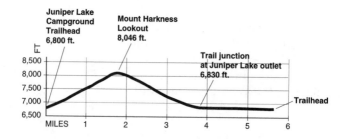

Mount Harkness

The hike: Gazing down into the seemingly benign crater on the top of Mount Harkness, where the soil is just beginning to show its fertility by supporting a smattering of scraggly silverleaf lupine, it's hard to imagine that this once was an active shield volcano. It oozed viscous lava of the type that pours out of the volcanoes on Hawaii, which has resulted in its broad stance. Once that relatively gentle phase of its volcanism ended, Mount Harkness birthed a cinder cone, which spewed the crumbling red rock that now adorns its slopes. These days, the mountain is a spectacular destination for hikers, its fiery past cloaked in stately evergreen forests and busy meadows of wildflowers.

A lonely fire lookout stands atop the mountain, on the southern rim of the sloping crater. From here, a park service sentinel watches the forested slopes surrounding Lassen Peak for signs of fire. Hikers enjoy the same 360-degree views, looking west to the barren hulk of Lassen, south past Lake Almanor, east to the distant Sierra Buttes, and north to the Cinder Cone and the twin Prospect Peaks.

Hikers at the Mount Harkness lookout.

The hike to the summit begins amid the thick red fir forest that skirts Juniper Lake. From the parking area, walk down the campground road to the camp's informational signs. Go left (southwest) at the signs, past Site 5, to the Mount Harkness Lookout Trail; it's 1.9 miles from here to the summit.

The trail begins by climbing gently, but the pitch soon gets more serious, switchbacking across a slope that supports a bloom of wildflowers beneath the shade of a mixed evergreen forest. The ubiquitous yellow dots on trees mark the route.

Continue to climb through the lovely open woodland, where the filtered sun nourishes a profusion of colorful plants, including vibrant green pinemat manzanita, which grows between the switchbacks just before the trail flattens. Gradually, the incline steepens again and the forest thickens; level sections that are all too brief provide respite in the otherwise relentless, though blissfully shaded, ascent.

The woods abruptly end as the trail reaches an open slope below the sloping north face of the mountain. The slope assumes a more ominous demeanor at its eastern edge, where it sharpens into a dark and jagged cliff face. In summer, when the clover and other wildflowers are at their thickest, this slope is abuzz with insects, especially bees, who emit a low hum like that of a distant motorboat or the family refrigerator. Traverse this slope, then switchback up through jumbled rocks into another meadow. At this point you will collect your first views of Lassen Peak to the northwest.

Reach a trail intersection on the west-facing slope of the mountain at 1.7 miles. Warner Valley and the Juniper Lake outlet lie down the trail to the right (west); you take this trail on the return if you choose to make the loop. To reach the summit of Mount Harkness, continue left (straight/south) and up, following the snaking, ever-ascending trail.

Round the last broad switchback and the lookout is in sight. The broad bowl to your left (northeast) is the crater, and a short spur trail leads west to an overlook of Lassen Peak. Sign the register at the base of the lookout's staircase; if you are lucky, the park service employee who mans the lookout will invite you up to survey the scene. Krista Watters, the lookout for the 1998 summer season, was a wealth of information on the history of the lookout and the natural history and highlights of the panorama.

You can return to the trailhead as you came, or complete the loop by going left (west) on the trail to Warner Valley and Juniper Lake 0.2 mile below the summit. This path takes you steeply down the west face of Mount Harkness for 1.7 miles, winding first through the lupine meadow and then through darkening woodlands, skirting and switchbacking through the occasional rocky gully or promontory.

Toward the bottom of the descent, the trail flattens for a stretch in a narrowing hollow, then climbs briefly over the manzanita-coated hummock that guards the hollow's western edge to a trail intersection at 3.8 miles. The left (south) fork leads to Warner Valley; the center (northwest) trail leads to Horseshoe Lake and Indian Lake (Hikes 48 and 49). The trail to the far right (looping back to the northeast) completes this loop, leading back to

A break in the trees on the slopes of Mount Harkness offers a glimpse of Lassen Peak.

the Juniper Lake Campground and the trailhead. The trail sign indicates that it is 1.8 miles back to the campground.

Yellow dots again mark the path to the lakeshore, which circles a fallen tree and briefly parallels the trail up Mount Harkness before bending northward toward the lake. You also pass a shallow pond (dry in late summer) on your way to the lakeshore.

Juniper Lake is lovely and placid, and, from a trailside perspective, has traded the deep blue it wore when viewed from the top of Mount Harkness for a forest green. The route rolls along the shoreline, dropping briefly at one point to a rocky beach. Enjoy the lake views and, if it is warm enough, take a dip in the cold waters before continuing northeast on the trail toward the campground. The route passes through a final swampy meadow before reaching the campsites; you re-enter civilization at Site 15 and at 5.6 miles. Follow the campground road right (northeast) back to the parking area.

43 Juniper Lake Loop

Highlights:	This flat, easy trail circumnavigates lovely Juniper Lake.
Type of hike:	Day hike; loop.
Total distance:	6.2 miles.
Difficulty:	Moderate.
Best months:	July–early September.
Maps:	USGS Mount Harkness quad; Lassen Volcanic National Park maps by the National Park Service, Earthwalk Press, and Wilderness Press; USDAFS Lassen National Forest map.
Special considerations:	There is no potable water along the trail. If you drink from Juniper Lake, first purify the water by boiling, filtering, or chemically treating it.
Parking and facilities:	There is a small parking lot at the trailhead. Toilets are available in the Juniper Lake Campground, and a picnic area lies at the northern tip of Juniper Lake, 1.7 miles north of the campground.

Finding the trailhead: From California 36 in the town of Chester, take the Feather River Road north for 0.7 mile to where the road forks. Go right on the Juniper Lake Road (Plumas County 318) at the fork, continuing north. Follow this road for 11.7 miles to the Juniper Lake Campground; the pavement ends after 5.5 miles and you'll pass the park entrance signs at 9.0 miles. Turn left (west) into the campground. After less than 0.1 mile, pull into the trailhead parking area on the right (north).

Key points:

0.0	Juniper Lake Campground Trailhead.
1.7	Reach the trail junction at the base of Mount Harkness's west slope.
2.2	Pass the junction with the trail to Indian Lake.
4.5	Arrive at the Juniper Lake picnic area on the lake's north shore.
6.2	Finish the roadside walk at the Juniper Lake Campground.

The hike: Though this by no means can be considered a wilderness trek, the loop around Juniper Lake is the perfect easy day hike for a family

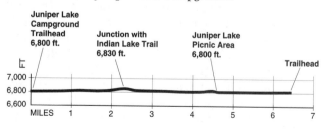

camping at Juniper Lake, for the angler, or for anyone who wants to enjoy the lake's environs without gaining a lot of altitude.

The trail begins alongside campsite 15, which can be reached from the trailhead parking lot by walking down the campground road for about 0.3 mile. A trail sign marks the spot. The trail begins by passing through a small

Juniper Lake Loop • Crystal Lake • Inspiration Point

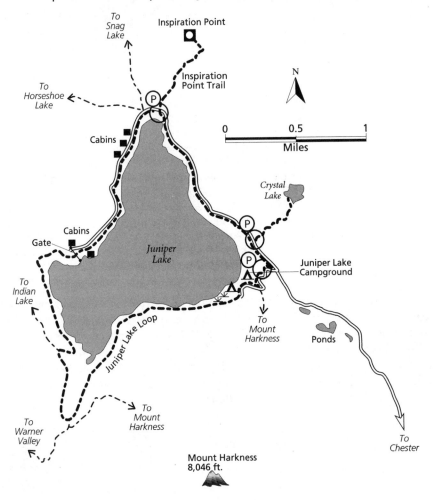

marshy meadow, then embarks on a traverse of the lake's south shore, closely tracing every wooded nook and tiny cove. Though basically flat, the footpath does twist in and out and dip up and down, a roller coaster without the wheels. About 1 mile into the hike, the trail drops down to a rocky beach right on the waterline, then heads back into the woods above the lake.

At about the 1.5-mile mark, the trail veers south, away from the lakeshore, and into the woods at the foot of Mount Harkness's western slope. Pass a vernal pool, often dry by late summer, and then, at 1.7 miles, reach a four-way trail junction. The center trail leads straight (southwest) to the Warner Valley; the route to the left (east) climbs to the summit of Mount Harkness (Hike 42), and the trail to the right (north) goes to Indian Lake. A trail sign makes all this abundantly clear.

The loop continues by following the northern trail toward Indian Lake. Climb over a sunny hillock spread with pinemat manzanita, drop through the skinny bed of a seasonal stream, then ford Juniper Lake's outlet stream to the next trail intersection at 2.7 miles. The left (northwest) fork leads to Indian Lake; you want to stay right (north) on the trail that leads to the Juniper Lake Ranger Station, which lies 2.3 miles ahead.

A short, steep section of trail leads out of the ravine that cradles the outlet stream and back onto a relatively flat cruise above the lakeshore. Again, yellow dots mark the footpath, which rolls through the forest as it heads north. Landmarks include a marsh on the right (east) side of the trail, a nice little bay and beach (also on the lake side of the trail), and a couple of steep ravines carved by creeks that are dry by late summer or early fall.

At about the 3.5-mile mark, encounter the first of a strip of private cabins along the west shore of Juniper Lake. The narrow trail dumps onto a rough road at this point, which serves as access for those lucky enough to have property with a lake view. A trail sign, a yellow dot, and a gate mark the terminus of the footpath.

Continue north on the roadway; easy and meditative walking leads past cabins scattered in the woods. I call this walk-and-talk terrain, where you can hike side-by-side with your partner and don't need to fear the consequences of a misstep if your attention wanders.

At 4.5 miles, you arrive at the Juniper Lake picnic area. From here, follow the Juniper Lake access road back to the campground—more walk-and-talk terrain, with gorgeous lake views and the occasional slow-moving automobile. The campground, and trail's end, is at 6.2 miles in the trailhead parking area.

Fishing at Jumiper Lake.

44 Crystal Lake

See Map on Page 168

Highlights:	This short, steep climb leads to a small tarn in a spectacular rock basin.
Type of hike:	Day hike; out-and-back.
Total distance:	0.8 mile.
Difficulty:	Easy.
Best months:	June–October.
Maps:	USGS Mount Harkness quad; Lassen Volcanic National Park maps by the National Park Service, Earthwalk Press, and Wilderness Press; USDAFS Lassen National Forest map.
Special considerations:	There is no potable water along the trail. Bring your own water, or purify water from Crystal Lake by boiling, filtering, or chemically treating it.
Parking and facilities:	There is only a small parking lot at the trailhead. For restrooms and picnic facilities, continue north on the Juniper Lake Road for 1.4 miles to the Juniper Lake picnic area. Restrooms are also available at the Juniper Lake Campground, which is 0.3 mile south on the Juniper Lake Road.

Finding the trailhead: From California Highway 36 in Chester, take the Feather River Road north for 0.7 mile to the road fork. Go right (northwest) on the Juniper Lake Road (Plumas County 318). Follow the Juniper Lake Road for 11.7 miles to the Juniper Lake Campground; the pavement ends after 5.5 miles and you pass the park entrance signs at 9 miles. Go 0.3 mile north of the campground access road to a small parking area at the trailhead, which is on the right (east) side of the road.

Key points:

0.0   Crystal Lake Trailhead.
0.4   Reach the shore of Crystal Lake.

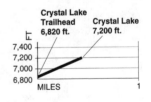

The hike: Crystal Lake is the perfect destination for the adventuresome family camped at Juniper Lake, or for the visitor with limited time or stamina (or both). The ascent to the small, sunny lake is short, with switchbacks doing an almost adequate job of moderating the steepness of the trail—it may be brief, but it is enough to get the heart pumping and the thighs burning.

Crystal Lake rests in a depression at the lip of a rock-rimmed valley. Folds of gray rock, which serve perfectly as seats for contemplation, spill into the clear water. The more ambitious can clamber over these rocks to explore the far shore of the lake, which is equally inviting.

The trail begins in the woods, and crosses the lake's outlet creek almost immediately. Yellow dots on the trees mark the easy-to-follow trail. The climb away from the Juniper Lake Road is moderate at first, gradually growing steeper (and steeper) as it snakes through young firs and pines.

The forest opens as the pitch of the trail abruptly sharpens, allowing greenleaf manzanita to grow beyond the "throw-rug" stage into shrubs standing two to three feet in height. Cross the creek again (dry in late season), and continue the upward traverse.

Climb one switchback, round a broader S-curve, and then ascend two more switchbacks before the final pitch leads alongside the lake's outlet stream. The trail veers right (northeast) onto the folded rock benches that guard the southern edge of the lake at 0.4 mile. Clamber about or contemplate for a spell, admiring the lake's smooth clear waters and the red cinder hummock to the northeast. You may also choose to circle the lake on social trails, which skitter over the rock outcrops and thread through the open woodlands that clothe the lakeshore.

When you are ready, return as you came, enjoying views of Mount Harkness and Juniper Lake as you begin your descent to the trailhead.

45 Inspiration Point

See Map on Page 168

Highlights: A spectacular circle of views can be enjoyed from Inspiration Point, including Lassen Peak, Prospect Peak, and Mount Harkness.
Type of hike: Day hike; out-and-back.
Total distance: 1.2 miles.
Difficulty: Moderate.
Best months: June–September.
Maps: USGS Mount Harkness quad; Lassen Volcanic National Park maps by the National Park Service, Earthwalk Press, and Wilderness Press; USDAFS Lassen National Forest map.
Special considerations: There is no water along the trail.
Parking and facilities: There is only a small parking area at the trailhead, but restrooms and picnic facilities are available at the adjacent Juniper Lake picnic area.

Finding the trailhead: From California Highway 36 in the town of Chester, take the Feather River Road north for 0.7 mile to the Y intersection. Go right (north) on the Juniper Lake Road (Plumas County 318); the left (northwest) fork leads to Drakesbad. Follow the Juniper Lake Road for 13.4 miles to the picnic area at the north end of Juniper Lake; the pavement ends after 5.5 miles, the park entrance signs are at 9 miles, and the Juniper Lake Campground is passed at 11.7 miles. The small parking area is to the right (north) of the road about 50 feet east of the picnic area parking lot.

Key points:
0.0 Juniper Lake Picnic Area Trailhead.
0.6 Reach Inspiration Point.

The hike: To the north, Prospect Peak hovers over the Cinder Cone, the Fantastic Lava Beds, and Snag Lake. The Red Cinder Cone and Red Cinder rise out of a broad expanse of forest that spreads northeast. Looking south, Juniper Lake lies cool and blue below the balding summit of Mount Harkness. And to the west, just visible through the crowns of the trees, Lassen Peak, barren and streaked with snow even as the season edges from summer to fall, lords over it all. These wonderful views are more than ample reward for making the quick climb to Inspiration Point.

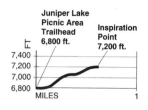

The trail begins at the northern edge of the parking area, and begins to climb immediately through a forest dominated by red firs and spotted with a patchwork of small meadows and plots of manzanita.

After 0.2 mile, the path steepens, winding upward through the woodland to an open, sunny bench. Traverse north and east across the bench; the incline of the trail moderates for the crossing. Once back in the forest, quick switchbacks lead up a final pitch that ends on the crest of a ridge, which is overgrown with manzanita. The trail veers left (west), climbing to the summit of the rocky knoll dubbed Inspiration Point at 0.6 mile.

The views are stunning, the exposure is sweet, and when the sun warms the rocks that serve as seats from which to contemplate the panorama, it's nearly impossible to tear yourself away. When you do, follow the same path back to the trailhead.

Lassen peeks through the trees on Inspiration Point.

46 Jakey Lake

Highlights:	Chances are that even in the height of the summer season, you'll have lonely Jakey Lake all to yourself.
Type of hike:	Day hike or backpack; out-and-back.
Total distance:	6 miles.
Difficulty:	Moderate.
Best months:	July–September.
Maps:	USGS Mount Harkness quad; Lassen Volcanic National Park maps by the National Park Service, Earthwalk Press, and Wilderness Press; USDAFS Lassen National Forest map.
Special considerations:	There is no potable water at the trailhead or along the route. Either pack in all water, or boil, filter, or chemically purify water from Jakey Lake. If you choose to backpack to Jakey Lake and points beyond, abide by the park's backcountry regulations by securing a backcountry permit and by setting up camp at least 100 feet away from water sources and trails.
Parking and facilities:	There is ample parking, as well as restrooms and picnic facilities, at the Juniper Lake picnic area. Camping is available at the Juniper Lake Campground, which is 1.7 miles south on the Juniper Lake Road.

Finding the trailhead: From California Highway 36 in the town of Chester, take the Feather River Road north for 0.7 mile to the Y intersection. Go right (north) on the Juniper Lake Road (Plumas County 318); the left (northwest) fork leads to Drakesbad. Follow the Juniper Lake Road for 13.4 miles to the picnic area at the north end of Juniper Lake; the pavement ends after 5.5 miles, the park entrance signs are at 9 miles, and the Juniper Lake Campground is passed at 11.7 miles.

Key points:

0.0	Juniper Lake picnic area Trailhead.
1.5	Reach the trail crossing above Cameron Meadow.
3.0	Arrive on the shores of Jakey Lake.

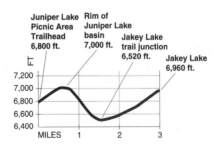

The hike: Jakey Lake is embedded so deeply in the backcountry that hiking to its shores is akin to stepping back in time. The route is so little used that the only signs of life I saw on the winding, overgrown trail were the scat of forest animals, and the prints of deer and something with claws—raccoon? Wildcat? Coyote? Baby bear? Regardless, there was nary a waffle stomp in sight, let alone a person in the flesh. If you thrive on solitude, this trail's for you.

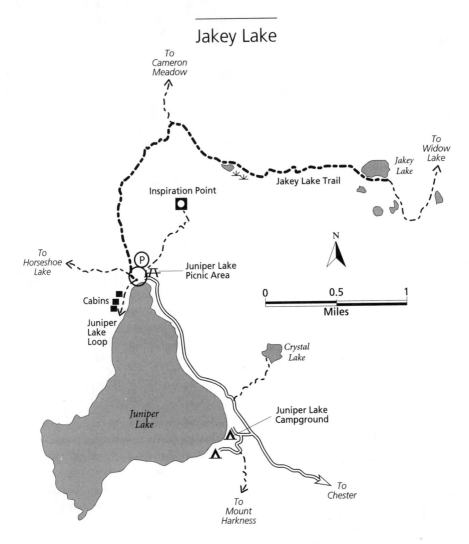

Jakey Lake

To Cameron Meadow

To Widow Lake

Jakey Lake

Jakey Lake Trail

Inspiration Point

To Horseshoe Lake

P

Juniper Lake Picnic Area

Cabins

Juniper Lake Loop

N

0   0.5   1

Miles

Crystal Lake

Juniper Lake

Juniper Lake Campground

To Chester

To Mount Harkness

Jakey Lake itself possesses all the charms typical of wilderness lakes. Open to the sky, its dark surface is rippled by winds. It is entirely circled by a thick woodland, which screens any sign of the park's mountainous landmarks, including Lassen Peak.

The route begins on the west side of the picnic area parking lot by the flagpole. A trail sign indicates the distance to both Jakey Lake and Snag Lake; go right (northwest) on the trail. The next sign and trail fork is about 50 yards beyond, where the potential destinations and corresponding mileages are detailed much more extensively. Go right (north) on the trail to Cameron Meadow and Jakey Lake, which is 2.8 miles distant.

Yellow dots mark the route through the open woodland; it's a fairly easy and straightforward uphill track through the rolling, fir-forested terrain that is common around Juniper Lake and other areas of the park.

Crest the ridge of the Juniper Lake basin; the trail flattens briefly before beginning a steep descent. Prospect Peak is just visible through the trees to the north. The path levels in a small meadow, then plunges down switchbacks to another meadow and a trail intersection at 1.5 miles.

The trail to Jakey Lake breaks off to the right (east); the trail to the left (northwest) leads to Cameron Meadow and Snag Lake (Hike 47). Yellow dots, sparse and sometimes rusted over, aid in route-finding. The Jakey Lake trail climbs gently through the woodland, crossing a small stream that is dry in late season, then proceeds another 0.1 mile to Jakey Lake's outlet stream. Continue to ascend, following the bed of the creek as both terrain and trail grow more rugged.

Cross the creek at about the 2-mile mark, and a meadow opens on the right (south) side of the trail. Broad, marshy ponds lie across the grasses—or perhaps it's the grasses that lie across the ponds—either way, the bugs can be extremely bothersome at this point. The trail skirts the left (north) side of the meadow, passing a copse of willow before climbing fairly steeply onto a bench, where a huge fallen tree blocks the path.

Climb over the deadfall; the trail flattens, and continues eastward until it returns to the bank of the stream. (Note: This stream doesn't appear on the USGS topographic map of the area.)

You have to scramble over another huge fallen tree before you make the final approach to Jakey Lake. The lake, tucked in its shallow, forested bowl and rimmed with a thin ribbon of verdant grass, is at the 3-mile mark.

A trail sign on the lakeshore indicates that Widow Lake can be reached by continuing on the path that skirts the south shore of the lake. Topographic maps of the area confirm this, but the trail becomes increasingly sketchy as you proceed, and eventually fades into the deadfall that blankets the forest floor below the Red Cinder Cone and Red Cinder. Unless you are a skilled cross-country traveler, I recommend that you return as you came. The trail between Jakey Lake and Widow Lake may be improved in future summer seasons: Check with a park ranger about trail conditions if you choose to follow this route.

47 Cameron Meadow and Grassy Creek Loop

Highlights:	The canyon that cradles Grassy Creek, sometimes steep and always lush with riparian plants, is a joy to travel along. Three good-sized lakes also spice the route.
Type of hike:	Day hike or backpack; loop.
Total distance:	7.4 miles.
Difficulty:	Strenuous.
Best months:	July–September.
Maps:	USGS Mount Harkness and Prospect Peak quads; Lassen Volcanic National Park maps by the National Park Service, Earthwalk Press, and Wilderness Press; USDAFS Lassen National Forest map.
Special considerations:	There is no potable water at the trailhead or along the route. Either pack in all water, or boil, filter, or chemically purify water from lakes or streams. If you choose to camp near Snag Lake, abide by the park's backcountry regulations by securing a backcountry permit and by setting up camp at least 100 feet away from water sources and trails.
Parking and facilities:	There is ample parking, as well as restrooms and picnic facilities, at the Juniper Lake picnic area. Camping is available at the Juniper Lake Campground, which is 1.7 miles south on the Juniper Lake Road.

Finding the trailhead: From California Highway 36 in the town of Chester, take the Feather River Road north for 0.7 mile to the Y intersection. Go right (north) on the Juniper Lake Road (Plumas County 318); the left (northwest) fork leads to Drakesbad. Follow the Juniper Lake Road for 13.4 miles to the picnic area at the north end of Juniper Lake; the pavement ends after 5.5 miles, and the Juniper Lake Campground is at 11.7 miles.

Key points:
- 0.0 Juniper Lake Picnic Area Trailhead.
- 1.5 Reach the intersection with the trail to Jakey Lake.
- 1.8 Pass the shortcut trail.
- 2.0 Cameron Meadow bounds the trail on the east.
- 2.9 Arrive at Snag Lake.
- 3.2 Reach the junction with the Grassy Creek Trail.
- 6.0 Arrive at Horseshoe Lake.
- 7.4 Return to the Juniper Lake Trailhead.

Cameron Meadow and Grassy Creek Loop

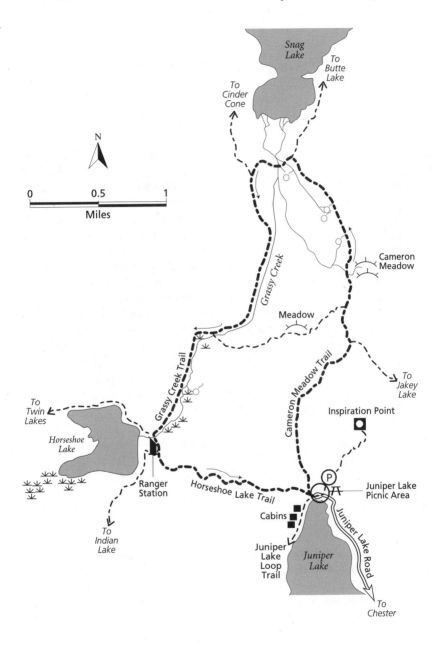

N

0   0.5   1
Miles

Snag Lake

To Butte Lake

To Cinder Cone

Grassy Creek

Cameron Meadow

Meadow

To Jakey Lake

Cameron Meadow Trail

Inspiration Point

Grassy Creek Trail

To Twin Lakes

Horseshoe Lake

Ranger Station

Horseshoe Lake Trail

P

Juniper Lake Picnic Area

Cabins

Juniper Lake Road

To Indian Lake

Juniper Lake Loop Trail

Juniper Lake

To Chester

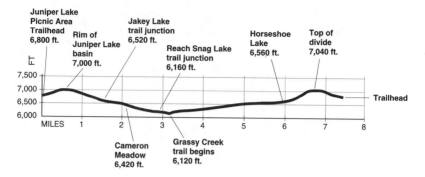

Juniper Lake
Picnic Area
Trailhead
6,800 ft.

Rim of
Juniper Lake
basin
7,000 ft.

Jakey Lake
trail junction
6,520 ft.

Reach Snag Lake
trail junction
6,160 ft.

Horseshoe
Lake
6,560 ft.

Top of
divide
7,040 ft.

Cameron
Meadow
6,420 ft.

Grassy Creek
trail begins
6,120 ft.

Trailhead

The hike: Sometimes spilling in dramatic cataracts, sometimes gurgling over jumbles of river cobbles, sometimes carving a sinuous path through luminously green meadows, Grassy Creek, like an energetic young child, presents many faces. It is the focal point of this trail loop, but the route, too, is multi-faceted, weaving through dense forest, passing the southern reaches of Snag Lake, and skirting the heavily wooded shores of Horseshoe Lake. You can even catch views of Lassen Peak on the final ascent—a gratifying parting shot before you rest on the beach at the north shore of Juniper Lake.

The loop is described here counterclockwise, but this is a purely arbitrary decision on my part—there are no serious steeps that make this choice wiser than the alternative. A cutoff trail lies midway between Juniper Lake and Snag Lake, offering a quick out for those who become footsore or run short on time.

The first part of this trail mimics the route to Jakey Lake (Hike 46); you can refer to that hike description if you need more details. The loop starts next to the flagpole on the west side of the Juniper Lake picnic area parking lot. Go right (northwest) on the trail to Snag Lake and Jakey Lake. Walk about 50 yards to the next sign and trail junction, and go right (north) on the trail to Cameron Meadow and Jakey Lake.

Hike north and uphill through an open woodland on the obvious path, which is marked by yellow dots on the trees, to the crest of the ridge overlooking the Juniper Lake basin. The trail flattens briefly as it crosses the ridge, then heads sharply down on a descent that is broken only briefly by a small meadow. You arrive at the junction of the trails to Jakey Lake and Cameron Meadow at 1.5 miles.

The trail to the left (north) leads to Cameron Meadow and Snag Lake; the Jakey Lake trail heads right (east). The Cameron Meadow trail is rough as it continues downhill to a stream crossing, then to the intersection with the shortcut trail (1.8 miles), which leads left (west) to Grassy Creek and up to Horseshoe Lake. Stay right (north) on the trail to Cameron Meadow, passing through an area thick with deadfall before you reach the grasses and marsh at the meadow's edge.

The heart of Cameron Meadow lies to the right (east) of the footpath at about the 2-mile mark. Cross one of the streamlets that waters the meadow— yellow dots mark the way—and continue on the now flat path. Enough light filters through the forest's canopy to propagate a lush green understory of ferns, grasses, and wildflowers.

A final descent through the woods lands you near the south shore of Snag Lake at 2.9 miles. The bulk of the lake can't be seen through the thick stands of timber; it shimmers bright and white between the trunks. At the trail intersection, go left (west) toward Horseshoe Lake; the right-hand (east) trail leads to Butte Lake (Hike 40 includes a description of the trail between Butte and Snag Lakes).

The trail leads through a marsh spanned in spots by rustic log boardwalks that both help protect the tender vegetation and keep your boots dry. Yet another chance to get soggy feet presents itself at the crossing of Grassy Creek. The pier that juts into the rocky creekbed is just decoration; you must test your balance on the logs to get to the west bank of the creek.

Continue west on the trail, which wanders through the woodland, then curves south and uphill to the next trail intersection at 3.2 miles. To continue the loop, turn right (south) on the trail to Horseshoe Lake and Juniper Lake. The trail to the left (north), leading to Butte Lake, is described in Hike 40.

The trail begins to climb now, though not painfully. At this point, your only clue that Grassy Creek is in the proximity is the whine of mosquitoes and the flutter of dragonflies in pursuit of their favorite prey. The trail levels in a small meadow, where the rumble of the stream becomes louder. About 0.1 mile farther, and you can see the creek below and to the left (east).

Tumbling cataracts enliven the route, which ascends into the deep shade of a draw. Ferns, willows, and other riparian flora line the creek's course—it's clear how it earned its name. Those handy yellow dots, once again, help you stay on the right track.

A steep pitch takes you up to an open spot where flat rocks offer an opportunity to sit and enjoy the cataract. Beyond, wander through willows

Grassy Creek supports a rich riparian zone.

and cross an area where the steep hillside has slid. The footing on the slide is tricky, but good.

At the 4.6-mile mark, the draw opens a bit and Grassy Creek has a chance to meander through a narrow meadow. The shortcut trail passed on the way down to Cameron Meadow reaches the Grassy Creek trail at this point, coming in from the left (east).

About 50 feet beyond the trail intersection, the meadow widens considerably, and the trail skirts its right (west) side before the draw closes in again. Continue up the creek for another quarter of a mile or so to the next opening, where meadow grasses again flourish, and again the trail sticks to the right (west) side.

Climb up and over a wooded hummock, then drop into more meadowlands. Trace the edge of the meadow to the trail crossing on the west bank of Grassy Creek at 6 miles. It's clear at this point that Grassy Creek is the outlet for Horseshoe Lake, which arcs south and west of the trail intersection, hidden behind a screen of evergreens.

The loop continues to the left (east), where the trail sign indicates that Juniper Lake—the end of the line—lies 1.4 miles distant. The trail to the right (west) leads around Horseshoe Lake and links to trails leading to Lower Twin Lake and the Warner Valley. Cross Grassy Creek on a split log bridge, then leave it behind as you hike past the Horseshoe Lake Ranger Station to the next trail intersection. The trail to Indian Lake (Hike 49) breaks off to the right (south); keep left (east) on the loop, which now follows an old roadbed.

The broad track climbs easily at first, but the pitch steepens as it rolls over benches below the crest of the saddle separating the Horseshoe Lake basin from Juniper Lake. As you approach the summit of the saddle, turn around and look west; Lassen Peak rises in the distance, framed by red firs.

The top of the saddle is nice and flat, with pinemat manzanita blanketing open spaces. After traversing the saddle, drop off toward Juniper Lake; the forest is much denser on this side of the pass. Juniper Lake quickly comes into view off to the right (south). The trailhead is reached at the 7.4-mile mark.

Option: If you choose to take the shortcut trail, this is what you see: Beginning on the Cameron Meadow Trail, the narrow path begins a steep ascent through the woods, then levels as it reaches a small, verdant, insect-infested meadow. Pass the meadow on its south side, then climb through widely spaced trees to cross a second tiny meadow. The trail rolls across the top of a knoll, then dives down through meadowy grasses to Grassy Creek. Cross logs to the trail intersection on the west side of the creekbed, where you can turn right (south) to Horseshoe Lake, or left (north) to Snag Lake. The trail is about 0.8 mile in length.

48 Horseshoe Lake

Highlights:	Hike from one pretty lake to the next, enjoying views of Lassen Peak at the trail's high point.
Type of hike:	Day hike; out-and-back.
Total distance:	2.8 miles.
Difficulty:	Easy.
Best months:	July–September.
Maps:	USGS Mount Harkness quad; Lassen Volcanic National Park maps by the National Park Service, Earthwalk Press, and Wilderness Press; USDAFS Lassen National Forest map.
Special considerations:	There is no potable water along the trail. Carry all you'll need; if you must drink from either of the lakes along the route, be sure to purify the water first.
Parking and facilities:	There is ample parking, as well as restrooms and picnic facilities, at the Juniper Lake Picnic Area. Camping is available at the Juniper Lake Campground, which is 1.7 miles south on the Juniper Lake Road.

Finding the trailhead: From California Highway 36 in the town of Chester, take the Feather River Road north for 0.7 mile to the Y intersection. Go right (north) on the Juniper Lake Road (Plumas County 318); the left (northwest) fork leads to Drakesbad. Follow the Juniper Lake Road for 13.4 miles to the picnic area at the north end of Juniper Lake; the pavement ends after 5.5 miles, and the Juniper Lake Campground is at 11.7 miles.

Key points:

0.0   Juniper Lake Picnic Area Trailhead.
0.5   Reach the top of the saddle.
1.4   Arrive at the Horseshoe Lake Ranger Station.

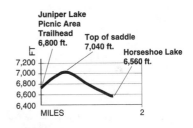

The hike: The phrase is hackneyed, but there's really no better way to put it: the hike from Juniper Lake to Horseshoe Lake is short and sweet. The track is wide and impossible to lose, the climbing is moderate, the view of Lassen Peak from the saddle is lovely, and there is a restful lake at either end of the trail. It is the perfect choice for a day hike with the family or a good buddy—you can walk side by side and discuss conservation or land preservation without fear of straying from the route or missing the vistas.

The trail begins at the trailhead near the flagpole on the west side of the Juniper Lake picnic area parking lot. Go right (northwest) on the trail to Snag Lake and Jakey Lake, walk about 50 yards to the next sign and trail junction, and turn left (northwest) on the old roadbed. The trail sign indicates that Horseshoe Lake is 1.4 miles ahead, and lists other destinations

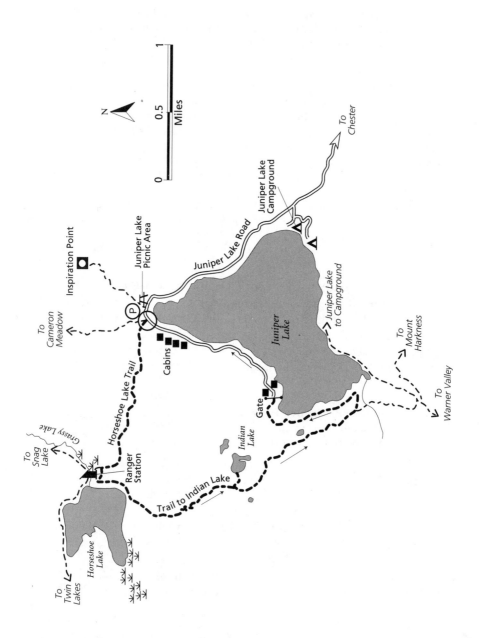

Little House in the Big Woods: The ranger station at Horseshoe Lake.

that can be reached via the trail. The trail to the right (north) heads out to Jakey Lake and Cameron Meadow (Hikes 46 and 47).

The initial uphill section is short and heavily shaded by a thick, red fir forest. You will reach the crest of the saddle between the two lakes at 0.5 mile, having hardly broken a sweat. The trees are more widely spaced on the broad saddle, and Lassen Peak rises directly west, its pink and white slopes sharply outlined against the deep blue of the high country sky, and framed by the browns and greens of the forest.

It's all downhill from the summit of the saddle to Horseshoe Lake. Though the trail winds through a more open forest, the vistas quickly disappear as you lose altitude. At 1.3 miles, the trail flattens in a clearing, where the trail to Indian Lake (Hike 49) breaks off to the left (south). The ranger station lies nestled in a stand of trees on the southwest side of the clearing. Continue west past the ranger station, crossing Grassy Creek, and, at 1.4 miles, you stand at a second trail intersection near the shoreline of Horseshoe Lake.

Good views of the lake are elusive; it pulls its cloak of trees right to its edge, tucking into a heavy woodland blanket. The trail that leads left (north and west) along its northern shoreline is your best bet if you want to find a place to sit at the waterside; the trail to the right (southeast) leads down the Grassy Creek drainage to Snag Lake. The clearing near the ranger station is more inviting as a picnic spot; it is open to the sunshine, though the lake is well-screened by the woods.

Unless you choose to continue to Indian Lake or some other destination, this is the end of the line. Return as you came.

49 Horseshoe and Indian Lakes Loop

See Map on Page 182

Highlights: Three lakes and vistas of two of the most prominent volcanoes in the park accent this loop. Pretty little Indian Lake is tucked in a shallow basin at the apex of the trail.

Type of hike: Day hike; out-and-back.

Total distance: 6.4 miles.

Difficulty: Moderate.

Best months: July–September.

Maps: USGS Mount Harkness quad; Lassen Volcanic National Park maps by the National Park Service, Earthwalk Press, and Wilderness Press; USDAFS Lassen National Forest map.

Special considerations: There is no potable water along the trail. If you must drink from any of the lakes along the route, be sure to purify the water first.

Parking and facilities: There is ample parking, as well as restrooms and picnic facilities, at the Juniper Lake picnic area. Camping is available at the Juniper Lake Campground, which is 1.7 miles south on the Juniper Lake Road.

Finding the trailhead: From California Highway 36 in the town of Chester, take the Feather River Road north for 0.7 mile to the Y intersection. Go right (north) on the Juniper Lake Road (Plumas County 318); the left (northwest) fork leads to Drakesbad. Follow the Juniper Lake Road for 13.4 miles to the picnic area at the north end of Juniper Lake; the pavement ends after 5.5 miles, and the Juniper Lake Campground is passed at 11.7 miles.

Key points:

0.0	Juniper Lake Picnic Area Trailhead.
0.5	Reach the top of the saddle.
1.3	Arrive at the junction with the trail to Indian Lake.
2.8	Drop down the spur trail to the shores of Indian Lake.
4.1	Reach the trail intersection near Juniper Lake's outlet stream.
6.4	Return to the Juniper Lake Trailhead.

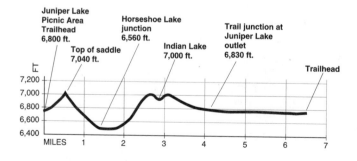

The hike: There is something invigorating about leaving the main route to reach a destination. And though Indian Lake lies within 0.25 mile of the security of a designated trail, you'll be treated to a whisper of that adventure. The path to the lakeshore is little more than a game trail, and, because the tarn is tucked in a rather steep-walled basin, out of sight of the park's familiar landmarks, you can imagine yourself in any wilderness, a trailblazer in the unknown. Of course, you can also simply savor the seclusion, soaking in quiet sunshine on the lake's narrow but welcoming beaches.

On the trail to and from the lake, those familiar park landmarks I've just referred to are in abundant evidence. You can enjoy views of Lassen Peak from the saddle between Juniper Lake and Horseshoe Lake, as well as on the climb to Indian Lake, and Mount Harkness dominates the southeastern horizon on the descent from the trail's apex.

As with all loops, this one can be hiked in either a clockwise or counterclockwise direction. It is described here counterclockwise, finishing with a flat and easy walk along the shores of Juniper Lake.

The trail begins near the flagpole on the west side of the Juniper Lake picnic area parking lot. Go right (northwest) on the trail to Snag Lake and Jakey Lake; walk about 50 yards to the next sign and trail junction, where you go left (northwest) to Horseshoe Lake, which is 1.4 miles ahead. The trail to the right (north) leads to Jakey Lake (Hike 46) and other destinations to the north and east.

The broad track climbs westward through a forest dominated by red firs to the crest of the saddle at 0.5 mile. Lassen Peak rises to the west, framed by the widely spaced trees on the saddle.

Continue down on the broad, winding track to the junction with the trail to Indian Lake at 1.3 miles, which is in a clearing near the western shore of Horseshoe Lake. The Horseshoe Lake Ranger Station is 100 feet west of the intersection. The trail to Indian Lake breaks off to the left (south), with the path to the right (west) leading to Grassy Creek and a second junction with trails leading north and east into other regions of the park.

The trail to Indian Lake is well signed—a "gold medal" trail, in which the yellow dots on trees seen elsewhere in the park have been replaced by metallic disks bearing the likeness of a hiker.

Though you are tracing the shoreline of Horseshoe Lake, a wall of thick trees hides the water. After 0.2 mile, reach another trail sign, indicating Indian Lake is a mile distant, and the big up begins.

A single flat bench breaks the steep ascent to the top of the ridge that borders Horseshoe Lake on its south side. Take advantage of this short rest, for above, the trail climbs out of the fir forest and onto more exposed slopes, where low-growing manzanita offers no shade from the sometimes brutal summer sun.

Widely spaced stands of evergreens occasionally shadow the trail as it tops out on the broad, wind-whipped ridge. The views are great: Scanning northwest to southwest, you can see West Prospect Peak, Hat Mountain, the Chaos Crags, Lassen Peak, the Pilot Pinnacle, and Mount Diller, among others.

Drop down the south side of the ridge over rolling terrain. Yellow dots have replaced the gold medals, and views of Mount Harkness have replaced views of Lassen Peak. At 2.8 miles, you reach the Indian Lake sign. The social trail to the lake, which lies in a rocky depression to the east, breaks off to the left, and drops about 100 feet in altitude and less than 0.2 mile in distance to the lakeshore. The evergreens, meadow grasses, wildflowers, and still water conspire to create a lovely setting for resting, contemplation, and picnicking.

When you're ready, climb back onto the main trail and go left (southeast), walking through open forest, passing a pond covered with lily pads, and a spill of talus as you continue. Skirt another little pond in a sink on the right (west), then begin to descend in earnest toward Juniper Lake and the base of Mount Harkness, the trail rolling over sunlit terraces as it drops.

Forest closes in on the path as you reach the trail intersection near Juniper Lake's outlet stream at 4.1 miles. Turn sharply left (north) to continue the loop; the right-hand trail leads east and south to Mount Harkness and the Warner Valley.

The climb away from the outlet stream is steep but short, and beyond, you will follow a relatively flat track along the shore of Juniper Lake. Yellow dots mark the footpath, which leads past a marsh, a small bay and beach, and a couple of steep ravines carved by creeks that are dry by late summer or early fall.

At about 5.5 miles, the trail spills onto a rough dirt road that serves as access to private cabins along the lake's west shore. A trail sign, gate, and yellow dot mark the end of the singletrack. Follow the roadway, which passes the cute cabins and offers nice views of the lake to the right (east) to the Juniper Lake Picnic Area, which is at 6.4 miles.

Drakesbad and the Warner Valley

Tucked near the head of the Warner Valley, the Drakesbad area of Lassen Volcanic National Park has long been a favorite destination of visitors to Lassen country. And for good reason. Though views of Lassen Peak, the park's centerpiece, are not dominant here, the presence of the volcano is felt in myriad ways. The pool at the Drakesbad Guest Ranch is filled with water warmed by volcanism; farther afield, that same volcanic activity fires up Boiling Springs Lake, Terminal Geyser, and the Devils Kitchen. On the cooler side, the spectacular mountain landscape is epitomized by the steepness of the walls of Warner Valley, the thickness of its mixed conifer forests, the snow-fed vigor of Hot Springs Creek, and the secluded peace of Drake Lake.

The area got its name from a late-nineteenth-century settler named Edward Drake, who, in addition to other activities, offered baths in the mineral waters of the area. Later, the Sifford family, which purchased the area from Drake, cultivated the area's resort status, building a formal, though rustic, bathhouse and offering other amenities, including camping facilities and meals. It was the Siffords, too, who coined the moniker "Drakesbad," or Drake's Baths.

In the early 1900s, Drakesbad played an important role in earning the Lassen country status as a national park. Though not as impressive as the 1914–15 eruptions that drew national attention to the future park's uniqueness, Drakesbad was a favorite vacation spot of Congressman John E. Raker, who championed the park's designation. While he campaigned to have the area preserved as a park, Raker and his family visited the area often, and it was from here that the U.S. Government sent out parties to conduct surveys in the area. Drakesbad was so key to the park's popularity, in fact, that it was once considered the obvious choice for the park's gateway.

The Drakesbad area itself, however, remained a private inholding in the park until the mid-1950s, when it was finally acquired by the National Park Service. Today, visitors can stay at the Warner Valley Campground, which, while fairly rugged, boasts 18 campsites, fire rings, tables, water sources, and restrooms. A $12-per-night fee is levied to camp here.

In addition, the park's concessionaire, California Guest Services, Inc., runs the Drakesbad Guest Ranch, which is a wonderful choice for folks who only want to take "roughing it" so far. To contact the ranch in the off-season, from October to May, call (530) 529-9820. During season, ask your long-distance operator to contact the Susanville operator in area code (530), then ask for Drakesbad Toll Station Number 2.

All hikes listed in this section are reached via the Drakesbad Road (Plumas County 312), which begins north of Chester and ends at the Warner Valley Campground, Warner Valley Trailhead, and Drakesbad Guest Ranch. The route is well signed; take the Feather River Road/Plumas County 312 north from California Highway 36/89 in Chester for 17 miles to the road's terminus at Drakesbad. The road is paved for most of its distance, then becomes a rough gravel road for the final 3 miles. It is not recommended for trailers.

50 Dream Lake

Highlights:	A short, easy hike to a small lake that offers some fishing and lots of splendid mountain atmosphere.
Type of hike:	Day hike; out-and-back.
Total distance:	1.4 miles.
Best months:	Late May–October.
Maps:	USGS Reading Peak quad; Lassen Volcanic National Park maps by the National Park Service, Earthwalk Press, and Wilderness Press; USDAFS Lassen National Forest map.
Difficulty:	Easy.
Special considerations:	There is no potable water available at the trailhead or along the trail. The lake's environs are perfect bug-breeding territory, so use insect repellent.
Parking and facilities:	You will find portable restrooms, an informational kiosk, and picnic tables at the trailhead. The parking area accommodates about 15 cars. More parking is available at the Warner Valley Campground Trailhead, located about 0.5 mile east, back down the road. The campground has restrooms as well.

Finding the trailhead: From Chester, take the Feather River Road north for less than 1 mile to the first fork in the road. Go left (northwest) on Plumas County 312, following the signs for Drakesbad; the right (northeast) road (Plumas County 318) leads to Juniper Lake. At the next road fork at about 5 miles, go right (north), again following the Drakesbad sign. Follow this narrow road for more than 10 miles; the road's surface changes from paved to gravel for the final 3 miles. The trailhead picnic and parking area is on the left side of the road, beyond the Warner Valley Campground and before the Drakesbad Guest Ranch.

Key points:

0.0	Warner Valley Trailhead.
0.4	Reach the trail fork and take the right (north) trail toward Devils Kitchen.
0.6	At the trail fork, turn left (west).
0.7	Reach Dream Lake.

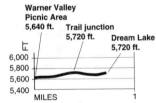

The hike: The trail to Dream Lake is a perfect romp for families with children—especially those who are beginning anglers. The route offers most of what a good hike in Lassen Volcanic National

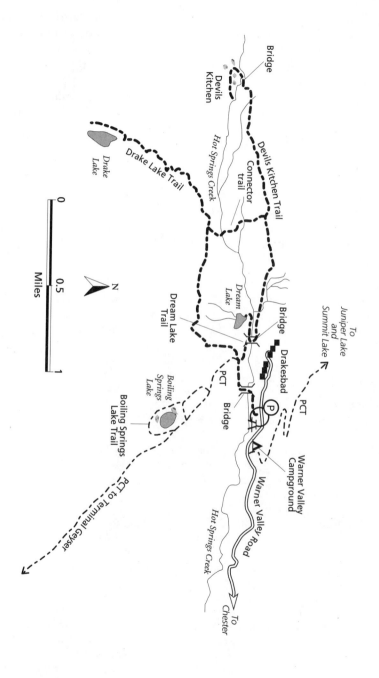

Park should, including a safe crossing over roaring Hot Springs Creek, a traverse over a meadowy slope wet with trickling hot springs water, and a serene lake as its final destination. Aaah.

Begin at the Warner Valley Trailhead, on the trail that also leads to Boiling Springs Lake and Devils Kitchen. The path winds streamside over small footbridges and boardwalks to the bridge that spans Hot Springs Creek. Cross the creek, and traverse through the meadow, crossing the small threads of warm water that flow across the trail.

At 0.4 mile, reach the first of two neighboring trail intersections. Go right (west) at the first trail intersection. The trail drops to cross a footbridge; orange dots mark the trees along the route. Stay right (west and meadowside), ignoring the path beaten through the grass by horses. Cross a second, then a third footbridge as the trail meanders through alternating forest and marsh. Two more small bridges span shallow streams before you reach a trail intersection at 0.6 mile. Take the left (south) trail, crossing the plank bridge, then climb a short distance to the placid, grass-lined shores of Dream Lake. There are plenty of places to explore or sit along the lakeshore, and while angling generally is not rewarding in any Lassen lake, this one offers as good a chance as any. Return as you came to the trailhead.

Options: You can reach both Devils Kitchen and the Drakesbad Guest Ranch from the plank bridge at the trail intersection below the lake. To reach Devils Kitchen, see the Hike 52 trail description. The guest ranch lies 0.3 mile north across the meadow, in plain sight of the trail intersection.

51 Drake Lake

See Map on Page 189

Highlights:	A steep hike to a secluded lake. The climb, fortunately, features stunning views of the Warner Valley.
Type of hike:	Day hike; out-and-back.
Total distance:	4.8 miles.
Best months:	Late June–early October.
Maps:	USGS Reading Peak quad; Lassen Volcanic National Park maps by the National Park Service, Earthwalk Press, and Wilderness Press; USDAFS Lassen National Forest map.
Difficulty:	Strenuous.
Special considerations:	This trail is very steep and dry. Bring plenty of water.
Parking and facilities:	Portable restrooms, information signs, and picnic tables are located at the trailhead. The parking area accommodates about 15 cars. More parking is available at the Warner Valley Campground Trailhead, located about 0.5 mile east, back down the road. Restrooms are also available at the campground.

Finding the trailhead: From Chester, take the Feather River Road (Plumas County 312) north for less than 1 mile to the first fork in the road. Go left (northwest), following the signs for Drakesbad; the right (northeast) road (Plumas County 318) leads to Juniper Lake. At the next road fork at about 5 miles, go right (north), again following the Drakesbad sign. Follow this narrow road for more than 10 miles; the road's surface changes from paved to gravel for the final three miles. The trailhead picnic and parking area is on the left side of the road, beyond the Warner Valley Campground and before the Drakesbad Guest Ranch.

Key points:

0.0   Warner Valley trailhead.

0.4   Turn right (west) at the second of two neighboring trail intersections.

1.4   Pass the connecting trail intersection; Drake Lake is 1 mile ahead.

2.0   Trail moderates above steep, exposed slope.

2.4   Arrive at Drake Lake.

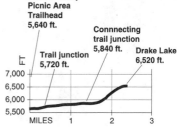

The hike: This is a lung and leg hike: Test your lung power on the way up, and your legs—especially your knees—on the way down. Fortunately, a lovely lake and fantastic views make the work more than worthwhile.

Drake Lake lies high above Drakesbad and the Warner Valley, and though the lower destinations in the area, like Boiling Springs Lake, get good traffic during the summer months, Drake Lake is seldom swamped. The shallow bowl that cradles the lake is rimmed in marsh grasses, wildflowers, and thick, mixed fir forest, so even if you do encounter other folks on the trail, you (and they) can find solitude and peace around the lakeshore.

The trail begins at the Warner Valley Trailhead. Walk up the valley to the west, crossing boardwalks in marshy areas. A bridge spans Hot Springs Creek, then the trail winds through the meadow above the Drakesbad pool, which is on the right (north). At 0.4 mile, reach the first trail intersection; go left (up and southwest) for about 50 yards to the second trail intersection, which is signed for Drake Lake. Go right (west) on the Drake Lake Trail.

Cross the first of many streams that bisect the trail as it heads west toward the head of the valley. This section of trail is frequented by horses (some might say thrashed by them), and just beyond the stream, you see where hooves have flattened the meadow grasses uphill to the left (southwest). Follow this up and into the woods. There are infrequent trail markers on the trees along the path, but the horses have guaranteed that it is easy to follow.

The trail is mainly flat through the forest, interspersed with a number of marshy areas and drainages that must be negotiated. Though you can't see it through the trees, the meadow that fills the upper reaches of Warner Valley, below and to the right (north), makes its presence known through fingers of grassland that pierce the forest, and a pervading moistness.

The climb is tough, but Drake Lake is a great reward.

At 1.4 miles, reach the trail marker for the connecting trail between the route to Drake Lake and the trail to Devils Kitchen (Hike 52). Stay straight (west) on the Drake Lake trail. About 0.1 mile ahead, the trail veers left (south) and begins to climb, crossing—you guessed it—yet another streamlet.

Emerge from the forest onto a dry, steep, manzanita-cloaked slope. Gear down and pump up your thighs: the climb is about to begin. A few switchbacks attempt to moderate the climb, with little effect. Eventually, Lassen Peak and Reading Peak peek above the northern ramparts of the Warner Valley. These views are obscured by trees once you climb a bit higher, but take heart: the encroaching woodland indicates lessening steepness and your proximity to the ultimate destination.

The incline becomes more humane as the trees thicken at about 2 miles, and the metallic hiking symbols that mark trees along the route vaguely resemble gold medals, which, after that climb, all hikers assuredly have earned. The rocky trail winds through the woods to the grassy lakeshore at 2.4 miles, where pausing to enjoy the pastoral setting—and rest quivering muscles—is a must.

Return as you came, enjoying spectacular views of the Warner Valley on the descent.

Option: A seldom-used, nearly cross-country trail leads south from Drake Lake to the park boundary, and beyond that, into the Rice Creek drainage.

52 Devils Kitchen

See Map on Page 189

Highlights: Climb through meadow and woodland to a thrilling hydrothermal area that straddles Hot Springs Creek.

Type of hike: Day hike; out-and-back.

Total distance: 4.2 miles.

Best months: June–October.

Maps: USGS Reading Peak quad; Lassen Volcanic National Park maps by the National Park Service, Earthwalk Press, and Wilderness Press; USDAFS Lassen National Forest map.

Difficulty: Moderate.

Special considerations: This trail visits one of the more secluded, varied, and volatile thermal areas in the park. Heed all warning signs, remaining on the trail at all times.

Parking and facilities: There are portable restrooms, information signs, and picnic tables at the trailhead. The parking area accommodates about 15 cars. More parking is available at the Warner Valley Campground Trailhead, located 0.5 mile east, back down the road. Restrooms are also available at the campground.

Finding the trailhead: From Chester, take the Feather River Road (Plumas County 312) north for less than 1 mile to the first fork in the road. Go left (northwest), following the signs for Drakesbad; the right (northeast) road (Plumas County 318) leads to Juniper Lake. At the next road fork at about 5 miles, go right (north), again following the Drakesbad sign. Follow this narrow road for more than 10 miles; the surface changes from paved to gravel for the final three miles. The trailhead picnic and parking area is on the left side of the road, beyond the Warner Valley Campground and before the Drakesbad Guest Ranch.

Key points:

0.0 Warner Valley Trailhead.

0.4 Reach the first trail intersection.

0.6 Pass the turnoff for Dream Lake.

1.2 Stay right (west) at the trail intersection for the cutoff trail, and continue climbing through the woods.

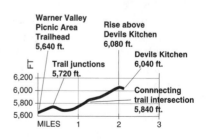

2.0 Crest the wooded hillside and look down into Devils Kitchen.

2.1 Loop through the footpaths that lace through the geothermal areas.

The hike: Belching fumeroles, boiling mudpots, steaming creeks, and rock outcrops in a dazzling array of fiery colors—the kitchen may be devilish and the stew may smell rotten, but the geologic pantry is full, and nature is cooking up a feast for the curious in this isolated spot.

The signs, sounds, and odors of the Devils Kitchen are served up from the safety of a safe network of pathways that wander through the area. Interpretive signs help decipher the sights. After a scrumptious appetizer that includes a pleasant, wildflower-spiced ramble through meadow and woodland, you'll find the main course more than satisfying.

As with most other hikes in this area, you depart from the Warner Valley Trailhead on the same trail that leads to Boiling Springs Lake. The path winds streamside over small footbridges and boardwalks to the bridge that spans Hot Springs Creek. Cross the creek, and traverse through the meadow to the first of two neighboring trail intersections at 0.4 mile. Go right (west) at the first trail intersection. Ignore the grassy path beaten down by horses after you cross the first stream, staying right (west). A series of footbridges through marsh and woodland leads to the trail intersection for Dream Lake at 0.6 mile. Go right (northwest) at this intersection, dropping toward the meadow.

Once in the meadow, the trail turns west toward the head of Warner Valley and rambles adjacent to meandering Hot Springs Creek. The grasses are dotted with wildflowers in midsummer and burnished gold in autumn; boardwalks make potentially soggy hiking a walk in the park. At the small bridge, look upstream at the miniature paddle wheels that turn with the flow—lazily if the stream is sluggish, more quickly if the flow is vigorous.

A crude bench marks where the trail leaves the meadow and climbs through transitional forest into the shady woodland. At 1.2 miles, reach a trail intersection: Drake Lake lies 1.4 miles to your left (south), and Devils Kitchen is 0.9 mile ahead (west).

Continue on the Devils Kitchen Trail, which climbs easily through the mixed fir forest. This woodland is quiet and peaceful; on a sunny autumn afternoon, I shared it only with a doe and her twins. The wind worked a lullaby in the branches, the melody punctuated by the muffled explosions of cones dropped from the trees by busy, harvesting squirrels.

After a steepening (but never terribly steep) climb, the trail dips through a grassy clearing watered by small, seasonal streams. The climb resumes, and if the wind is just right, you may catch the Halloween scent of sulfur emanating from the volcanic area that lies ahead and out of sight.

Skim the margin of a meadow as the trail flattens and threads between two grand incense cedars. Drop through another seasonal stream, then climb past a hitchrail to the rim of the kitchen at 2 miles.

Switchbacks lead down through singed trees, passing danger signs, to a bridge that spans cloudy Hot Springs Creek. The water spills into a steaming pool amid the denuded, opalescent rock.

An interpretive trail threads through the wonderland of the Devils Kitchen. For safety's sake—and to learn something about the geology of the area— remain on the trail at all times. Boiling cauldrons and steaming vents abound. One of the viewpoints overlooks the granddaddy of the area's mudpots; the earth vibrates with its furious boiling. A nearby fumerole has steamed the pink volcanic rock pea-green. After making a circuit of the kitchen, retrace your steps to the trailhead.

Option: A trail with a rather serious creek crossing links the Devils Kitchen trail and the trail to Drake Lake and the Boiling Springs/Terminal Geyser area. This link can be used to connect Devils Kitchen to Drake Lake, or to make a short loop around the meadow at the head of Warner Valley. It also can be used as an alternative to the horse-trod path that serves as the first 1.4 miles to Drake Lake, offering instead the Warner Valley meadow and the woodlands below Devils Kitchen as a warm-up for the climb.

The link is described here from east to west, beginning at the Devils Kitchen trail and ending on the Drake Lake Trail. Keep in mind, however, that you can traverse the trail in either direction. The description of the hike to Drake Lake (Hike 51), as well as this hike description, provide more details.

Begin by following the trail toward Devils Kitchen. At 1.2 miles, you will reach the connecting trail: Drake Lake lies 1.4 miles to your left (south), and Devils Kitchen is 0.9 mile straight ahead (west). Turn left (south) on the footpath, which drops from the Devils Kitchen Trail into grasses and willows, meandering through the dense thicket to a small stream crossing. Beyond, the trail reenters the woods.

The second creek crossing, which lies at about the midpoint of the trail, is more challenging: the water of Hot Springs Creek moves swiftly here, and the slick log crossing requires that you take care placing your feet. Once across, meadow grasses briefly encroach on the trail as you climb gently through the trees.

At 0.4 mile, you will reach the Drake Lake Trail. Drake Lake is 1 mile to the right (south), and the Warner Valley Campground and Trailhead is 1 mile to the left (east). Choose your destination and carry on.

53 Boiling Springs Lake

Highlights:	A short hike through dense forest to a geothermal lake.
Type of hike:	Day hike; out-and-back.
Total distance:	1.8 miles.
Difficulty:	Easy.
Maps:	USGS Reading Peak quad; Lassen Volcanic National Park maps by the National Park Service, Earthwalk Press, and Wilderness Press; USDAFS Lassen National Forest map.
Best months:	June–September.
Special considerations:	Remain on the trail once you reach the geothermal area surrounding Boiling Springs Lake. As with all geothermal and hydrothermal areas within the park, straying from the trail may result in serious burns.
Parking and facilities:	You will find portable restrooms, an informational kiosk, and picnic tables at the trailhead. The parking area accommodates about 15 cars. More parking is available at the Warner Valley Campground Trailhead, located about 0.5 mile east, back down the road. Restrooms are also available at the campground.

Finding the trailhead: From Chester, take the Feather River Road (Plumas County 312) north for less than 1 mile to the first fork in the road. Go left (northwest), following the signs for Drakesbad; the right (northeast) road (Plumas County 318) leads to Juniper Lake. At the next road fork at about 5 miles, go right (north), again following the Drakesbad sign. Follow this narrow road for more than 10 miles; the road's surface changes from paved to gravel for the final three miles. The trailhead picnic and parking area is on the left (south) side of the road, beyond the Warner Valley Campground and before the Drakesbad Guest Ranch.

Key points:

0.0   Warner Valley Picnic Area Trailhead.

0.4   Reach the first trail intersections. Go left at the second trail intersection.

0.9   Arrive at the shore of Boiling Springs Lake.

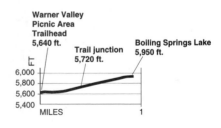

The hike: The milky green waters of Boiling Springs Lake are a relatively gentle example of the volcanic forces at work in Lassen Volcanic National Park. Set in a deep bowl, surrounded by steep cliffs topped by evergreens, the lake simmers peacefully, seeming to belie the warning signs that surround it.

The trail to the lake used to be interpretive, with signposts that corresponded to information provided in a small pamphlet describing both geothermal activity and the area's ecosystems. Since the area was deemed part

Boiling Springs Lake

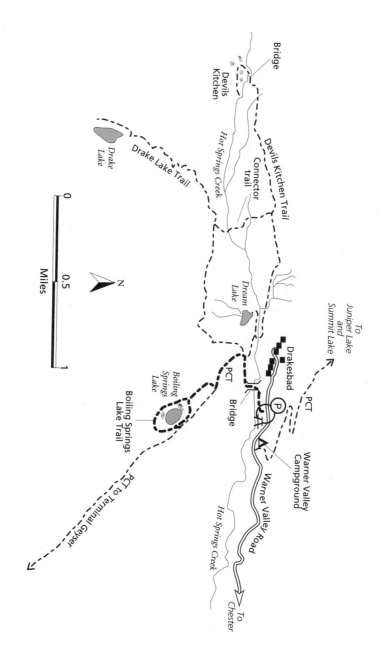

of the designated wilderness that comprises much of the park's backcountry, signposts and interpretive materials have been removed.

The trail, which is part of the Pacific Crest Trail (PCT) at this point, begins by rambling along boardwalks through the marshy area that forms the eastern shore of Hot Springs Creek. Cross a rustic bridge, then traverse above the creek on the hillside overlooking the Drakesbad Guest Ranch pool. Small, warm streams lined with algae intersect the route.

Two trail intersections follow in quick succession at 0.4 mile; stay left (south) at both, following the signs for Boiling Springs Lake and Terminal Geyser. The lake lies 0.5 mile ahead.

The trail climbs easily through thick forest to another trail intersection at 0.7 mile; Terminal Geyser is to the left (southeast) on the PCT, and the Boiling Springs Lake circuit trail begins 0.2 mile to the right (south). The trail flattens in the thick woodland alongside the lake's outlet stream, which is dry in late season and painted white by minerals.

As you approach the lake, signs appear warning of the dangers of the thermal area, and the trail forks. Go right (west), across the streambed and up to the lakeshore at 0.9 mile. Climb to the rim of the pastel-green lake and go right, circling the shoreline in a counterclockwise direction. At different points, you can stop and observe belching fumeroles and boiling mudpots, which thump persistently like the heartbeat of the earth. In early season, when water is plentiful, the thick, gray mud in the pots bubbles like hot cereal on a stovetop; in late season, they are more mysterious, their orifices crusted over, the source of the thumping hidden beneath a deceptively placid surface.

On the southeast shore of the lake, amid the trees that abut the steep embankment bordering the water, you encounter another couple of trail intersections; stay left (northward) on the circuit trail. At the north end of the lake, drop back to the start of the circuit. Retrace your steps from here back to the trailhead.

54 Terminal Geyser

Highlights: A ramble through dense forest and over a saddle to a secluded geyser.

Type of hike: Day hike; out-and-back.

Total distance: 5.4 miles.

Difficulty: Moderate.

Best months: June–early October.

Maps: USGS Reading Peak quad; Lassen Volcanic National Park maps by the National Park Service, Earthwalk Press, and Wilderness Press; USDAFS Lassen National Forest map.

Special considerations: This hike leads to a hydrothermal feature of the park, which, for safety's sake, necessitates that hikers heed all warning signs and remain on the trail.

Parking and facilities: You will find portable restrooms, an informational kiosk, and picnic tables at the trailhead. The parking area accommodates about 15 cars. More parking is available at the Warner Valley Campground trailhead, located 0.5 mile east, back down the road. Restrooms also are available at the campground.

Finding the trailhead: From Chester, take the Feather River Road (Plumas County 312) north for less than 1 mile to the first fork in the road. Go left (northwest), following the signs for Drakesbad; the right (northeast) road (Plumas County 318) leads to Juniper Lake. At the next road fork at about 5 miles, go right (north), again following the Drakesbad sign. Follow this narrow road for more than 10 miles; the road's surface changes from paved to gravel for the final three miles. The trailhead picnic and parking area is on the left (south) side of the road, beyond the Warner Valley Campground and before the Drakesbad Guest Ranch.

Key points:

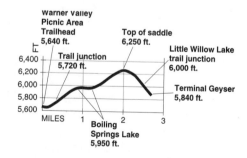

0.0 Warner Valley Picnic Area Trailhead.

0.4 Pass the first trail intersections.

0.9 Skirt the shores of Boiling Springs Lake.

1.2 Turn left (southeast) toward Terminal Geyser from the southeast shore of Boiling Springs Lake.

2.5 Pass the trail intersection with the Pacific Crest Trail to Little Willow Lake.

2.7 Reach the Terminal Geyser.

The hike: Despite its name, Terminal Geyser is not a geyser but an especially vigorous fumerole, a cleft in the surface of the earth hidden by a thick and perpetual cloak of hot steam. The geyser's white plume can be seen

Terminal Geyser • Little Willow Lake

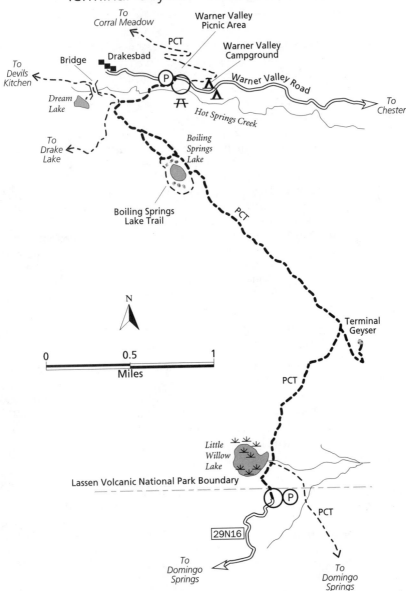

To Corral Meadow

Warner Valley Picnic Area

PCT

Drakesbad

Warner Valley Campground

To Devils Kitchen

Bridge

Warner Valley Road

To Chester

Dream Lake

Hot Springs Creek

To Drake Lake

Boiling Springs Lake

Boiling Springs Lake Trail

PCT

N

Terminal Geyser

0   0.5   1
Miles

PCT

Little Willow Lake

Lassen Volcanic National Park Boundary

PCT

29N16

To Domingo Springs

To Domingo Springs

from many high points in the eastern reaches of the park, rising above the thick green of the forest that surrounds it.

The route begins by following the Boiling Springs Lake Trail (Hike 53) for 0.9 mile, first tracing the course of Hot Springs Creek, then arcing left (southwest) at the trail intersections at 0.4 mile and climbing through the forest. At 0.7 mile, the trail forks again; stay left (south) on the Terminal Geyser Trail, which wanders through the woods to intersect the Boiling Springs

Lake trail at 0.9 mile. Go left (southeast and clockwise) on the lake's circuit trail to the trail intersection at 1.2 miles. Go left (southeast) and up on the Terminal Geyser trail, which is also the Pacific Crest Trail (PCT). The geyser lies 1.5 miles ahead.

The climb shortly mellows amid big Jeffrey pines. The trail is narrow, but clear and well traveled, snaking up onto a more exposed slope carpeted with pinemat manzanita. Cross the top of a ridge, with views of the wooded crests to the west opening briefly, and then begin a gentle descent.

Drop to a double trail junction. At the first, with the horse trail that parallels the PCT to the Terminal Geyser, go right (southwest) and down to the second sign for the Terminal Geyser at 2.5 miles. At this trail intersection, you will leave the PCT, which goes right (southwest) to Little Willow Lake (Hike 55). Take the left (southeast) fork, dropping through gullies and forest toward the steam that rises in great white clouds through the trees. Pass a red danger sign, heeding its warnings of the dangers posed in areas of thermal activity, as well as more signs for Terminal Geyser. Switchbacks lead steeply down to a sharp leftward bend in the trail. The trail flattens as it borders a ravine and edges to the clearing at the base of the geyser.

The spot is secluded and spartan, with the geyser's spout of steam emitting from the gold- and orange-stained rocks of a steep gully. A narrow path leads over two steaming streams to narrow overlooks of the geyser's mouth. Be cautious: a misstep could result in serious burns.

This area was restored to its natural state in the summer of 1999. A geothermal well, known as the "Walker O" well, was capped, and the access road that served the well was removed, resulting in a much more pristine setting.

Enjoy the solitude for a spell, then return to the trailhead via the same route.

Hikers gather at the Terminal Geyser.

55 Little Willow Lake

See Map on Page 200

Highlights: A rolling hike that follows the Pacific Crest Trail (PCT) past two hydrothermal areas to an isolated lake on the southern boundary of Lassen Volcanic National Park.

Type of hike: Day hike or backpack; out-and-back or shuttle.

Total distance: 8 miles.

Difficulty: Moderate.

Best months: June–early October.

Maps: USGS Reading Peak quad; Lassen Volcanic National Park maps by the National Park Service, Earthwalk Press, and Wilderness Press; USDAFS Lassen National Forest map.

Special considerations: There is no potable water available at the trailhead or along the trail. Either pack in all water, or purify water from Little Willow Lake. The lake is both boggy and buggy through most of the hiking season. The PCT is marked with white diamonds between Little Willow Lake and the Terminal Geyser Trail intersection.

Parking and facilities: You will find portable restrooms, an informational kiosk, and picnic tables at the trailhead. The parking area accommodates about 15 cars. More parking is available at the Warner Valley Campground Trailhead, located about half a mile east, back down the road. Restrooms and water also are available at the Warner Valley Campground.

Finding the trailhead: From Chester, take the Feather River Road (Plumas County 312) north for less than 1 mile to the first fork in the road. Go left (northwest), following the signs for Drakesbad; the right road (Plumas County 318) leads north to Juniper Lake. At the next road fork at about 5 miles, go right (north), again following the Drakesbad sign. Follow this narrow road for more than 10 miles; the road's surface changes from paved to gravel for the final three miles. The trailhead picnic and parking area is on the left (south) side of the road, beyond the Warner Valley Campground and before the Drakesbad Guest Ranch.

Key points:

0.0	Warner Valley Picnic Area Trailhead.
0.4	Pass the first trail intersections.
0.9	Skirt the shores of Boiling Springs Lake.
1.2	Turn left (southeast) toward Terminal Geyser from the southeast shore of Boiling Springs Lake.
2.5	Pass the trail intersection to Terminal Geyser.
4.0	Arrive at Little Willow Lake.

The hike: Little Willow Lake is "out there." Secluded and pristine, it lies just off the Pacific Crest Trail (PCT) near where the trail crosses the southern border of the park. The shallow waters evaporate to small marshy pools that hold clusters of

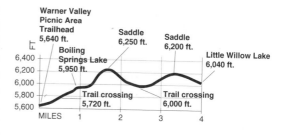

lily pads in late season, all cradled in a thickly forested basin. The lake is the perfect launching point for a trek along the PCT through the park, and the perfect destination for the Lassen explorer seeking a site less visited.

Begin the hike on the Boiling Springs Lake Trail, following its course along Hot Springs Creek to the trail intersections at 0.4 mile, and bearing left (south) to the lake itself at 0.9 mile (see Hike 53 to Boiling Springs Lake or Hike 54 to the Terminal Geyser for details). Circle the lake in a clockwise direction to the Terminal Geyser trail intersection at 1.2 miles, and go left (southeast), following the PCT toward the geyser.

Climb up and over a gentle ridge carpeted with pinemat manzanita and shaded by a park-like scattering of large firs and Jeffrey pines, then head down the wooded, west-facing slope to the trail intersection at 2.5 miles, where the Terminal Geyser trail and PCT diverge. Go right (southwest) on the PCT to Little Willow Lake.

The trail wanders through a mature, mixed fir forest, a rolling traverse that dips in and out of shallow drainages. You will gain more altitude than

Thick grasses line the shores of Little Willow Lake.

you'll lose over the next half-mile, but the climb is easy and shaded, and so very benign. At about 3.2 miles, crest a gentle ridge, cross a flat stretch of path through sun-dappled woodland, then begin an equally benign descent. After 4 very enjoyable miles, reach the northeast margin of Little Willow Lake and the PCT register box. The bucolic lake lies amid grasses and marsh to the right (north), inviting contemplation and photography, if not swimming and fishing.

Options: To exit the park, or to continue on the Pacific Crest Trail (PCT) south to Domingo Springs and beyond, skirt the southern shore of the lake. The trail arcs sharply left (south) near the southwestern tip of the lake, and climbs fairly earnestly to the park boundary and a small parking area that can be reached using Forest Service roads that originate near the Domingo Springs Campground and Domingo Springs PCT Trailhead.

---

56 Warner Valley to Corral Meadow

Highlights:	A challenging climb leads to a peaceful meadow and the banks of Kings Creek.
Type of hike:	Day hike; out-and-back.
Total distance:	4.8 miles.
Difficulty:	Strenuous.
Best months:	June–early October.
Maps:	USGS Reading Peak quad; Earthwalk Lassen Volcanic National Park map; Lassen Volcanic National Park map; USDAFS Lassen National Forest map.
Special considerations:	The first part of this hike is very steep, so bring plenty of water, keep a pace within your limits, and rest as you need to.
Parking and facilities:	The trailhead is in the upper parking lot of Warner Valley Campground, where you will find a small parking area, restrooms, an informational kiosk, and campsites. More parking facilities, as well as picnic sites are available at the Warner Valley Picnic Area Trailhead, located about half a mile west on the Drakesbad Road.

Finding the trailhead: From Chester, take the Feather River Road (Plumas County 312) north for less than 1 mile to the first fork in the road. Go left (northwest), following the signs for Drakesbad; the right (northeast) road (Plumas County 318) leads to Juniper Lake. At the next road fork at 5 miles, go right (north), again following the Drakesbad sign. Follow this narrow road for more than 10 miles; the road's surface changes from paved to gravel for the final 3 miles. The Warner Valley Campground is located about 0.5 mile east of the Warner Valley Trailhead and the Drakesbad Guest Ranch.

Warner Valley to Corral Meadow

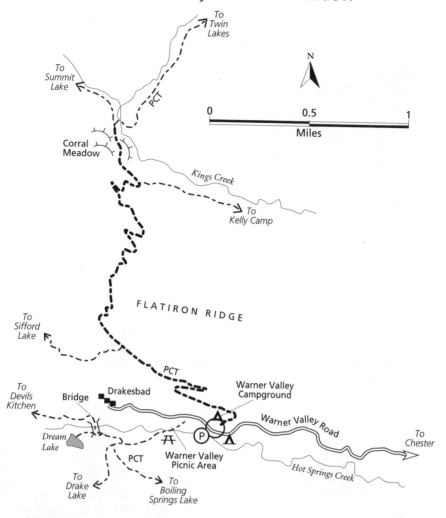

Key points:

0.0   Warner Valley Trailhead.
1.0   Reach the top of the climb out of Warner Valley, and the trail intersection.
2.4   Arrive at Corral Meadow.

The hike: The Pacific Crest Trail (PCT) climbs steeply out of the Warner Valley, and the hardy hiker will revel in the ascent. Steep switchbacks, rocky, exposed terrain, and views like those from an eagle's aerie invigorate the soul, legs, and lungs. From perches along the trail,

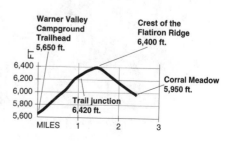

you can look south onto the rolling slopes of Sifford Mountain, west into the head of the valley, and east past Kelly Mountain.

Then the woods grow thick, and don't part until you reach Corral Meadow. This mature strip of wildflowers and dense grasses straddles Kings Creek just below its confluence with the creek that flows out of the Grassy Swale. The meadow, and the stretch of creek that waters it, sees little traffic; it is insulated from all but the most ambitious hikers by the difficulty of the terrain that surrounds it.

From the Warner Valley Campground, the trail heads up and east through the dense fir forest to the first of three switchbacks that link long traverses up the south-facing wall of the valley. Beyond the first switchback, the trail climbs a rugged stone and log staircase. The path is etched into a cliff of folded, globular, gray and black rock.

Round the second switchback, which offers great views of the Drakesbad area. The rock changes its nature, laid down in shaly sheets where manzanita and a few evergreens have gained a foothold. Continue the climb, rounding the third switchback and climbing west onto the Flatiron Ridge, which forms the northern bastion of the Warner Valley.

The forest is thick atop the ridge. At 1 mile, reach the intersection with the trail that leads left (west) to Sifford Lake and Kings Creek Falls. The trail to Corral Meadow goes right (north), and begins a rolling climb over the contours of the Flatiron Ridge. After a brief flat stretch on the crest of the ridge, the trail begins to drop into the Kings Creek drainage, descending three switchbacks to a deadfall-clogged drainage, then another three switchbacks to a trail intersection on the southern edge of the meadow.

The climb out of Warner Valley offers great views.

Kelly Camp lies 3.7 miles to the southeast, down the Kings Creek drainage; the rest of Corral Meadow lies along the more defined path to the left (north).

The boggy, buggy meadow offers few opportunities for rest, refreshment, or contemplation, but the rocky shores of Kings Creek, at the northern edge of the meadow at 2.4 miles, are very inviting. At the next intersection, with the trail that branches off the PCT and leads left (north) to Summit Lake, there is a large, open area, where the trees part to allow access to the watercourse; this is the perfect turnaround spot. Return as you came.

Options: From Corral Meadow, you can continue northwest to Summit Lake (Hike 19) or to the Kings Creek Falls area (Hike 17). You also can continue north on the PCT through the Grassy Swale (Hike 57).

The Pacific Crest Trail

A lovely 18-mile stretch of the Pacific Crest Trail (PCT), one of the premier hiking trails in North America, passes through the heart of Lassen Volcanic National Park. It winds through some of the park's most remote territory, as well as some of its busiest, serving both as a microcosm of all that makes the park great, and a link to all that is great along the West Coast of the United States.

The Pacific Crest Trail), designated a National Scenic Trail by Congress in 1968 and dedicated in 1993, extends for some 2,650 miles, spanning some of the highest points in the lower 48 states as it rambles from Mexico to Canada. In Lassen country, the PCT crosses the southern boundary of the park near Little Willow Lake, and departs the park in the north near Badger Flat. It avoids most of the park's tourist centers, passing well east of both the Southwest Entrance Station and Manzanita Lake, as well as to the east of Lassen Peak itself. It cruises instead right through the park's center, an almost perfect bisection, with its midpoint at the Twin Lakes. The closest it comes to civilization while within the park is in the Warner Valley, where it passes within a quarter of a mile of the Drakesbad Guest Ranch.

Part of the PCT is merged with the Nobles Emigrant Trail, another long-distance track that, rather than serving recreational and environmental purposes, served as a highway for migrants to California in the mid-nineteenth century.

The PCT can be hiked in either direction, in segments, or as part of other trail hikes or loops within the park. I've chosen to describe it here as a shuttle hike beginning in the north, where the trail enters the park near Hat Creek, about 2 miles west of Badger Flat, and running to the south, where it exits the park near Little Willow Lake. Though the hardy hiker could cross the park on the PCT in a long day, most choose to make the trip in two or three days, spending one night near the Twin Lakes and a second, if needed or desired, in the Warner Valley.

If you wish to camp overnight in the backcountry, please abide by the park's backcountry regulations by securing a permit and setting up camp at least 100 feet from water sources and trails. Complete backcountry regulations are listed in the introduction to this guide.

There are no potable water sources along the trail, save at the Warner Valley Campground, so you should be prepared to purify water that you collect from streams or lakes by boiling, filtering, or chemically treating it. There are no amenities other than minimal parking areas at either trailhead; pack in everything you need.

To reach the northern trailhead from within the park, begin at the Hat Creek Trailhead, which is located 9.5 miles south and east of the Manzanita Lake Entrance Station, and 18.5 miles north and east of the Southwest Entrance Station. Hike north on the Nobles Emigrant Trail, which is described in Hike 28, to its intersection with the PCT, and follow the trail as it proceeds east and south.

To reach the northern trailhead from outside the park, follow California 44/89 north and west from the Manzanita Lake Entrance Station to Lassen Forest Road 32N12, which heads right (east) to Twin Bridges and West Prospect Peak. The Pacific Crest Trailhead is about a quarter of a mile west of Twin Bridges, on the southeast side of Hat Creek near Plantation Loop Road.

To reach the southern trailhead from within the park, begin at the Warner Valley Trailhead, which is located about 17 miles northwest of Chester on Plumas County 312. From the Warner Valley Trailhead, hike south, passing Boiling Springs Lake, on the trail described in Hike 55 for Little Willow Lake.

To reach the southern trailhead from outside the park, you will again begin in Chester, following the Feather River Road (Plumas County 312) northwest to its intersection with Plumas County 311, north of the High Bridge Campground. Go left (northwest) on CR 311, following the signs for the Domingo Springs Campground. The PCT intersects the county road opposite the campground entrance.

You can also hop on the PCT closer to the park boundary at Little Willow Lake. To reach the park boundary from Domingo Springs, continue on CR 311 to Forest Road 29N18, which leads west to Forest Road 29N16. Turn right (north) on FS 29N16, which is marked with a sign for Little Willow Lake. Stay north on FS 29N16 for about 3 miles to where it dead-ends near the park's southern boundary. Hike north and over the hill to Little Willow Lake; the trail register is located on the lake's southeastern edge. The Lassen Forest Service map is a good guide.

For more information on the PCT itself, contact the Pacific Crest Trail Association, 5325 Elkhorn Blvd., PMB #256, Sacramento, CA 95842-2526; (916) 349-2109. The website is at www.pcta.org.

57 Pacific Crest Trail—Badger Flat to Little Willow Lake

Highlights:	The pleasures of this trek are numerous, including the meadow at Badger Flat, the Twin Lakes, the Grassy Swale, and the hydrothermal features around Drakesbad.
Type of hike:	Backpack; shuttle or out-and-back.
Total distance:	18.3 miles.
Difficulty:	Strenuous.
Best months:	Late June–September.
Maps:	USGS West Prospect Peak, Prospect Peak, Reading Peak, and Mount Harkness quads; Lassen Volcanic National Park maps by the National Park Service, Earthwalk Press, and Wilderness Press; USDAFS Lassen National Forest map.
Special considerations:	Be prepared to boil, filter, or chemically purify water collected from lakes and streams.

Pacific Crest Trail—Badger Flat to Little Willow Lake

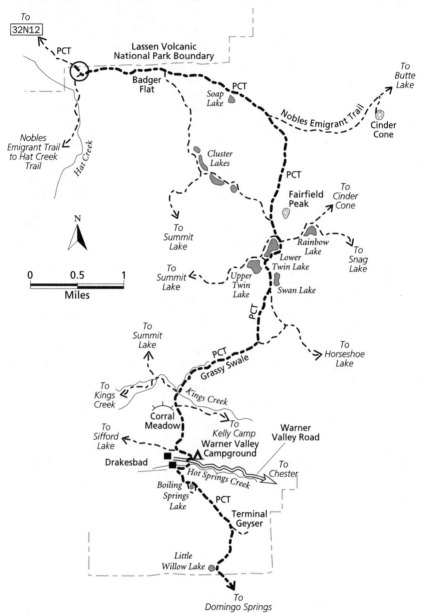

Key points:

- 0.0 Lassen Volcanic National Park boundary near Hat Creek.
- 2.0 Arrive at Badger Flat.
- 4.5 Turn south, diverging from the Nobles Emigrant Trail.
- 7.3 Reach Lower Twin Lake.
- 12.1 Pass Corral Meadow.
- 14.5 Reach the Warner Valley Trailhead.
- 15.4 Pass Boiling Springs Lake.
- 18.3 Finish at Little Willow Lake.

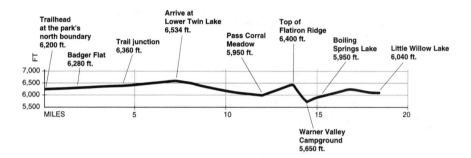

The hike: End to end, the Pacific Crest Trail (PCT) passes through some of the most rugged and scenic parts of Lassen Volcanic National Park. From the seclusion of Badger Flat and the Grassy Swale to the relatively busy, but lovely, Lower Twin Lake and Warner Valley areas, the route is relatively easy, delightful, and will no doubt tempt you to venture onto other segments at various points along its scenic route.

From ground zero—where the PCT passes into the north part of the park near Hat Creek—the trail strikes off in an easterly direction, following the track originally laid down by pioneers traveling the Nobles Emigrant Trail in the 1850s and 1860s. The path, a doubletrack set by wagon wheels, rolls through easy and mostly flat terrain through thick stands of timber as it cruises east toward Badger Flat. There are few travelers on this part of the trail, which lends itself to meditative walking.

After 1.5 miles, the living forest is transformed into a graveyard of deadfall and standing dead; evergreens that once were grand now bear the black scars of fire. The barren heights of Lassen Peak are visible to the southwest.

At 2 miles, arrive at Badger Flat, a lovely meadow with more views of Lassen Peak. At the eastern end of the meadow, you reach a trail intersection. Stay left (east) on the merged Pacific Crest and Nobles Emigrant Trails; the trail that goes right (south) leads to the Cluster Lakes and Summit Lake.

The wagon track, which fades a bit in this stretch, continues eastward, following the bed of a seasonal stream as it rolls over hills blanketed with a mixed evergreen forest. Pass Soap Lake, which lies behind a curtain of trees on the right (south) side of the trail, and continue to the next trail intersection at 4.5 miles, where the merged trails diverge. The Nobles Emigrant Trail continues eastward around the base of Prospect Peak to the Cinder

Cone and Butte Lake, while the PCT now bends right (south). The trail designation is scratched in black ink on the sign at the junction.

The trail continues south as a doubletrack, passing through open woodland and making a beeline for Fairfield Peak, which can be seen through the trees. The path climbs through a fragrant understory of herbs and wildflowers, but so gently that it's hardly noticeable. As the PCT skirts the western flank of Fairfield Peak, the forest deepens, and the path narrows to singletrack, then blossoms back to doubletrack, as it works around deadfall and living trees.

The PCT swings to the southwest side of Fairfield Peak, then drops to the junction with the trail that goes right (west) to the Cluster Lakes. Stay left (south) on the PCT, which leads to the shore of Lower Twin Lake at the 7.3-mile mark.

The PCT hugs Lower Twin Lake's eastern edge, passing the trail that breaks off to the left (east) to Rainbow Lake, and continuing south to the next trail junction. Here, the PCT goes left (south) away from the shore of Lower Twin Lake (the trail sign indicates that Swan Lake lies along this track), while the right-hand path continues the circuit of Lower Twin Lake, then heads west to Upper Twin Lake, Echo Lake and Summit Lake.

Follow the PCT up onto a bluff, from which you can look down and west onto Upper Twin Lake. Roll through open terrain past Swan Lake, which lies on the left (east) side of the track. Scrubby meadows parallel the route, offering wonderful camping opportunities that are a convenient distance from the lake.

Continue through more open woodland to a Y intersection. The trail to the left (southeast) circles the base of Crater Butte as it heads down to

The Pacific Crest Trail leads south toward Twin Lakes.

Horseshoe Lake; the PCT heads right (southwest), toward Corral Meadow. The track stays fairly level, passing into a burned area where grasses and wildflowers thrive in sunshine admitted by an absent canopy. The dead, standing trees also make good homes for a variety of birds, whose songs ring in the otherwise still air.

The path drops into a gully filled with charred and living trees. At the bottom of the gully, you will follow the lush track of a small, tumbling stream. Cross the streamlet and veer west into more open terrain. The stream waters a meadow tucked in the trees to the left (south).

At the next trail junction, stay right (southwest) on the PCT; the marginal trail to the left (east) leads to Horseshoe Lake. Corral Meadow lies 2.4 miles ahead.

The PCT now drops alongside the Grassy Swale, a narrow swath of meadow that parallels the trail on its left (south) side. Red diamonds, which are few and far between, help mark the narrow but clear trail. The stream comes into view only when the swale narrows and crushes it against the track; otherwise, it is white noise in a quiet wilderness.

About a mile below the last trail intersection, you will cross the stream on rocks, then the trail veers south and away from the water. You are no longer caressed by the grasses of the swale, but enveloped in a forest of large firs. Firs also border the small patch of meadow that the trail soon meets and crosses. Indeed, on the stretch of trail leading down to Kings Creek and Corral Meadow, forest, meadow, and bog mingle and alternate, with the nameless companion stream growing more raucous on your right (northwest) as it descends to its confluence.

Quick switchbacks lead down to the cobbled banks of Kings Creek. The Kings Creek crossing is a bit challenging: You must either ford the brisk waterway, or use a precarious bridge of deadfall that lies downstream from the trail. Once across, you stand at another trail junction. Summit Lake lies up to your right (northwest), and Corral Meadow and the Warner Valley lie down the trail to the left (south).

Corral Meadow, at 12.1 miles, is colorful, narrow, and boggy. The little-used path to Kelly Camp breaks off the PCT to the left (southeast) before you begin to climb switchbacks that lead onto the Flatiron Ridge, which separates Corral Meadow and the Kings Creek drainage from the Warner Valley.

The switchbacks lead to an ascending traverse, which leads to more switchbacks, which finally deposit you on the rolling crest of the Flatiron Ridge. Descend from the ridgetop to the intersection with the trail that leads right (west) toward Sifford Lake. At this point, you stand near the brink of the Warner Valley, which falls away to the south.

The PCT arcs left (southeast) from the trail intersection, and begins the steep descent to the valley floor. The drop down the north wall of the valley is precipitous and exposed, but the views of the Drakesbad area and the upper valley are superlative. A sun-splashed rock on the edge of the second switchback offers the perfect place from which to take in the vistas. A long traverse leads to the final of three switchbacks, and you pass through thick trees into the Warner Valley Campground at 14.5 miles.

Walk down through the campground to the Warner Valley Road, and head about a quarter of a mile west to the Warner Valley Trailhead, where the PCT resumes its march to the south.

From this trailhead, the PCT and the trail to Boiling Springs Lake and Terminal Geyser are merged. Cross Hot Springs Creek, then traverse westward above the waterway to a couple of back-to-back trail intersections that lie 0.4 mile from the Warner Valley Road. Stay left (south) at both, hiking up to the striking hydrothermal lake, complete with thumping mudpots and sulfur-scented steam, at 15.4 miles. Circle the lake in a clockwise direction to the intersection with the trail to the Terminal Geyser and go left (southeast), following the PCT toward the geyser and Little Willow Lake.

Climb up and over a gentle ridge carpeted with pinemat manzanita and shaded by a park-like scattering of evergreens, then head down through denser woods to the final trail junction, where the route to the Terminal Geyser and PCT diverge. Go right (southwest) on the PCT toward Little Willow Lake.

The PCT wanders through a mature fir forest, dipping in and out of shallow drainages as it climbs. Crest a gentle ridge, cross a flat stretch through sun-dappled and viewless woods, and then begin an easy descent to the east margin of Little Willow Lake and the PCT register box. The lake, seemingly in the terminal stages of its existence as such, lies amid thick, marshy grasses on the right (north) side of the path.

The Pacific Crest Trail leaves the park at this point, heading south over the boundary and continuing to Domingo Springs and beyond. Take a year off work, and continue, if you choose.

The Nobles Emigrant Trail

In the mid-1800s, several emigrant trails crossed the Sierra Nevada to the gold-rich foothills on the range's western slopes and fertile valleys of central California. The hardships encountered by travelers along the routes were notorious—unpredictable weather, scarce water and food, and terrain that was nearly insurmountable in travel-worn wagons. Witness the gruesome fate of the Donner Party on the central Sierra pass that bears the same name, and the infamous Lassen Trail, which meandered so wildly through the mountains of northern California that some of those who arrived at trail's end wanted to do away with trailblazer Peter Lassen.

Not so the Nobles Emigrant Trail, forged by William H. Nobles and touted as the easiest route over the Sierra Nevada into California's Great Valley. Nobles, a native of New York who came to California, like so many others, looking for gold, established his trail in the early 1850s. His story, and the story of the trail he founded, is detailed in Robert Ames' booklet *Nobles' Emigrant Trail*, which is available through the Lassen-Loomis Museum Association (see Appendix C: Further Reading).

A portion of this emigrant trail passed through what would later become Lassen Volcanic National Park. The park has preserved much of the original route, with the exception of a couple of miles that lie buried beneath the debris that filled the Lost Creek and Hat Creek drainages after the eruptions of Lassen Peak in May of 1915. Sections of the old emigrant trail link to other parts of the trail network in the northern reaches of the park, where Lassen's backcountry is, arguably, at its wildest. The trail offers secluded and relatively easy hiking for anyone who ventures onto it. It won the praise of weary pioneers traveling with loaded wagons through unknown territory . . . imagine how pleasant it is for the modern hiker, laden only with backpack and bedroll, seeking solitude, beauty, and a touch of history.

The trail is described here in two sections. The first section is from Butte Lake, where it entered the present-day park, to the Hat Lake Trailhead. The mudflows and eruptions of 1915 obliterated the trail between Hat Lake and the northern reaches of Anklin Meadow. The second part of the trail is described from near its intersection with Lost Creek to Summertown, at the park's western boundary. Shorter portions of the trail, which make good day hikes, are described in other sections of the book (Hike 28 in the Emigrant Pass and Hat Creek chapter, Hike 35 in the Manzanita Lake chapter, and several hikes in the Butte Lake chapter). The description here describes the trail in its entirety, for those who may want to follow the wagon tracks on an overnight odyssey.

58 Nobles Emigrant Trail— Eastern Section

Type of hike:	Backpack; out-and-back or shuttle.
Total distance:	12.5 miles.
Difficulty:	Moderate.
Best months:	July–September.
Maps:	USGS Manzanita Lake, West Prospect Peak, and Prospect Peak quads; Lassen Volcanic National Park maps by the National Park Service, Earthwalk Press, and Wilderness Press; USDAFS Lassen National Forest map.
Special considerations:	Please abide by the backcountry regulations set forth by park administrators, including securing the proper backcountry permits and camping at least 100 feet away from water sources and trails. Be sure to boil, filter, or chemically treat water from streams or lakes along the trail.
Parking and facilities:	The campground at Butte Lake is equipped with pit toilets, fire pits, and bear-proof food cabinets. At the time of this writing, there was no potable water source at the lake, but the park plans to have water available for the 2001 or 2002 summer season.
	While there are no amenities at the Hat Creek Trailhead proper on the western end of the trail, nearby Manzanita Lake Campground is fully equipped with water sources, restrooms, a visitor center/museum, and a camper store with laundry facilities and showers.

Finding the trailhead: To reach the Butte Lake Trailhead from the Manzanita Lake Entrance Station, backtrack west for 0.5 mile on the Lassen Park Road (California Highway 89) to the intersection of CA 44 and CA 89. Turn right on CA 44/89, and follow it north and west for 13.6 miles to Old Station, where CA 44 makes a sharp right (east) turn and breaks from CA 89. Turn right (east), and continue on CA 44 for another 11 miles to a right (south) turn onto the road to Butte Lake. The gravel road leads for about 7 miles to the campground and picnic area. The trailhead is on the west side of the boat ramp area.

The Hat Creek Trailhead is located about 9.5 miles south and east of the Manzanita Lake Entrance Station, and 18.5 miles north and east of the Southwest Entrance Station.

Key points:
- 0.0   Butte Lake Trailhead.
- 1.2   Pass the Cinder Cone.
- 4.5   Merge with the Pacific Crest Trail.
- 5.5   Skirt Soap Lake.
- 7.1   Arrive at Badger Flat.
- 8.6   The Nobles Emigrant Trail diverges from the PCT.
- 12.5   Reach the Hat Lake Trailhead.

Nobles Emigrant Trail—Eastern Section

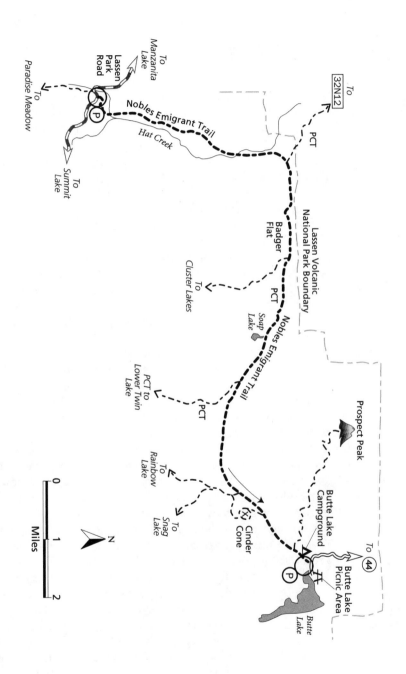

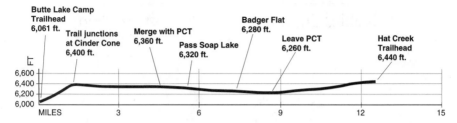

Butte Lake Camp Trailhead 6,061 ft.
Trail junctions at Cinder Cone 6,400 ft.
Merge with PCT 6,360 ft.
Pass Soap Lake 6,320 ft.
Badger Flat 6,280 ft.
Leave PCT 6,260 ft.
Hat Creek Trailhead 6,440 ft.

The hike: This section of the Nobles Emigrant Trail no doubt inspired awe and wonder in the travelers 150 years ago, who had to pass the stark Cinder Cone, the ominous Fantastic Lava Beds, and the colorful Painted Dunes before plunging back into the more familiar forest. The terrain is no less awesome and wonderful today, enhanced by our modern understanding of the powerful volcanic forces that sculpted the landscape.

The trail begins on the southwest side of the Butte Lake Picnic Area. The first section of the emigrant trail doubles as the Cinder Cone Trail. The route is wide and soft with cinders, bordered on the east by the black basalt of the Fantastic Lava Beds, and on the west by the forest of Jeffrey pines that has colonized the lower slopes of Prospect Peak.

The junction with the trail to the summit of Prospect Peak is at 0.5 mile; stay left (southwest) on the Nobles Emigrant/Cinder Cone Nature Trail. The trail veers away from the lava beds as the Cinder Cone looms on the southern horizon, then climbs to the junction with the steep trail that leads to the summit at 1.2 miles.

Stay right (southwest) on the Nobles Emigrant Trail, which skirts the west-facing side of the Cinder Cone to a Y intersection at 1.6 miles. The left-hand trail leads south to Snag Lake; the right-hand is the emigrant trail, which leads southwest, to yet another trail intersection. Again, follow the right-hand trail, heading southwest on a narrowing swath of footfalls etched in the cinder fields at the base of Prospect Peak.

The two tracks that harken back to the wagon wheels that once passed this way don't become apparent until you enter the woodlands that clothe Prospect Peak's south-facing flanks. The tracks trace a westerly course through the cinders, which support a feathery growth of grasses and wildflowers as the Jeffrey pines give way to lodgepoles and firs.

The route rolls through the woods to its intersection with the Pacific Crest Trail (PCT) at 4.5 miles. Stay right (west) on the now-merged Nobles Emigrant Trail and PCT; the trail to the left (south) leads to the Twin Lakes.

The surface of the trail gradually becomes less sandy and is littered with deadfall. The forest is broken with small grassy meadows. At 5.5 miles, you will pass Soap Lake, screened by a curtain of evergreens on the left (south) side of the track. Beyond the lake the trail becomes more exposed and a bit hillier, and the double track, which sees relatively little traffic, loses some definition. Cross, and then follow, the bed of a seasonal stream. The trail arcs northward, then curves back southwest, going around a small hill, to the picturesque expanse of the Badger Flat meadow at 7.1 miles.

218

The Cinder Cone as seen from the Nobles-Emigrant Trail.

In addition to the lovely meadow, camping opportunities, and the best views thus far of Lassen Peak, you will also find a trail intersection at Badger Flat. Stay right (west) to continue on the Nobles Emigrant Trail; the trail to the left (south) leads to the Cluster Lakes, and eventually to Summit Lake.

The trail proceeds through an area that was damaged by fire in 1984; though the huge, mature trees are blackened, the lack of a canopy permits great views of Lassen Peak. The living forest gradually begins to dominate again, and the rolling path continues west to the next trail intersection, where the PCT diverges from the Nobles Emigrant Trail at 8.6 miles.

The PCT heads right (north) and out of the park. Stay left (south) on the Nobles Emigrant Trail, dropping on the old roadbed to parallel the eastern bank of Hat Creek. About a quarter of a mile south of the junction with the PCT the double track widens and, in addition to the wagon ruts, may also bear the mark of a modern vehicle. The trail veers right (west) to cross Hat Creek; choose a log or a logjam as your bridge, and cross with care. A trail sign indicates the distances to Badger Flat and other points east.

Continue south, following the west bank of Hat Creek and passing a cluster of buildings that sits on private property. The trail is now a well-defined roadway that leads gradually upward through the thick lodgepole forest cloaking the lower slopes of Raker Peak, which guards the west side of the route. Cruise through an aspen grove, then an open area with a great view of Lassen Peak, before reaching a second, fairly treacherous Hat Creek crossing. You can either rock-hop, or negotiate a tightrope log crossing that lies a bit downstream, to reach the east side of the creek. The trail climbs to its end along the shoulder of Lassen Park Road at the Hat Creek Trailhead at 12.5 miles.

59 Nobles Emigrant Trail—
Western Section

Type of hike:	Day hike; shuttle or out-and-back.
Total distance:	5.5 miles.
Difficulty:	Easy (shuttle); moderate (out-and-back).
Best months:	July–September.
Maps:	USGS Manzanita Lake and West Prospect Peak quads; Lassen Volcanic National Park maps by the National Park Service, Earthwalk Press, and Wilderness Press; USDAFS Lassen National Forest map.
Special considerations:	There are no potable water sources along the trail. Be sure to treat water from stream or lakes by boiling, filtering, or chemically treating it.
Parking and facilities:	There are no amenities, nor is there adequate parking, at the Lost Creek end of the trail. The nearest parking is at the Hot Rock, located 0.7 mile south of the trail's terminus. There is a nice parking area at the midpoint of the hike, near the summit of Nobles Pass at Sunflower Flat. This is located on the south side of the Lassen Park Road (California Highway 89) 3 miles south and east from the Manzanita Lake Entrance Station. There are no restrooms or other facilities at this location. The Summertown Trailhead also offers no amenities, but the area around nearby Manzanita Lake Campground is fully equipped with water sources, restrooms, a visitor center/museum, and a camper store with laundry facilities and showers.

Finding the trailhead: To reach the Nobles Emigrant Trailhead at Lost Creek from the Manzanita Lake Entrance station, follow the Lassen Park Road (CA 89) east and south for 7.5 miles to the parking area at the Hot Rock. Head north, backtracking on the Lassen Park Road, for a little more than 0.5 mile to the unmarked trail, which is on the right (northeast) side of the road.

The Summertown Trailhead is at the Manzanita Lake Entrance Station. The closest parking is at the Loomis Museum/visitor center, which is 0.5 mile east of the entrance station on the Lassen Park Road (CA 89). Park at the museum, then follow the trail that traces the shoreline of Manzanita Lake west to the entrance station. The trailhead lies up the gated service road on the north side of the entrance station.

Key points:

0.0	Lost Creek Trailhead.
2.0	Cross the Lassen Park Road.
3.2	Reach the second crossing of the Lassen Park Road.
4.0	Hike over Nobles Pass.
4.5	Enter the Chaos Jumbles at the base of Table Mountain.
5.5	Reach the Summertown Trailhead.

Nobles Emigrant Trail—Western Section

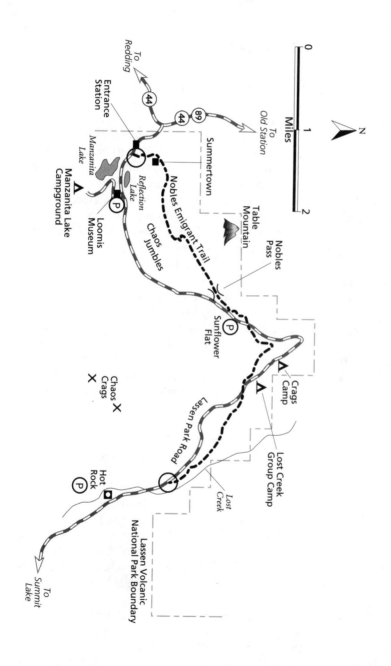

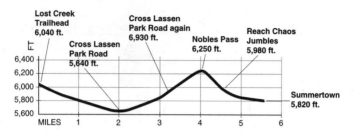

The hike: The western reaches of the Nobles Emigrant Trail are a mixed bag. The segment described here, from Lost Creek to Lassen Park Road, was the site of a controlled burn in 1999, and is littered with firefighting equipment and the detritus of construction and maintenance. While this may be interesting to some hikers, it is a less than pristine experience.

As you begin to climb toward Nobles Pass, however, the path takes on a mantle of both natural beauty and historical richness. A marker at Sunflower Flat, just below the pass, commemorates the pioneers that used this trail. Once over the summit, you will pass through the Chaos Jumbles, remnants of a massive avalanche off the Chaos Crags that now fosters an open woodland of Jeffrey pines. A few artifacts and a little imagination lend poignancy to the remains of Summertown, at trail's end near the western boundary of the park.

As mentioned above, the Lost Creek section of the trail offers little in terms of scenic value and is seldom used. In addition, access may be restricted; check with a park ranger before embarking on your hike.

To locate this section of the trail from the Hot Rock parking area, backtrack along the Lassen Park Road for 0.7 mile to a service road with a sign marked DP-4. Turn right (northeast) on the service road, and head down through the thick forest to the double track trail, which is unmarked but looks like other parts of the wagon-cut route. Veer left (northwest) on the trail, and proceed to the start of the Lost Creek Diversion Flume, with its dam, pipe, and shack. The flume dates back to the turn of the century, when the Shasta Power Company attempted to harness hydroelectric power from Lost Creek. The flume, which roughly parallels the Lassen Park Road to Sunflower Flat, was abandoned after being damaged by the 1915 mudflows.

A service road provides the easiest passage through this heavily wooded area, though this may or may not be the actual emigrant trail, which appears to weave to and from the roadway. The next quarter of a mile of the road is strewn with gravel deposited by the stream. Beyond, the road enters the burn area, descending along shallow benches to a pump house and water tank. The forest is heavily burnt on the west side of the track, less affected on the east.

Climb out of the forest to the Lassen Park Road at about the 2-mile mark. The Nobles Emigrant Trail continues on the opposite (west) side of the road about 200 yards to the northwest. There is a turnout along the road at this point.

A flat section of the path leads through an open forest of mature trees, with a meadowy understory littered with deadfall. You will begin to climb shortly, passing a jumble of rocks on the left (south) side of the trail. The trail is secluded, littered with pine needles, until it emerges from the forest to ascend a hillside carpeted with pinemat manzanita. The trail is now close to the park road, and you can hear the highway noise as you climb.

As the trail nears the second road crossing, the double track plunges into a thick, mixed fir and lodgepole pine forest. Emerge from the woods on the roadside at 3.2 miles.

A small rock cairn, or "duck," marks the trail's passage back into the woods on the opposite (northwest) side of the road. It is a gentle climb from here to the summit of Nobles Pass; it is also abundantly clear that this is a wagon road, its two tracks leading through a colonnade of trees.

Top out on Nobles Pass at 4 miles. From the pass, the trail drops into the open woodland that has found a foothold amid the pinkish soil of the Chaos Jumbles. The bald pates of Lassen Peak and the Chaos Crags peek over the rubble hummocks on the south side of the route. Yellow triangles with red trim mark this section of the route.

Switchbacks lead down into easier terrain, with the trail tracing broad curves through the pines until it settles into a depression between the Chaos Jumbles on the south and the base of Table Mountain on the north at about 4.5 miles.

Continue down and west, passing through a gully clogged with deadfall. At the 5.5-mile mark, the emigrant trail ends in a large clearing, where old foundations and pieces of pottery and glass recall the settlement that once was Summertown.

To continue to the Manzanita Lake Entrance Station, follow the gravel road that leads west, then southwest, toward Manzanita Lake. Trail markers line the road, which becomes paved. Stick to the pavement, avoiding gravel roads that branch off left and right. Pass through a park maintenance area; the Lassen Park Road is 0.1 mile beyond. A gate blocks access to the road, which is directly opposite the entrance station and the northwestern shores of Manzanita Lake. The Loomis Museum is 0.5 mile east of the entrance station, and can be reached by crossing the park road and following the footpath that traces the shore of Manzanita Lake.

Appendix A: Hiker's Checklist

Always make and check your own checklist!

If you've ever hiked into the backcountry and discovered that you've forgotten an essential, you know that it's a good idea to make a checklist and check the items off as you pack so that you won't forget the things you want and need. Here are some ideas:

Clothing
- ☐ Dependable rain parka
- ☐ Rain pants
- ☐ Windbreaker
- ☐ Thermal underwear
- ☐ Shorts
- ☐ Long pants or sweatpants
- ☐ Wool cap or balaclava
- ☐ Hat
- ☐ Wool shirt or sweater
- ☐ Jacket or parka
- ☐ Extra socks
- ☐ Underwear
- ☐ Lightweight shirts
- ☐ T-shirts
- ☐ Bandanna(s)
- ☐ Mittens or gloves
- ☐ Belt

Footwear
- ☐ Sturdy, comfortable boots
- ☐ Lightweight camp shoes

Bedding
- ☐ Sleeping bag
- ☐ Foam pad or air mattress
- ☐ Ground sheet (plastic or nylon)
- ☐ Dependable tent

Hauling
- ☐ Backpack and/or day pack

Cooking
- ☐ 1-quart container (plastic)
- ☐ 1-gallon water container for camp use (collapsible)
- ☐ Backpack stove and extra fuel
- ☐ Funnel
- ☐ Aluminum foil
- ☐ Cooking pots
- ☐ Bowls/plates
- ☐ Utensils (spoons, forks, small spatula, knife)
- ☐ Pot scrubber
- ☐ Matches in waterproof container

Food and Drink
- ☐ Cereal
- ☐ Bread
- ☐ Crackers
- ☐ Cheese
- ☐ Trail mix
- ☐ Margarine
- ☐ Powdered soups
- ☐ Salt/pepper
- ☐ Main course meals
- ☐ Snacks
- ☐ Hot chocolate
- ☐ Tea
- ☐ Powered milk
- ☐ Drink mixes

Photography
- ☐ Camera and film
- ☐ Filters
- ☐ Lens brush/paper

Miscellaneous
- ☐ Sunglasses
- ☐ Map and a compass
- ☐ Toilet paper
- ☐ Pocketknife
- ☐ Sunscreen
- ☐ Good insect repellent
- ☐ Lip balm
- ☐ Flashlight with good batteries and a spare bulb
- ☐ Candle(s)
- ☐ First-aid kit
- ☐ Your FalconGuide
- ☐ Survival kit
- ☐ Small garden trowel or shovel
- ☐ Water filter or purification tablets
- ☐ Plastic bags (for trash)
- ☐ Soap
- ☐ Towel
- ☐ Toothbrush
- ☐ Fishing license
- ☐ Fishing rod, reel, lures, flies, etc.
- ☐ Binoculars
- ☐ Waterproof covering for pack
- ☐ Watch
- ☐ Sewing kit

Appendix B: Glossary

Andesite: An intermediate type of lava between basalt and dacite, andesite can range in color from gray to brown, and is often flecked with small crystals so that it resembles granite. Found throughout Lassen Volcanic National Park.

Basalt: A common, black or dark-colored lava that often turns red when exposed to the weather. Composes the Fantastic Lava Beds.

Cinder cone: Steep-sided volcanoes formed when magma under high pressure erupts explosively. Usually symmetrical in shape. Example: Cinder Cone.

Cinders: Material ejected from a volcano that is the size and consistency of sand.

Composite volcano: Built by piling layer upon layer of lava from successive eruptions, this is the common structure for most of the Cascade volcanoes. Examples: Mount Shasta, Mount Tehama.

Dacite: Similar to andesites, but containing more silicon dioxide, dacites range in color from pink to gray to brown. Often, they are also flecked with smaller crystals. Composes Lassen Peak.

Fumerole: A vent in a volcanic area from which gas and steam escape.

Hydrothermal areas: Areas where water and magma conspire to create mud pots, steam vents, and boiling pools or hot springs. Examples: Bumpass Hell, Devils Kitchen.

Lava: Magma, or molten rock, that escapes from volcanoes.

Plug dome volcano: A steep-sided volcano that is formed when extremely viscous masses of lava emerge rapidly from a vent. Example: Lassen Peak.

Pyroclastic flow: An explosive and extremely destructive eruption of gas and steam from a volcano.

Shield volcano: Viscous, free-flowing lava builds these volcanoes, which have low, broad-based profiles and resemble shields. Example: Prospect Peak, Hawaiian volcanoes.

Appendix C: Further Reading

Eruptions of Lassen Peak, B. F. Loomis, Lassen Loomis Museum Association. 3rd Revised Edition 1971.

Footprints in Time: A History of Lassen Volcanic National Park, Douglas Strong, Lassen Loomis Museum Association. 1973.

His Life & Legacy: Peter Lassen, Ruby Johnson Swartzlow, Lassen Loomis Museum Association. Revised Edition 1995.

Ishi in Two Worlds, Theodora Kroeber, University of California Press. 1961.

Lassen Place Names, Paul E. Schulz, Lassen Loomis Museum Association. 1949.

Lassen Volcanic: The Story Behind the Scenery, Ellis Richard, KC Publications, Inc.

Lassen Volcanic National Park and Vicinity, Jeffrey Schaffer, Wilderness Press. 1981.

Nobles Emigrant Trail, Robert Amesbury, Lassen Loomis Museum Association. 1967.

Road Guide to Lassen Volcanic National Park, Robert and Barbara Decker, Double Decker Press. 1997.

Roadside Geology of Northern California, David B. Alt and Donald W. Hyndman, Mountain Press Publishing Company. 1975.

Through Vulcan's Eye; Geology of Lassen, Phillip S. Kane, Lassen Loomis Museum Association 1980.

Trees and Shrubs of Lassen, Raymond Nelson, Lassen Loomis Museum Association. 1962.

Other titles available from the Lassen Loomis Museum Association:

Books
  Flowers of Lassen Volcanic National Park
  Butterflies of Lassen
  Aquatics of Lassen
  Indians of Lassen

Pamphlets
  Teachers Guide to Lassen
  Trail Guide to Lassen Peak
  Trail Guide to Bumpass Hell
  Trail Guide to Lily Pond

Index

Page numbers in *italics* refer to photographs.

About the Author

Tracy Salcedo-Chourré is always on the trail, whether hiking, mountain biking, or skiing. When she's not outdoors, she can be found at her computer, writing, or volunteering at her local school. In addition to working as a newspaper reporter and editor, and authoring a number of magazine articles, she has written fifteen hiking guides covering areas in Colorado, where she lived for 12 years, and California, where she currently resides with her husband, three sons, and the family pets.

The author with her sons at the Terminal Geyser.